The Marriage Clinic CaseBook

A NORTON PROFESSIONAL BOOK

THE MARRIAGE CLINIC CASEBOOK

Edited by

Julie Schwartz Gottman

W.W. NORTON & COMPANY
New York ■ London

W. W. Norton & Company has been independent since its founding in 1923, when William Warder Norton and Mary D. Herter Norton first published lectures delivered at the People's Institute, the adult education division of New York City's Cooper Union. The Nortons soon expanded their program beyond the Institute, publishing books by celebrated academics from America and abroad. By mid-century, the two major pillars of Norton's publishing program—trade books and college texts—were firmly established. In the 1950s, the Norton family transferred control of the company to its employees, and today—with a staff of four hundred and a comparable number of trade, college, and professional titles published each year—W. W. Norton & Company stands as the largest and oldest publishing house owned wholly by its employees.

Copyright © 2004 by W. W. Norton & Company, Inc.

All rights reserved.
Printed in the United States of America.

The text of this book is composed in Sabon
with the display set Franklin Gothic
Composition by TechBooks, Inc.

Manufacturing by Quebecor World—Fairfield Division.
Production Manager: Ben Reynolds.

Library of Congress Cataloging-in-Publication Data

The marriage clinic casebook / edited by Julie Schwartz Gottman.
    p. cm.
"A Norton professional book."
Includes bibliographical references and index.
ISBN 0-393-70413-0
1. Marriage counseling—United States—Case studies.   2. Marital psychotherapy—United States—Case studies.   I. Gottman, Julie Schwartz.
HQ10.5.U6M37   2004
616.89′1562—dc22   2004049251

W. W. Norton & Company, Inc., 500 Fifth Avenue, New York, N. Y. 10110–0017
www.wwnorton.com

W. W. Norton & Company Ltd., Castle House, 75/76 Wells Street, London W1T 3QT

1 2 3 4 5 6 7 8 9 0

Contents

Foreword

John Gottman

The creation of this volume has been part of a journey born of a collaboration between a researcher who did some clinical work and a clinician who did some research. When Julie and I began collaborating to integrate clinical research and clinical practice, the challenge was to forge an approach that was based on genuinely respectful two-way communication. The academic orientation that I began with was arrogant and superior. If Julie told me about something that had worked with her cases, I would usually smugly ask her, "Where's your data?" That attitude led to quite a lot of marital conflict. But it was also very productive. As we started working together I began learning from Julie and also learning what an amazingly talented clinician I had married. We both began to see that an integration of research and practice required mutual respect and the mutual acceptance of influence.

We began building a marriage clinic. We clinicians took years to develop trust and affection among the eighteen of us. It also took years before we could build a climate in which we could honestly talk about our treatment failures. As we did, we all started learning from one another, and the research itself broadened both in focus and in scope.

We started with a group of clinicians who came from many perspectives, from object relations to behavioral to systems, and who came from many disciplines as well. We built a clinic without walls, meaning that everyone had his or her own office but we had a central screening, referral, and triage service.

We were looking for dialogue, not a group of true believers. We were working from certain principles, theory, and data, but not from dogma. We welcomed and celebrated the work of others, both clinical, such as that of Dan Wile, and research-based, such as that of Donald Baucom, Andrew Christensen, Dan O'Leary, Doug Snyder, and Susan Johnson. We also began working with same-sex relationships, based on our 12-year longitudinal study. The relationship clinic we built became an exciting base from which to work.

The marketing of our workshops led us to call our approach, which was based on the Sound Relationship House theory (Gottman, 1999), "Gottman Method Couples Therapy." However, we have always felt uncomfortable with that term and the amount of ego it suggested. The approach we have developed is integrative and broad. We cite and celebrate the work of others and give credit where it is due. We see ourselves engaged in a quest for the best treatment we can devise for couples. As is characteristic of people in our field, we keep searching. We are now engaged in basic research, as well as intervention and prevention research, and have been working to extend our clinic to include national membership. The research has become more applied and the clinical work has become more experimental. We want to do research and clinical work that affects families everywhere and supplies good information based upon state-of-the-art research and practice.

The dream is for a national and international community of researchers and clinicians who will dialogue, share ideas, and network from many perspectives, so that we can offer the best service to couples—one that is based solidly on high-quality research and on high-quality practice and the collaborative interplay of the two. The real goal is understanding. This book is the first product of that collaborative interplay.

REFERENCES

Gottman, J. M. (1999). *The marriage clinic: A scientifically based marital therapy.* New York: Norton.

Contributors

MICHAEL T. CLIFFORD, STM, M.DIV., LMFT, the Gottman Institute Relationship Clinic, Seattle, WA, and private practice, Everett, WA.

REGINA DELMASTRO, RN,C CEDC THTP, the Gottman Institute Relationship Clinic, Seattle, WA, and private practice, Bellevue, WA.

CYNTHIA H. ERVIN, PH.D., the Gottman Institute Relationship Clinic and private practice, Seattle, WA.

CONNIE FEUTZ, M.A., CMHC, the Gottman Institute Relationship Clinic, Seattle, WA, and private practice, Bellingham, WA.

JULIE SCHWARTZ GOTTMAN, PH.D., the Relationship Research Institute and the Gottman Institute, Seattle, Washington.

ANDY GREENDORFER, M.S.W., the Gottman Institute Relationship Clinic and private practice, Seattle, WA.

BARBARA JOHNSTONE, M.A., the Gottman Institute Relationship Clinic and private practice, Seattle, WA.

SARAH L. RATTRAY, PH.D., the Gottman Institute Relationship Clinic, Seattle, WA, and private practice, Shoreline, WA.

TRUDI SACKEY, M.A., LMFT, the Gottman Institute Relationship Clinic, Seattle, WA, and private practice, Kirkland, WA.

RUTH SAKS, PH.D., the Gottman Institute Relationship Clinic and private practice, Seattle, WA.

MAUREEN SAWYER, MSW, ACSW, the Gottman Institute Relationship Clinic and private practice, Seattle, WA.

TERRY STERRENBERG, M.DIV., MSW, the Gottman Institute Relationship Clinic, Seattle, WA, and private practice, Kirkland, WA.

MIRABAI WAHBE, M.A., the Gottman Institute Relationship Clinic, Seattle, WA, and private practice, Seattle and Bellingham, WA.

The Marriage Clinic CaseBook

Chapter 1 ❋

Introduction: An Abbreviated History and Overview of Gottman Method Couples Therapy

Julie Schwartz Gottman

One summer 10 years ago, John and I sat in our canoe off the shore of Orcas Island. The sea rippled as we paused from paddling to sit and gaze into the deep forest descending to the shore.

"I wonder what would happen if we created a workshop that helped couples," John said. "We've got this beautiful data. It shows we can create change...."

"Wouldn't that be *incredible?*" I replied in my usual hyperbolic style. "To actually use this to *really* help people instead of just a few in the lab?"

"We'd have to build a workshop. We'd explain the theory and do exercises to lead couples through the interventions from the lab. We'd start with building friendship, forming a base for their working with conflict the next day. Only this time they'd learn different skills, the ones that work."

We both knew from Jacobson's (1984) analysis of his behavioral couple therapy outcome that one year after therapy only 33% of couples in therapy were in the nondistressed range of marital satisfaction, and that 35–50% of those couples relapsed after 2 years, leaving a dismal 17% success rate. What if we could improve on that?

We were very excited and with atypical speed paddled quickly back to shore, trudged back up the hill to our cabin, climbed up to the loft, and set to work.

A month later the manual was completed. But we'd forgotten one detail: Where were the couples supposed to come from? We heard about someone who was a master program developer and between jobs. Thus Etana Dykan entered our lives, the Gottman Institute was born, and the first workshop was given in March of 1996 to 30 couples.

Meanwhile, we also created a workshop to train clinicians how to do couple therapy based on John's research and my years with clients. It was clear that we had to have a group of advanced-level clinicians who understood our methods intimately enough to skillfully help the couples needing more than the 2-day couple workshop. We also needed their help during the couples' workshops we gave, because our participant numbers were growing beyond what the two of us could easily support during the workshop exercises. In 1998, advanced trainings were offered, and from the clinicians who participated, 16 were asked to form the Marriage Clinic.

Referrals were made, clients were seen, and in our bimonthly consultation meetings, we wrestled with the dilemmas our couples faced—affairs, childhood trauma, depression, outbreaks of violence, attention deficit disorders, chronic ill-nesses, troubled children, distressed stepchildren—in short, the problems that you as a clinician face daily when you walk into your office.

Three years ago, John suggested to the group that we write a book for clinicians. It would describe case studies, the most difficult ones, and guide clinicians through the complexities of applying what we came to call "Gottman Method Couples Therapy" (GMCT) to their work. We were aghast. Most of us felt we didn't know enough. In characteristic fashion, at 3 A.M. one night, John wrote up a tentative book proposal, handed it to me the next morning, and said, "Look, it's easy, you can do it." I blanched.

The Marriage Clinic group also hesitated, wanting to wait and learn more first.

Another 2 years passed. Finally, after collectively ushering nearly 4,000 couples through workshops and/or therapy, we agreed to write up some cases. Those cases are presented here.

BASE PRINCIPLES

Following is a brief summary of some basic principles. (For an in-depth description, see Gottman, 1999.) GMCT is based on the Sound Relationship House theory (SRH; formerly known as the Sound Marital House theory). Following a 14-year longitudinal study of over 700 couples, John Gottman learned that the couples who successfully kept their relationships together worked on three primary objectives: They sustained their romance through the fundamentals of friendship, they managed their conflicts well, and they created a shared sense of meaning that knitted their lives together. There were also a number of corrosive forces that they tried to squelch, namely, the "Four horsemen of the apocalypse": criticism, contempt, defensiveness, and stonewalling. They worked hard to honor each other's dreams and laugh when perpetual issues raised their hoary heads. They also balanced the negative and positive interactions they had, so that there were five times as many positive as negative interactions during conflict and nearly 20 positive interactions to every negative one during peaceful times. From the study of these couples internally through physiological readings and externally through second-by-second videotaped coding, we learned the details of the SRH theory.

Imagine a house subdivided into seven levels, bottom to top. We begin with the foundation, which consists of the first three levels. These levels sustain friendship and depth of connection, which in turn fuel romance, passion, and good sex.

The First Level: Love Maps

Love maps represent our knowledge of our partner's internal world. Who are our partner's best friends, colleagues, enemies, allies? What are our partner's favorite books, movies, restaurants, travel destinations? What are our partner's dreams, hopes, nightmares, aspirations? What are our partner's most embarrassing moments from childhood? Their funniest moments? Couples who have distanced from one another don't know the answers, or what they know may be years old and outdated. In GMCT, clinicians give couples a list of questions to ask one another that help them update their love maps. In the workshop these questions are printed on cards, and couples play with the cards, guessing at the answers to the questions and gently correcting each other when wrong answers are given. By asking the questions, couples encounter each other as constantly changing and growing new worlds to be explored.

The Second Level: Fondness and Admiration

This level involves voicing our feelings of care and respect for our partners. As human beings, we need to feel loved, just as we need food and water. Yet many couples neglect to express their love. Consequently, partners feel lonely, uncared for, and invisible. Criticism and contempt compound the problem. Some couples think their partners will appreciate "constructive advice" or criticism—that it will foster improvements in their partners and in their relationships. The reality is that it does quite the opposite—it tears at the fabric of the partners' beliefs that they are loved and respected. It mirrors back to the partners negative reflections of themselves. Contempt, or criticism poisoned with superiority and sarcasm, name calling, or mockery, is worse still. Contempt is the antithesis of respect; thus it destroys feeling loved and shreds self-respect. Contempt even predicts infectious illness in its recipient. Couples in distressed relationships often feel battered by contempt. Expressions of fondness and admiration can help to heal these relationships. In GMCT, couples are taught to change their habit of mind. Rather than looking for their partners' flaws, sins, and omissions, couples are taught to watch for the positives in their partners—the behaviors, words, and glances that should be appreciated but are more often overlooked. Then they are coached to voice their appreciations in either words or touch. The more fondness and admiration are expressed, the more partners see one another as a refuge from the harsh realities of the world outside. The relationship begins to feel like a port in a storm, not the storm itself.

The Third Level: Turning Toward

This level contributes the small nuts and bolts that hold the SRH together. These are those moments when one partner makes a bid for connection to which the other partner positively responds. For example, look at the following turning toward moment between a couple named Joe and Adele.

Joe: Wow, look at those whitecaps on the sea.
Adele: Yeah, they sure are huge.

That was a bid for attention that the partner turned toward. Bids for attention can be negatively responded to as well, by either turning away or turning against. Turning away might sound like this:

Joe: Wow, look at those whitecaps on the sea.
Adele: (*reads her book without looking up*)

Turning against could be like this:

Joe: Wow, look at those whitecaps on the sea.
Adele: Would you stop interrupting me? I'm trying to read!

The bids may be for attention, affection, conversation, humor, emotional support, and so on. The number of these moments and the way they are responded to predict with good accuracy whether or not a couple will stay together or separate. Successful couples usually turn toward one another when bids for connection are made. Couples who separate don't. When seeking to heal their relationships, couples must learn to recognize when these bids for connection are made and how to respond to them positively. Often when couples finally reach therapists (usually, 6 years after first noticing the distress in their relationships), so many bids for connection have failed that couples no longer trust each other enough to even attempt another bid. The therapist can begin by gently interceding, structuring conversations in which couples write down the specifics of how each partner would prefer to receive attention. Couples can also try to do one positive thing for their partner each week, while the recipient guesses what that one thing was. Slowly, couples can rebuild the third level of their SRH by increasing the frequency of turning toward one another.

Together, love maps, fondness and admiration, and turning toward form a solid foundation of trust that underlies friendship and intimacy. Love maps help partners to feel individually known and interesting; fondness and admiration nourish partners' feeling loved and respected; and turning toward moves couples closer together as responders to each other's needs. When these three levels are strong, there is room for passion and sexual intimacy to grow and deepen.

The Fourth Level: Positive Sentiment Override

Also known as the positive perspective, this level is the bonus achieved when the first three levels have been solidly built. It is a concept originally suggested by Weider and Weiss (1980). It describes an overall color or mood of the relationship. It also refers to the way in which one partner interprets neutral statements made by the other partner. For example, if Joe says, "You left the fan on in the bathroom again," Adele might reply, "Oh, right. I'll go switch it off" (positive sentiment override), or "Stop trying to control me, as if you never leave anything on" (negative sentiment override). In the first case, the response is acceptance; in the second, it's counterattack and defensiveness. In *negative sentiment override* a person has "a chip on the shoulder" and is hypervigilant for negativity from the partner. When positive sentiment override is in place, even negative statements can be responded to with neutrality; in other words, one partner gives the other partner the benefit of the doubt. If Joe says, "I hate how you burned this toast," Adele might reply, "Whoa, what side of the bed did you get up on this morning?" The attribution is entirely different; a temporary emotional state of the partner is presumed to underlie negativity, not a lasting negative partner trait. Sentiment Override, positive or negative, is determined by the quality of friendship and intimacy. If partners have been trampled by the four horsemen, haven't asked each other a personal question in many months, and typically ignore each other's bids for connection, negative sentiment override will sour the relationship. On the other hand, if partners have continually updated their love maps of one another, frequently expressed fondness and admiration, and regularly turned toward one another in the small moments, positive sentiment override will sweeten it. Negative sentiment override can be reversed by strengthening the first three levels of the SRH and minimizing the presence of the four horsemen.

The Fifth Level: Managing Solvable Problems

The fifth and sixth levels of the SRH focus on the regulation of conflict. Gottman (1994) found that only 31% of couples' problems were solvable; the remaining 69% were perpetual and had to do with lifestyle and personality differences embedded in the relationship. This fifth level concentrates on solvable problems. Solvable problems can be successfully negotiated to resolution. However, five skills are needed. The first has to do with issue "start-up." How a problem is initially raised determines its course. For example, if Adele uses "softened start-up" to raise an issue, she starts her sentence with "I," states her feeling or thought without blame, describes the situation that troubles her in neutral terms, and clearly expresses her need. If she uses "harsh start-up" instead, she starts off with "you," blames Joe for what's wrong, and neglects to express her need. For example, suppose that Adele's mad that Joe never initiates sex. Using harsh start-up, she might say, "You're so friggin' passive . . . you call yourself a man?" With softened start-up she'd say, "I'm feeling upset that I seem to be doing all the initiating in our lovemaking. It makes me wonder if you're still attracted to me. Would you please let me know when you want to make love? Maybe give me a signal of some kind?"

Obviously, it is much easier to respond to a softened start-up than to a harsh one. In fact, the first 3 minutes of a problem discussion predict the entire course of the discussion, simply by what kind of start-up is used. Without intervention, there is only a 4% chance of natural reversal of a harsh start-up. Clinicians begin to improve conflict regulation for their clients by teaching the skills of softened start-up. This creates a huge potential change.

A second skill used by successful partners is "repair." Repair refers to the phrases couples use to get off-track conversations back on track. For example, suppose that, despite his best intentions, Joe says to Adele, "Are you sure you want to wear that dress? You look kind of big in it." He knows the minute the words leave his mouth that he's blown it. To repair things he might quickly add, "Oh, honey, I'm sorry. What a dumb thing to say," to which Adele might enthusiastically agree and, with some positive sentiment override, laugh a little and reply, "Maybe I do look big in it, but what's wrong with that? I like it, so I'm going to wear it. So there." A train wreck has been averted.

GMCT clinicians use the "repair checklist" of phrases to teach their couples repair skills. When partners discuss an issue, they have a written-out repair checklist on hand. If they negatively escalate and get derailed, they can refer to the repair checklist for phrases that will deescalate and refocus the discussion. It's also important that the listening partner accepts the repair; otherwise, the repair effort spins off into space, taking the couple with it. If in our earlier example Adele had replied, "Yes, you are stupid. Just leave me alone. I don't want to go anywhere with you tonight," the repair would have failed and she and Joe would have become emotionally distant. Adele might need a little time to express her hurt feelings before being able to accept Joe's repair, but acceptance of the repair is crucial.

A very important third skill is the ability to physiologically self-soothe. John Gottman found that people who experienced diffuse physiological arousal (DPA) were unable to listen to their partners or clearly articulate their own feelings. Partners whose pulses elevated above 95 beats per minute (bpm) were more likely to be in a state of DPA. Their conversations often contained the four horsemen, especially stonewalling. Gottman hypothesized that stonewalling was an attempt to self-soothe because it was most often seen in heterosexual men with high pulse rates during conflict discussions. Once pulse rates declined to normal resting levels, the nature of conversations completely changed, becoming calmer and more easily negotiable.

Clinicians use simple instruments to measure heart rate, especially when their clients have difficulties with negative escalations and stonewalling. Clinicians also work with their clients to help them recognize early on when they are becoming physiologically aroused. Then, by using biofeedback, deep relaxation, diaphragmatic breathing, and other techniques, they teach clients to soothe their tense bodies. Clients are also encouraged to take breaks from each other for at least 20 minutes when they are physiologically aroused so that they have the space and time to self-soothe before continuing their conversations. During these breaks it is important that the physiologically aroused person not rehearse distress-maintaining thoughts (thoughts of righteous indignation or innocent victimhood). With these techniques of physiological self-monitoring and regulation, many catastrophic collisions can be avoided.

A fourth skill necessary for solving problems is "accepting influence." When conflict discussions become entrenched, it is often because one partner is refusing to acknowledge the validity of his or her partner's position and to be influenced by it. Let's say that Joe needs to work late one evening. Adele, however, wants him home to help her prepare for her mother's visit that weekend. Using softened start-up, Adele might say, "Joe, will you please find another time to work late? I really need you to help me clean up the house. You know how mom loves everything to be spick-and-span." Joe might refuse to accept her influence and reply, "No, Adele. My work comes first. You'll have to do it by yourself." Adele will probably feel a little shut down and unimportant to Joe. She may also resent that her housework has less priority than his job work. The next time Joe asks for a favor, Adele will be less likely to respond positively to him. If Joe instead replies, "OK, I'll help you. But I may have to stay late at work tomorrow night," Adele will be more likely to acquiesce in turn and to appreciate Joe for his flexibility. In GMCT couples are reminded of the power of accepting influence. In the Japanese martial art of aikido, a powerful way of moving is to "yield to win." In relationships, yielding to influence often results in a cultivation of trust and intimacy.

The final skill needed for solvable-problem regulation is the ability to compromise. Compromise isn't easy, but it can be aided by a technique called "the two ovals." Partners draw two concentric ovals. In the inner oval, they list the points of their position on an issue that they cannot compromise on or give up. These are like the bones of the issue; if partners were to compromise on these they would feel some loss of their core identity. An example might be Joe wanting Adele to cook less red meat for dinner. In his inner oval he might write, "Must eat less meat to avoid future heart disease," a point on which he would not compromise. In the outer oval couples write down points on which they can be more flexible. Joe might write, "Can take Adele out to dinner more, so she doesn't have to cook as much at home." Then, as couples bring their ovals to the table for discussion, there is more clarity in where compromises can and cannot be made. Couples discuss several questions: Where is there overlap in our feelings, ideas, and beliefs? On which points can we both be flexible? And how can we honor each other's essential needs? As these questions are discussed, solutions to problems can be drawn up.

Conflict regulation is easier when the aforementioned five skills are used. However, patterns of attack-defend may persist and render even the simplest conflict negotiation overwhelmingly difficult. GMCT clinicians employ a number of methods to reverse attack-defend. One is video playback, in which the couple interaction is videotaped, played back, and discussed with the couple. Another is analyzing the "anatomy of the fight," or how each statement leads to the next negative response and to the cycle's inevitable disharmony. A third method is to understand each partner's "internal working model," or his or her intrapsychodynamic world and how it plays out during the couple interaction. Past traumas, important relationships from childhood, and beliefs about the self are more deeply understood here. An additional technique is Dan Wile's method of restatement. The therapist restates the partner's words with more personal self-reflection and emotion in order to create a joint platform from which both partners can better understand each other. Another method is to help partners identify their own "enduring vulnerabilities"—that is, the words or issues that trigger past pain so intense that conversation becomes impossible. Finally, therapists can help couples identify the "conversation they never had"—the underlying issues that weren't spoken. Once these issues surface, couples have discussions that distinctly differ from their initial fights.

If couples fail in converting fights into discussion, two other methods can be used to process the failures and move on. Both are questionnaires, titled respectively "The Aftermath of a Marital Argument" and "The Aftermath of a Failed Bid." The questionnaires ask couples to identify the feelings and behaviors that contributed to the fight. They also explore the setting conditions in which the fight occurred. Most importantly, they help couples to express their own subjective reality of what took place. When each partner answers these questions out loud, the listening partner is encouraged to simply listen rather than defend his or her position or disagree with the partner. Finally, couples also define what both they and their partners could do differently the next time the situation arises to make the discussions go more smoothly.

The Sixth Level: Dialogue with Perpetual Problems and Honoring Each Other's Dreams

The aforementioned five skills don't solve all problems. Some problems are very different; we call them "gridlocked conflicts." The sixth level of the SRH focuses on those 69% of problems that are perpetual and often gridlocked. It contains the most existential aspects of GMCT. John Gottman found that, when perpetual problems became gridlocked, clients' deepest dreams and values lay hidden at their center. Using a method called "the dream-within-conflict intervention," couples are guided to take turns being speaker and listener. The speaker voices his or her position on the issue. The listener then interviews the speaker, asking existentially based questions like "What does this mean to you?"; "Is there some underlying value in your position?"; "Is there a story behind this for you?"; "Is there a future hope you have or a sense of purpose in this issue for you?"; or "How about some disaster scenario?" In other words, listeners become interviewers who learn about their partners' hidden histories, beliefs, values, and dreams. After a set amount of time, the roles are reversed, and the speaker becomes the listener. When these feelings, experiences, and values are revealed, the thick wall separating the partners begins to crumble. Partners no longer view each other as the enemy. Instead, they come to see each other as dreamers and philosophers with fathomless levels to explore. Rigidly held stances soften, arrows are shelved, and at least partial compromises can sometimes be reached. In addition, once partners' dreams are revealed, this time with no swords drawn, it's much easier for the couple to find ways to honor both sets of dreams. In sum, this level helps make relationships safe enough for both partners to more fully be themselves and to realize their own dreams.

The Seventh Level: Creating Shared Meaning

Again adopting an existential perspective, couples in this level explore the roles, values, and symbols that give their lives meaning. Using either a questionnaire or discussion, couples clarify their beliefs. For example, they examine what it means to be a wife, husband, father, mother, lover, son, daughter, worker, and so on. Gay and lesbian couples may also talk about the meaning of coming out or commitment or choices involving parenting within the context of life in a homophobic culture. Couples are also supported as they explore their religious and spiritual values, as well as their beliefs about work versus play, parental discipline versus permissiveness, and autonomy versus togetherness. The beauty of the seventh level lies in the fact that it takes partners back to the beginning, to knowing one another on a deeper level—in short, back to the love maps. Thus, movement through the levels is circular and can be eternally expanded upon, forming a whole universe of relationship.

OVERVIEW OF BOOK

The following chapters expound upon how GMCT can be integrated into a clinical setting, how it is practiced with particularly difficult cases, and how it is used to conduct couple therapy follow-up.

In Chapter 2, Ervin explains how she integrated SRH assessment and intervention methods into an already-eclectic framework. She describes the difficulty of sitting with a couple in their "emotional maelstrom" and how SRH methods aided her in maintaining equanimity in the midst of it. She focuses on an especially difficult couple whose "fire and ice" seemed immutable. Yet with frequent and skilled use of the dream-within-conflict intervention, she helps this couple begin to change.

Delmastro takes on an especially difficult case in Chapter 3, telling the story of a couple struggling with trauma-related domestic violence. Delicately combining individual work and GMCT methods, Delmastro helps the partners to understand the connection between their early trauma and current dysfunctional patterns, thereby forging new paths on which the couple can travel toward intimacy.

In Chapter 4, I describe the particularly rocky issue of extramarital affairs. Gleaning wisdom from the work of the late Shirley Glass, I combine GMCT with the treatment of posttraumatic stress disorder engendered by sexual betrayal.

Sterrenberg looks at the seemingly ubiquitous problem of depression in Chapter 5. By exploring the internal working model of the depressed partner in the case example and helping him to become more accepting of his wife's love, Sterrenberg rekindles the marital fire.

Johnstone takes on what appears to be an impossible case in Chapter 6. Working with two partners diagnosed as suffering from borderline psychopathology, Johnstone must deal with extreme oscillations between idealization and vilification. Employing GMCT interventions and tremendous patience, she teaches the couple self-soothing, the belief in two subjective realities (which nearly breaks apart the therapy), and how to process a fight. She also knits together individual work and couples therapy to help each partner heal from terrible childhood trauma. Over the course of 2 years, the couple transforms.

Sexual problems often plague relationships and are one of the top three perpetual problems listed as gridlocked. In Chapter 7, Saks delineates a therapy to help an older couple suffering from sexual difficulties. By first working on the four horsemen and then building the couple's fondness and admiration system and exploring their internal working models and dreams for their marriage, Saks helps to move the couple toward sex's being tenable. From there care is taken to slowly introduce sexuality and the balancing of influence until finally passion and peace enter the couple's sexual world.

In Chapter 8, Feutz helps an emotionally distant couple by increasing the presence of affect—both positive and negative. Bridges of connection are built by strengthening the three levels of friendship of the SRH and by creating new rituals of connection. Conflict skills are built and techniques are developed to limit the four horsemen and to manage flooding. Emphasis is placed on building a new SRH on the foundation of the shared meaning system that already exists. Finally, she helps the couple to access personal feelings in order to reconnect them with each other.

In Chapter 9, Sackey details the complexity of working with a stepfamily. Damaged relationships between biological parents, ex-spouses, stepparents, and stepsiblings must be carefully managed. Sackey helps heal the couple and family through SRH theory and methods, stepfamily developmental models, and couples and family therapy in different interpersonal combinations. Methods are used to counter the couple's conflict-avoidant style and open up old conflicts and histories. The four horsemen are diminished and deeper understanding of family dreams is accomplished. Through the therapy, the family grows more inclusive, stronger, and ultimately healthier.

In Chapter 10, Rattray offers a number of analogies and metaphors that can augment GMCT. Central to the work of most therapies is the translation of abstract concepts into symbols and stories that can be more easily embraced. Rattray details metaphors, such as the idea of "two subjective realities," that help couples understand SRH concepts.

In Chapter 11, Greendorfer describes "Marathon Couples Therapy"—a condensed and intensified version of GMCT. This type of therapy reduces months of standard GMCT into 3 to 6 days of therapy with 4- to 6-hour-long sessions. Sessions are packed full of interventions, videotaped dialogue review, and individual historical exploration as couples work intensively on their relationships. Often the outcomes are powerful and surprisingly long-lasting.

In Chapter 12, Sawyer takes on the daunting task of bridging psychoanalytic couples therapy and GMCT. She reviews, concept by concept, the SRH theory and reveals the underlying affect regulation that also underlies psychoanalytic work. In a vignette taken from her work, she also reveals the thinking that helps her to interweave the two theories.

In Chapter 13, Wahbe wrestles with one of the toughest marital crises: What to do when partners are split on whether or not to have children? Wahbe describes a case in which a child represents both a blessing and a curse. After the child's arrival, the marriage deteriorates into a battle ground. By reducing flooding and replacing attack–defend with appreciation, the couple can finally embrace their child, and each other.

Clifford discusses termination and follow-up in Chapter 14, describing a methodical and careful plan that follows couples through their first 2 years after therapy termination. It is based on a review of gains on ten SRH criteria. Routine checkups are held every 6 months over a 2-year period. In these sessions, the therapist meets with couples to review maintenance of the gains they have made. Through these four sessions, couples are provided with a way to sustain their gains and troubleshoot if relapse appears on the horizon.

These chapters are offered as a glimpse into the practice of GMCT. We hope that you will come away with more faith in your own work, as well as a desire to build upon and refine these methods. As we all know, the world of relationships is endlessly complex and full of mystery—there is always room to learn more.

REFERENCES

Gottman, J. M. (1994). *What predicts divorce?* Hillsdale, NJ: Erlbaum.

Gottman, J. M. (1999). *The marriage clinic: A scientifically based marital therapy.* New York: Norton.

Jacobson, N. S. (1984). Variability in outcome and clinical significance of behavioral Marital therapy: A reanalysis of outcome data. *Journal of Consulting and Clinical Psychology, 52*(4), 497–504.

Weider, G. B., Weiss, R. L. (1980). Generalizability theory and the coding of marital interactions. *Journal of Consulting and Clinical Psychology, 48*(4), 469–477.

C h a p t e r **2** ❁

The Gottman Model's Effect on the Equilibrium of the Couples Therapist

Cynthia H. Ervin

Have you ever longed to jump into the bullring and get between the bull and the matador? Practicing couples therapy can be equally dangerous to your serenity. Both Bowen (1978) and Minuchin (1981) described the various triangles that can form among people. The coziest is when three people all like each other and get along nicely. Other triangles are less comfortable. It's stressful to be in a triangle in which two people are allied and the third is on the outs, especially if the third person is you. But the real killer is when one person is trying to remain allied to two people who are in conflict with each other. This is the dilemma of the child whose parents hate each other and the worker whose two bosses are feuding. So what does the hapless couples therapist, fool that she is, do but deliberately walk into that role. She inserts herself between the bull and the matador, keeping them from killing each other while maintaining a loving relationship with both, and talking to them until they finally decide that they not only don't want to kill each other, but also, in fact, want to go to the movies together and make love. At any point along the road to that transformation, they may aim their swords or horns at the therapist. Your job as a therapist is to remain balanced, not take sides, be accepting and supportive (even when they attack more fiercely), and use your training and brains to help them. But keeping your equilibrium in the middle of such an emotional maelstrom is a daunting challenge.

I have been fascinated by couples for years and have used many models to work with them. But GMTC has provided me with a clearer working model of couples therapy than I have had to date, giving me a level of clarity and perhaps confidence that I had not enjoyed in working with couples before. Gottman's model has helped me keep my equilibrium while maintaining compassion and the capacity to think clearly in the emotionally intense field of couples therapy.

A SAMPLING OF PREVIOUS CONTRIBUTIONS AND SRH AS A COMPREHENSIVE MODEL

In my years as a therapist I have had many teachers who helped me to achieve a greater ability to stay peaceful and thoughtful when the situation in therapy is difficult. Some of them have been highly respected innovators in their field and I've learned from their writings. Others have been colleagues, supervisors, and consultants. On one particular occasion, I was feeling very low and sure that my negligence had led to terrible consequences for a client. "You're a bit player," my consultant said softly, "in a large drama." I cannot count the times that mantra has helped me through a session.

Murray Bowen (1978) said that the most important thing a couples or family therapist can do is maintain a "nonanxious presence." In order to do this, he suggested, the therapist must deal with her own family-of-origin issues. Similarly, the analysts claimed you had to be analyzed first, if you were to successfully avoid countertransference. Having one's own therapy and dealing with one's own family-of-origin issues–or at least knowing what they are and when they come up—is important.

Working on knowing when I'm being triggered has been another great help. But the journey continues. Somehow, I'm still not immune to the stomach-wrenching triangle that can happen in work with couples. This is because it's not solely about the individual therapist. It's about the situation. Some of my best therapist friends are very individuated people, and they still get overwhelmed by very distressed couples. Dealing with family-of-origin issues is a lifelong process. Most of us want to practice our trade before we're dead. And working on your "issues" is complicated. How do you know when you've done it? I confess I still need more than the promise of resolved personal issues if I am to stand comfortably in the maelstrom.

The Milan school contributed circular questions and Cecchin (1987) invited us to be curious. The idea of taking a stance of great curiosity has been very helpful to me in working with couples. When in doubt, get really curious. The people before you are remarkable and fascinating. Circular questions are another great tool. To ask a good circular question, you must have a nonjudgmental view and take several perspectives into account at once. While you are helping a family or a couple see the world from each other's perspectives, you are doing the same for yourself. The questions can be a path to understanding the idea of holding more than one subjective reality. As any of us who have experienced almost any kind of human relationship know, understanding someone else's subjective reality without feeling that one's own is being threatened can be very difficult indeed.

Complex skills and attitudes are involved, which the SRH addresses. I still try to be curious and I still use circular questions, but couples are intense on many levels. The SRH adds a complex and flexible framework within which I can be curious, use circular questions, or try any number of other therapeutic techniques.

Narrative therapy is another great approach. According to narrative therapy, we are socially constructed beings. We have stories told about us—about who we are and what our potential might be. Some stories are productive and even fun. But some are not. They constrict us and make us believe debilitating things about ourselves (White & Epston, 1989). According to the narrative view, therapists also can be recruited by stories—about themselves and their clients. They can believe stories which depict them as inadequate and incompetent, and they can buy into the negative and constraining stories clients tell about themselves. After going to narrative workshops, I often feel very uplifted. I see heroes everywhere. I see people whose relationships have been invaded by disrespect, not disrespectful people. Narrative therapists encourage us not to pathologize ourselves or our clients. Thinking of a warring couple as two heroes stuck in cruel stories gives me a really useful image. I also find it helpful to think of myself as a hero trying not to get caught in unhelpful stories of inadequacy. Narrative therapy provides a method for questioning clients in systematic and freeing ways. So far, for me, narrative therapy has provided a big map made with beautiful broad strokes. The SRH gives me a more detailed map—one compatible with narrative concepts— that provides both structure and choices.

Guerin (1987) described a four-point assessment system for couples. He evaluated the seriousness of the problems and the likelihood of the marriage flourishing. A "one" was a couple who needed some education about relationships and would blossom from there. A "four" was a couple who had already consulted a lawyer. I found the system helpful. It highlighted the idea that couples present different levels of distress and, once again, I am not responsible for that, nor is it helpful for me to *try* to be responsible for it. If I am not weighed down by the presenting problems, I am in a better position to be helpful, even if the distress level is very high.

A friend and colleague of mine once said that when families would get into fights in his office, he would rub his hands together and think, "Oh goody, enactment!" He drew this highly helpful concept from structural family therapy. My friend tried to use this mental trick to find a place to stand in the midst of the emotional intensity of families. But many therapists never shed the feeling of being overresponsible. This is understandable: Haley (1976) told us that, if the therapy failed, it was entirely the therapist's fault. Certainly when we find ourselves wandering aimlessly and blaming our clients' resistance when the work does not go well, we do indeed need to face our own responsibility. But Haley's message was not good for my friend, and it's not good for me. I need a sound model to guide me. Hearing that I am responsible without feeling that I have a clear path seems rather like the position of the parentified child.

Certainly, there are excellent and useful models of family therapy. But working with a couple is different from working with a family, and it is definitely different from working with an individual. Skills from both therapies are applicable, and we try to apply the models we know. However, they often fail to give us the guidance we need when we face the complex emotional territory that couples present.

DISCOVERING THE GOTTMAN MODEL AND UNWITTINGLY ENTERING A LONG STRUGGLE

Gottman materials provide a detailed map consisting of many paths. It's the kind of straightforward map people like me can use. When John Gottman gives workshops for clinicians, he says he wants people say to themselves, as they leave, "This is no big deal. I can do this." I often left workshops feeling that the presenter was brilliant and that I had seen videos or role plays of fine therapy. I also felt that perhaps I was not as brilliant as the presenter. I always learned something, but I didn't necessarily grasp clear methods, concepts, and stances that I could apply.

The underpinning for Gottman's work is years of research, which is what drew me into my first workshop. The workshop did not prompt me to stop doing everything else I already knew. Like many of my esteemed colleagues, I hate fads. But I left that first workshop thinking what Gottman hoped I would think—that I could do this and it could be really helpful. I also saw him as a researcher who was respectful of clinicians and wanted to interweave clinical work and research. Researchers—and many clinicians, for that matter—often lament that clinicians don't apply research findings to their work. Gottman presented a way to do that. He offered a clear compendium of materials from which I could choose, depending on the situation. Nevertheless, I did not jump in and use them all. Rather, the relationship between my work and GMCT has been a process of mutual growth. Initially I simply responded positively to research-based therapy with a manual that does not ignore the importance of the client-therapist relationship, the judgment of the therapist, the highly emotional nature of the couple relationship, and the heart in therapy. The amusing thing about "the manual" is that it keeps changing. I have at least six versions lined up in my office. I hope it changes forever.

THE ASSESSMENT: A BASIS FOR EQUILIBRIUM AND PILES OF PAPER

The assessment includes an initial session with both partners, detailed questionnaires about the relationship, for both partners to fill out, individual time with each partner, and a feedback and planning session. The therapist sees the couple together the first time. They get to tell their stories, and a detailed oral history of their relationship is taken. Then the clients get to talk to each other while the therapist sits apart and videotapes the discussion for 10 minutes or so. Then the therapist asks if this is pretty much how it is at home. Usually it is. Some people dislike using videotape. I found implementing that part a hassle, but I could see the value in it right away. It immediately gave me a way to stand back and evaluate—a way to stay out of the fray, especially in the beginning, while I was getting to know the couple and finding my compassion for them.

I did, however, definitely balk at the big pile of paperwork handed out at the first session. With much trepidation, I actually tried using all the questionnaires at first. More than one client said that filling out the paperwork made them feel so resentful of their partner that they were afraid to do it. That spooked me. I didn't want to be afraid of the clients' feelings, but I also didn't want to blow them out of the water before they started. As I continued to use the SRH framework, however, I began to feel that the information would really help. I struggled with the question of responsibility. If the questionnaires were painful to fill out, did that mean I should be "gentler" and move into such painful territory slowly? I began to wonder if I wasn't taking too much of the wrong kind of responsibility again.

Although I cannot verify with absolute certainly that it happened, I remember a Gottman Institute Marriage Clinic discussion about first sessions and having the couple leave with a feeling of hope. My memory is that John Gottman maintained that giving hope was "not my job." Then he said something about evaluating, collecting information, and being ready to give feedback, letting the couple know what needs to be done. John has since told me that he doesn't remember saying that giving hope isn't part of the job. But I want him to remember. I know there are psychotherapists out there who do not tend to feel overresponsible, but I am not one of them. Leaving a couple feeling hopeful is a good thing, but the hope does not come from me feeling heavily responsible for them feeling hopeful. It comes from their sense that I really see and understand their problems and that I can handle the emotions with which they themselves have so much trouble.

Eventually I tried giving couples the whole wad of questionnaires with their many detailed questions about personal symptoms, violence, and emotional abuse. I get a great deal of information up front about the history and functioning of the relationship. I know how they feel about their handling of money, raising children, and having fun. I get information about their sex lives and substance use and much more.

I've developed a patter about all these papers that is based on my now-extensive experience with many couples filling them out. I mention that the packet is very thick and that different people approach it in different ways, which is fine. I tell my clients that some people are irritated by the yes-or-no questions because they feel they can't answer so simply. I emphasize that the packet is for me to get a lot of information quickly, so they can go ahead and write on it and explain things to me and I will read it. I assure them that the information will be useful and will make our work more effective.

As I mentioned earlier, the assessment includes individual meetings with the partners. What initially convinced me to see each partner alone was our discussions of domestic violence. I came to know that I had to ask each partner about violence without the other partner there. After I began to do it more routinely, I also began to confess that this session was very useful in many ways. It gives me an opportunity to join with each partner and hear his or her story of the relationship as well as of family of origin without having to worry about the other person's reaction. I find that the individual session is a good time to ask about alcohol and other drugs, in addition to violence, as well as depression and suicidal feelings, concerns about affairs, and even a history of abortion or miscarriage. These are all issues that can turn out to be vitally important. Providing the safety to discuss such personal matters during the assessment saves time and avoids unhappy surprises later.

The feedback session follows the individual sessions. We discuss the state of things, where the strengths are, what we will need to work on. I tell them about the four horsemen, the behaviors that are bad for marriage: criticism, stonewalling, defensiveness, and contempt. I tell them that research shows that successful couples have some of the first three horsemen, but they have virtually no contempt. They do, however, have anger, longing, love, disappointment, and all those feelings that need to be talked about. We make a contract. We have an agreement about what we will be working on. I get permission and agreement that I will be able to stop destructive behaviors and recommend better ones. "These are the areas you will need to work on," I say. "Are you willing to enter into this contract?"

This process is not always tidy. One couple took several sessions to decide to accept the contract to work on couples therapy. They were hurt and not sure they wanted to agree to anything. They had some feelings to talk about first. They were separated and also needed to talk about child-sharing arrangements right away. I could go with their need. I still had the model in my head. I could accept the idea that this couple was still in the evaluation process, even though it was taking longer than usual. I could even take a bit of a detour and still come back to the basic structure. Knowing that we were still assessing the situation, that we had not yet contracted for therapy, gave me the freedom to explore with them and follow their lead without feeling as if I had to get something going. We'd get something going if and when they were ready. I could face the sessions without that awful feeling that I personally had to make something happen.

I find that the evaluation process directly addresses the issue of responsibility and overresponsibility. In the feedback session I can make it clear that I am sympathetic and respectful and, at the same time, I can simply show them their work. It is not my work. I have a base from which to reach out when I do the evaluation, but I am not in the middle of it. I am not the cause of the problem. Nor am I the cure. They bring the problem and the process can offer them paths, as it does me. There is a map of these paths, and I can plan my route. With a good working model, I can do my work and have a much-increased chance of maintaining my own equilibrium.

The Gottman approach helps provide a path. This is not to say that I follow a rigid line; the path has many inlets and outlets and diversions.

MIKE AND ALICE

Mike and Alice were both pleasantly attractive people in their early forties. During our first session together, I learned that Alice's family had a rigid structure and dished out a lot of criticism in the guise of helpfulness. There was sexual abuse in the extended family. Mike's family was chaotic and emotionally abusive. He spent as much time away from them as possible.

The couple presented with Alice looking frustrated, critical, and cold. She was obviously in negative sentiment override. Mike looked beleaguered and stonewalling. I soon figured out that he was in negative sentiment override as well.

The First Session

In our first session, I learned that the couple had been married for 9 years and had a 7-year-old girl and a 5-year-old boy. Alice had a son from a previous marriage. He had his own apartment, but was welcome at Mike and Alice's home and visited periodically. Alice was a teacher, but found it difficult to work the full schedule with two young children. So she taught preschool two mornings a week and sometimes substituted for public schools to augment her income. She was feeling burned out on mothering and trapped in her work and her life. She was ready for adventure and change. She wanted to move out of the city and maybe raise horses, but she said she'd be open to change of any kind. She wanted Mike to join her in figuring out how to go about it together. Mike was a lawyer who worked for a nonprofit organization that provided low-fee legal services. He also sometimes provided legal assistance pro bono on the side. He agreed that he worked long and unpredictable hours, although the couple disagreed about the number of hours and how unpredictable they were. Mike was pleased with his job and felt he was on a productive career path. He was sympathetic to Alice's needs and agreed that living in a less populated area would be great, but he still wished Alice would find a less disruptive way to fulfill herself.

Their courtship was lovely, but the wedding was painful. Mike was in the middle of a trial and had very little time to plan. They cut their celebration off and canceled the honeymoon. To top it off, Alice had the flu during the ceremony. They were both glad they lived through it but had no fond memories of it. Alice felt like Mike was distracted and unconcerned about both her health and her dreams. Mike felt like this was very old news and wondered why Alice couldn't forgive and move on.

Mike and Alice agreed that the summer before they came for therapy was relatively pleasant. There had been fewer demands on their schedules and less stress with the children. Their daughter had trouble focusing on her homework and their son was difficult to get going in the morning. With school in session for the children and Alice back to work, the couple was fighting much more. The issues they said they needed to work on were: "organizing our daily lives, parenting, intimacy, conflict resolution, and anger management," as well as Alice's desire to make a change.

I asked them to discuss a problem during this first session, and they chose to talk about her wanting a big change in their lives. The following dialogue may sound sparky, but the tone of both partners was actually cold and low-key.

> Alice: I want to move. I'm tired of my life here. I'm not enjoying my job. I need something more in my life, but I can't just go to school or something, because of the kids. I can't leave them, and if I have to work and study and take care of kids, I'll go under. I'm sick of the city. I've been so depressed. I'm tired of being depressed. I can't talk about my dreams. You won't talk to me.
>
> Mike: I know you're sick of being here. You talk to me all the time. You're down on this place first thing in the morning, every weekend. You're

always frustrated. (with sarcasm) So that's my problem that I can't just go find a job and support us in some out of the way place.

Alice: We really can't talk about it. You say I'm angry at you, but you're angry all the time, including now. And you're always busy. I feel like we've never pulled together. Our lives haven't meshed.

Mike: Well, whenever there's a conflict, there's never any forgiveness. We hang onto anger and never let go.

Alice: If I have a different opinion, you go into conflict. You close off and remove yourself. It makes me crazy. Eventually you come back, but we never resolve it.

Mike: I could be better at communicating, but nothing is ever enough. You barrage me with questions about jobs in smaller towns. I can't answer your questions.

Alice: You don't want to.

They continued to argue, back off, begin arguing again, and so on. Eventually they looked helplessly at me. I had the freedom of knowing that this was their "problem discussion," and I didn't have to *do* anything about their interaction. I was mentally and emotionally available to witness it and appreciate the difficulties they had.

"Is that about the same as what happens at home?" I asked.

"Sometimes. Other times it escalates into a shouting match and slammed doors. Sometimes the children are around to hear it." During that first session, I had a hard time imagining them shouting at each other. My feeling about this couple was that, if they came apart, it would be through ice, not fire. But when it comes to couples, there is plenty of fire somewhere within the ice—or at least a time when there used to be. Given Mike and Alice's description of the fights they had at home, I had reason to believe the fire was still there. That was good.

I did not follow a script in this session. The Sound Marital House structure allows for conducting sessions in many ways. I was aware of thick tension, longing, and unspoken pain in the marriage and about their families of origin. But I was relieved of the responsibility for changing it that day. It was just the first session and the beginning of the assessment. This session was an example of how not feeling obligated to give the couple hope left me free to experience them in a way that, paradoxically, probably gave them—and me—more hope. I had access to my own evaluating mind and could use my emotional responses as information without getting tied up in trying to get something to happen too soon. At the end of the session, Mike and Alice both said they were glad they had come and had told the story and glad that I saw what happens to them. I have come to believe that being really seen, really understood, and really witnessed is a powerful human need and a wonderful experience for both the understander and the understood.

Having a map in my head about what I want to accomplish in the first session gives me a firm place to stand. Having this particular structure in my head has given me a path toward the freedom to feel strongly and to care about my new clients without feeling swamped by their pain. Another very important aspect of the work for me is not following a model in a slavish way. In this session I was not using the specific list of questions in the oral history for research purposes. I did not videotape the problem discussion, because Mike and Alice preferred not to. (I did videotape a discussion later.) Hearing a couples' story, getting their history, and seeing how they interact are not unique to this approach. But there is a solid underlying structure, a multifaceted path.

During this first session I was also doing the first assessment of their "fondness and admiration." I was watching for signs of affection. How did they look when they recalled their meeting and courtship, when they mentioned their children? Did they show pride in each other's work? What could I see in their faces? I was also looking for criticism, stonewalling, defensiveness, and contempt. Any quick eyerolls? Contemptuousness in the mouth? Any subtle expressions of inherent superiority? I saw and heard plenty of criticism, stonewalling, and defensiveness. I didn't pick up contempt, so I asked them about it. I described the four horsemen, told them a little about the research, and asked if my perception fit theirs. They said it mostly did, but that they did have contempt at home. My assessment in that first session was that Alice tended to speak very critically and that Mike tended to defend and stonewall. They hooked each other in all the predictable ways. But I didn't know them well yet. I was looking forward to seeing them again and learning more about them.

Continuing the Assessment: The Pile of Paper

At the end of the first session, I gave Mike and Alice the whole packet of assessment forms, and both of them brought the completed forms back to their individual sessions. The paperwork revealed that neither Mike nor Alice was seriously considering divorce, but they showed a great deal of unhappiness. I picked up an interesting discrepancy, which was revealed only because I had all that diagnostic paperwork. Mike seemed more unhappy than Alice on paper. He recorded more problems as "perpetual," whereas Alice left a few blank and said the rest were solvable. They agreed that their love maps were not terrible but could be better and that their fondness and admiration system was in very bad shape. He gave a bleaker picture of their negative perspectives, gridlock, four horsemen, and flooding, although she was not positive about any of those areas either. He reported having a very hard time with her start-up. They agreed that they were both fairly open to influence but feeling extremely lonely and disengaged. They had not been intimate emotionally or sexually for a long time. Regarding conflict tactics, she looked more insulting and he more withdrawing. Neither of them had many personal psychopathology symptoms. He was aware of irritability and a tendency to feel guilty. She had some irritability and agitation. There was no violence, although she had slammed doors and thrown things down. The interesting part was that Mike was dissatisfied whereas Alice reported more strengths. This intrigued me because Alice verbally expressed much more unhappiness in the relationship. When they had come in together, it looked like Alice was the only one who was at the end of her tether. The paperwork revealed much more negativity in Mike. That was good to know. It helped later, when I felt his unspoken anger. I had information that allowed me to understand what I was experiencing rather than feel confused, uncertain, and frustrated. It was like having a sign on a winding road letting me know that a stop sign was coming up. I had a chance to feel in control and slow down instead of coming to a screeching, heart-pounding stop.

Individual Assessment Sessions

During the individual sessions, I got more information about the couple's levels of commitment to the marriage, what they each hoped for in the relationship and their lives, and about their families of origin. I also ruled out domestic violence, any kind of substance abuse, suicidality, and affairs. She had had a miscarriage before she met Mike, and the pregnancies with their two children were very difficult. Mike was kind to Alice's older son, but sometimes felt left out when he was visiting. They both indicated that they were committed to trying to work out the marriage. Mike was more vague, just expressing the wish to live in a harmonious, nurturing home. He did not have more specific hopes or fears. Alice was much clearer that she needed Mike to be more responsive and more willing to "deal with things."

Mike was the oldest of four children. His father was an attorney with an "anger management problem." His mother was alternately depressed and angry. Mike's parents and siblings got into shouting fights. Neither parent hit the children, but they hit each other and the children hit each other. He was not aware of his mother's (or father's) being injured. Usually his parents' fights ended with his father storming out of the house and his mother remaining in her room. The siblings would fight until someone was seriously in tears. Mike described his father as difficult and temperamental but more predictable than his mother. Sometimes his mother was loving, but she was also increasingly erratic and depressed. Mike's youngest brother was often in trouble and Mike picked him up from the police station on two occasions. Mike's response to the chaos at home was to spend as much time away as possible. He did a lot of fishing and other solitary activities. His schoolwork was spotty at best and he barely made it through high school. In the middle of all this, Mike's mother had a crisis, left the family, remarried, and was rarely seen again. Mike said that, on the one hand, he was relieved. The house was quieter. On the other hand, the children were left with his father, which meant often being left alone, and taking care of his siblings. They resented him and Mike felt guilty about leaving them too much. He and his siblings ended up alienated from each other and Mike had not seen any of his family of origin in years. He expressed feeling very torn and felt he should be able to "get over it" and spend time with them.

Alice grew up as an only child in a semirural area. She described her father as very strict and distant and not home very much. When Alice started school, her mother went to work full-time and was also away from home a lot. Alice was often alone, but also spent time with her aunt and three cousins, who were older by several years. Her recollection was that her parents got along with each other, but she didn't see them interact very much. Her experience was that communication in the family often included a lot of criticism. She didn't really understand why, but her three cousins all got into some kind of serious trouble. Alice avoided them and played mostly by herself. One of her older cousins was sexually abusive to his younger sister. He had tried to molest Alice once. She did not know why it was only once, and she did not think of the incident as very serious, although she remembered she thought it was odd and wrong. She said she probably told him to get off and cut it out. She said she was a "scrappy" child and not likely to put up with being hurt.

Alice had felt attached to her mother, whose death from a long, progressive illness a few years earlier was a tremendous loss. Her father was in his nineties and Alice took care of his finances. Alice felt completely alienated from her cousins. She lived far away from them and had no desire to be around them. She felt that they resented her because of their perception that she was "special" and "rich" and always got "everything she wanted." Alice missed her mother and felt sad about rarely seeing her father, but said she had just let it go. It wasn't worth getting into. She also talked about the miscarriage which happened before she was with Mike. She said it was one of the hardest things she ever experienced. Alice reported feeling somewhat depressed. She hoped that improving or leaving her marriage and being able to make the changes in lifestyle she wanted would lift her mood. I believed her, but I also wondered how much the losses she'd experienced in childhood and adulthood contributed to her restlessness, dissatisfaction with the relationship, and depression.

Feedback and Getting to Work

During the feedback session, Alice and Mike were attentive and agreed that they both needed to decrease contempt. Alice would especially need to look at her tendency to criticize and Mike would need to show less defensiveness and stonewalling. I explained *flooding* to them and Mike readily agreed that he was flooded when he stonewalled. This conversation was perhaps the first time Alice began to see Mike's behavior in a more sympathetic light. They also agreed that they needed to blow some life into the positive side of their relationship, or, in other words, work on their fondness and admiration. They left with the assignment to do something nice for each other and guess what they each did at the next session. They were very earnest about this assignment. He brought her flowers. She gave him a card and also came home early from a night with friends, so he could do some work. She identified the flowers and he identified the card. He missed her coming home early as a nice thing to do, which reinforced her feeling that he felt fine about working all the time and took for granted that she would be home with the children. Mike and Alice showed that they were willing to try things and to work, but the exercise felt a little hollow. I didn't get a toasty feeling. It was like they had been good students but couldn't quite grasp the main point.

During the next four sessions, we spent some time on love maps and fondness and admiration. They took the love map cards home and, unlike many couples, used them and brought them back the following week. They said it was nice to do, but I still didn't see any sign of a warming trend. Nevertheless, they said they were fighting less, which was a relief. I do find that sometimes the volume needs to be turned down before couples can get to the heart of the matter. So although

I could see we had much more work to do, they did feel some relief. And I had barely touched the possibilities available to me in the SRH. I saw that Mike and Alice could show more appreciation and fight less. They still felt distant and cold, which let me know I needed to continue further along the many paths.

Using the Lower Floors of the SRH

We discussed softened start-up and being open to influence. They both actually agreed that Alice already used softened start-up and that Mike didn't usually start emotion-laden interactions. They agreed that Alice was open to influence and that Mike was as well, but he sometimes didn't follow through when it felt crucial to Alice. We spent some time talking about making and responding to bids for connection, showing appreciation, and rituals of connection. They went home with assignments to work on these behaviors. They tried. They even rather enthusiastically agreed that their ratio of positive communications to negative ones was pretty bad. They were eager to improve it. She understood that she needed to consciously reduce her criticisms and increase her appreciations. He was quite clear about making bids and consciously responding to bids. They did the appreciations checklist with no trouble. It still felt pro forma to me but they were having fewer negative interactions.

During these early sessions, we also worked a great deal with flooding. Mike was particularly prone to flood and then either get very angry or stonewall. He readily acknowledged that he flooded and tried to address the problem with conscious breathing and time-outs, but mostly he forgot in the heat of the moment. A colleague of mine once talked about using bubble-blowing with anxious children. I wondered if it would help flooded adults. To blow bubbles, you have to breathe slowly, the bubbles are kind of relaxing to watch, and you really can't take yourself too seriously while you're blowing bubbles. Not all adults will go for it, but Mike was willing. He blew some bubbles in the office and said it was nice and that he felt better. The problem came up at home. On one or two occasions, when Alice perceived Mike ratcheting up emotionally, she recommended—not too nicely as I understood it—that maybe he had better just go blow some bubbles. Bubbles lost their luster after that, but he continued to practice breathing deeply and slowly.

Meanwhile, I was also learning more about Mike and Alice's interactions and how they got stuck when they tried to talk about important subjects like their kids, their lives, and their dreams. Mike claimed that Alice could say really nasty things. Alice complained that she couldn't get anything going with Mike emotionally or any way. He didn't participate in the home. He spent his evenings working on the computer, while she kept the routines going with the kids by herself. He wasn't available to her son when he was home and he was not supportive when she was pregnant with their children. He wasn't romantic and never wanted sex with her. He wouldn't talk to her about her deep restlessness. She felt hurt, abandoned, and disappointed. Then we came full circle to his complaint about her criticisms.

They agreed that their behaviors needed to change. He agreed to be available in the evenings when he got home from work, instead of immediately disappearing into his office and losing himself on the computer. She agreed to be mindful of her critical comments, decrease them, and increase complementary statements. I believe they tried. But he forgot what he had promised during the session, in spite of honestly meaning to stay around at least some evenings. She didn't forget. She felt fully justified in being critical at the time, even though, on reflection, she could see that her criticism was getting her nowhere.

Relentless Loopy Arguments

Like many couples, Mike and Alice came in wanting to talk about the fights they had at home. Without actually pulling out the written exercise, I walked them through the steps of the "aftermath of a marital argument." They were each able to say how they felt during the fight. They each told their story. They were actually able to tell me that they could see how a reasonable person could feel the way their partner did. When they got to the part about what they might do differently, they faltered. They started to talk about it but had a hard time staying out of what their partner should do differently. The exercise had the same feeling that the fondness and admiration work had. They were trying to be good students, but little was happening on an emotionally helpful level, and the same arguments resurfaced in the same form 5 minutes later.

These relentless, loopy arguments are like an eternal whirlpool that engulfs the couple and threatens to overwhelm them, the therapist, and maybe even the furniture. What appeared on my mental billboard again were the words "negative sentiment override" and "perpetual problems." I didn't know what was or was not perpetual problem at that point. I just realized how unhelpful working directly on fondness and admiration can be in the face of negative sentiment override. If you don't have a "climate of appreciation," repairing fights is also going to be an uphill job. Alice had presented looking brittle, cold, and negative. Mike had seemed softer, but I remembered his paperwork. His negative override was at least as severe as hers and, even if I was too insulated in my cozy office to feel it, surely she did. And he felt hers as well. They had found ways to take breaks and to hurt each other less, but to progress further, we were going to have go to the next level.

I tried using the dream-within-conflict intervention with them in the way it is written in the manual, because it was clear that we were going to have to get to deeper meanings. They worked hard at interviewing each other, and it did take them to another level. It didn't take them to the level they would need to get to the first time, but it was a step along the way. They interviewed each other with some sympathy. The problem was that they were both still trying to make their point. He wanted to be sure that she dealt with the fact that her family was very critical and that she still tended to communicate that way. She wanted him to deal with his learned tendency to withdraw emotionally and in every other way. They tripped over another source of conflict. She pretty much agreed that her extended family was useless and felt his family was as well. He didn't think she should write off her family and didn't want to write off his either (even though he never saw them). She saw his willingness to "overlook" things in their families as part of the general pattern of his obliviousness and he saw her willingness simply to remove her family from her life as part of her rigidity and tendency to be judgmental.

But they did each hear some about each other's experiences and they were able to sympathize with the other's story. It wasn't perfect, but it did create some warming and was a good step.

Using Videotape to Intervene in Attack-Defend Cycles

During the session, Alice was still very upset about not being able to talk about changing their lives and she said she felt pressured by the children's growing up. She wanted to get settled. So, plunging in, we worked on "having the conversation they needed to have" (Wile, 1993) again. As soon as they began talking about her wish to relocate and change their lives, they moved into "attack-defend" (Wile) mode. "Every time I try to bring it up, you block it," Alice complained, "and you never tell me your dreams." "Well, I don't have a 5-year plan," Mike shot back, in a tone somewhere between righteous and whiny. I asked to videotape the conversation so we could look at it together, and they agreed this time. This was another time I was glad to have a map. Being in the middle of an attack-defend argument is not easy, and, of course, occurs frequently with distressed couples, which is partly why some colleagues would rather not deal with couples. But I had the road sign in my head: "Attack-defend on the horizon—steer clear." Videotaping is a great way to get some distance. I happen to have a big, old camera from the 1980s, so I can literally stand behind it and remove myself.

Alice opened with what was wrong with what Mike had been doing up to this point. He responded with a whining kind of defensiveness. ("I *am* trying.") Then her criticism got more global, about his general lack of interest in her wishes.

Alice: You never want to talk. You're always too busy.
Mike: I am not. Just this week I looked at the Internet, but I didn't see any good jobs anywhere else. What do you want?
Alice: You say you want to look into living somewhere with more space, but you never actually do anything about it.
Mike: I looked at the Internet just last week.
Alice: I feel alone, as if my concerns are not worth your time.
Mike: I told you, I *am* looking. I don't know what you want from me.

Even with the big camera to hide behind, I didn't stay out of the conversation completely. I asked them if they thought they were progressing. No, they replied, they didn't. I asked them to try having a different conversation. I reminded them about flooding and criticism and defensiveness. The conversation changed a little.

Alice: *(taking a big breath)* Okay. What kind of work would you consider doing?
Mike: I could do anything. I'd clean stalls in Montana.
Alice: What?
Mike: I could just look around and think about it.
Alice: I can't figure out what you're saying. It's too nebulous.
Mike: What can I do to convince you I want to do it?

Alice: If I saw you motivated. You have trouble putting any real time or motivation into it.

Mike: Okay, let's plan an afternoon a week to work on it.

Alice: But you never even want to talk about it, much less do research.

Mike: You have a hard time seeing where I'm coming from. I have a stable spot here, where we live now, where I'm working.

Alice: I understand. You're digging in. For me, it's a trap. And something better isn't just going to present itself.

Mike: Well, let's set aside some time.

Alice tried to get Mike to be realistic and clearer by asking more questions, while Mike tried to convince her he was motivated to change their lives without being specific. He insisted they need to set aside time to talk about it at home, but neither of them really believed that would happen.

Before we replayed the videotape, I asked Mike and Alice to observe their own behavior and to avoid watching and judging their partner. The wonderful thing about videotape is that the clients take the responsibility for describing what happened, not me. I can avoid that nasty triangle. They can engage with themselves and each other.

"It was painful to watch," Mike lamented after seeing the tape. "I see myself stonewalling—not engaged."

"I was ineffective," Alice replied. "And I was negative, even my posture was negative. I was kind of trying to connect, but there was no spark."

I asked what they thought they might want to change.

"I'd have to change the way I said things," Alice responded. "I'd have to be more positive and have more enthusiasm. More warmth."

"I need to be more proactive," Mike said, "and not just reactive."

They gave themselves homework. He decided to make three bids for connection each day and she chose to show five appreciations.

Back to Basics

I wish I could say the videotape intervention was so powerful that Mike and Alice lived happily ever after. But, in fact, they proceeded to have a terrible couple of weeks. Couples often step back after a step forward. Alice was away part of the time and called to see how things were going. According to her, Mike was yelling at the kids while she was on the phone with him and handling their daughter's homework frustration very poorly. After she got home, they fought about it and he disappeared into work again. He didn't see why she couldn't be supportive about his having a hard time with their daughter, especially because she sometimes had a hard time, too. He also said he had a lot of work to do when she got back. She didn't see why she couldn't leave him with the children for a few days without a big blowup.

I began again to work with them on processing the fight. I already knew that, with massive intervention, they could barely process a fight without getting flooded and back into the fight. In this case, they were about to get back into the fight. I just didn't let it happen. I felt them going back into the patterns that hurt them. I could have gotten frustrated and impatient. After all, we'd been here before. I could have felt hopeless about Alice's inability to see that her approach was critical and Mike's defensiveness and placating behaviors. Instead, I saw the aftermath of a marital argument format in my head again, and I led them through it. They each said how they felt. They each told their story. I could see the first signs of flooding. So I decided to tell them a story about one of my own marital bloopers to make them laugh and to let them know that they were not alone in finding it difficult to see one's own part in a fight. I was looking for ways to normalize arguments, reduce shame, and bring down the emotional escalation without either of them feeling blamed. Laughter is a great way to reduce flooding. Flooded people don't often feel very humorous, but, when I told them the story, they did laugh, and they laughed again when I said marriage is not for the faint-hearted. Then they each took the step of owning a piece of the fight. I think that happened for two reasons. First, I had just owned a bit of misbehavior of my own, which perhaps helped with their shame. Second, they felt calmer after laughing and breathing for a few minutes. Though it was difficult, they were beginning to see the loops in their arguments. They recognized flooding and their tendencies to withdraw and criticize.

The Dream-Within-Conflict Intervention

The dream-within-conflict intervention flashed before my eyes again. I thought it might help provide Mike and Alice with more space and promote compassion, which was needed if they were to ever own a piece of the fight. It also provided me with another signpost. I had a map, so I didn't get lost and frustrated. I hoped we could get further this time. But I also decided not to let this be a dyadic experience. I participated in guiding the conversation and asking questions. Gottman often says that couples therapy should be mostly dyadic, not triadic. In other words, it's mostly between the couple, not individual therapy between the therapist and each partner. The couple bears the responsibility—they do the real work. But the model has to adapt to the situation. Some couples need more from the therapist. With Mike and Alice, I chose to modify the intervention and take a greater role. With questions and encouragement, Mike talked more about his experience growing up, his ways of distancing and tuning out the distress in his family. We found out about his guilt both then and now. He talked about how he felt he should have been taking care of his parents and brothers and sisters and how helpless he felt without really knowing it. Finally we got into Mike's self-criticism and verbal self-abuse and how much more wicked they were than Alice's criticism of him. He was self-critical; his defensiveness was protecting him from his self-criticism. Toward the end of the session, Mike suddenly broke into wracking sobs about his guilt and his ambivalence about his family. He and Alice were both shocked by his intense and open emotion.

At the beginning of the next session, we acknowledged Mike's experience. He again communicated his surprise about his own emotion and said that he preferred that we interview Alice next. She described how she was close to both of her parents but not to her aunt and cousins. She felt hurt by them and distant from them. Much of her late childhood and adolescence was spent alone. She didn't have much more to say about the time her cousin "bothered her." She just put it in the category with her family not being very worthwhile. Alice owned that she tended to cut people off when they hurt or angered her. She had done that with family and with friends and she was not pleased with herself about it. She could see herself doing it with Mike. She could see that her behavior came from fear.

The dream-within-conflict discussions led to looking at fights in the light of what they had experienced and heard from each other. I walked them through looking in detail at what they were feeling each step of the way. Mike's self-criticism and defensiveness became clear again. Alice commented, in a truly heartfelt manner, that she had no idea that Mike was so critical of himself. She had only seen him fend her off and argue with her. Then she would just cut him off and get icier.

After the sessions that focused on dream within conflict, Mike and Alice went back to discussing more current issues. They were able to do so with much less pain than they had experienced earlier. Mike was clearly more engaged. He wasn't any more proactive about moving, but he was more engaged in honestly discussing his ambivalence about the idea. They discussed the children and strategies for working with them. All this went fairly well, but I still had a strong sense of Alice's distance and Mike's difficulty staying engaged over time. They even talked about his "numbing" and her "stainless steel exterior." They could see it and wanted to explore further. So we went back to dream-within-conflict.

This time Alice was able to interview Mike. Her questions led back to his family again. They talked about his experiences at length, and suddenly he became very agitated. He said he felt as if he were in his childhood house. He also knew he was in my office and I was able to soothe him fairly quickly. I then spoke softly about the traumas he experienced and how time doesn't diminish the feelings. We were able to talk about how understandable it was that Mike would need to withdraw and get away when he was on the verge of a frightening emotional response. I think Mike was as fascinated by his own process as he was frightened.

The remarkable part, however, was that Alice's compassion did not visibly kick in. She was sympathetic, but still in a very detached sort of way. So we turned to her side of the dream-within-conflict. She talked about her family and acknowledged again the hurt and the tendency she had to cut people off and distance herself when she felt hurt. But she still felt far down the "cascade of distance and isolation" to me. I have a mental image of this cascade. The person caught in it is falling down a waterfall in a barrel. The barrel is halfway down. The person in the barrel says, "Okay, I'll come to therapy and see if I can get this barrel back up to the top of the waterfall, at which point maybe I can decide if I want to improve this marriage. Right now I feel a bit out of control of those feelings." Naturally this is hard on the person seeing his or her partner fall away. Alice acknowledged her fear and lack of trust again.

I encouraged Mike to keep going, to keep asking Alice questions not only about her family of origin, but also about their relationship. Eventually they arrived at the time when she had needed surgery and a long recovery period. She was terrified for her health, the welfare of her children, and also of the boredom she anticipated during recovery. She felt stuck and helpless. And she felt that Mike was not there for her, that he didn't understand. She told Mike she had tried to talk about it but he would never hear her.

"We've talked about it a lot," he replied.

"Just a couple of times and you never really got it. You didn't understand what I was feeling."

"Well, we did talk about it, but I guess I was always trying to get you to see that I hadn't done anything wrong. I think I was defensive. I don't think I ever did understand."

Alice was tearful. They were becoming closer and gentler toward each other.

THE GOTTMAN MODEL AND MY OWN EQUILIBRIUM

I'd like to report a final success with Mike and Alice. In truth, I am still working with this couple. I expect to work more with Mike on his experience of trauma and how it affects his interactions with Alice. And I expect to work more with Alice on the events in the relationship that led to her falling back on her tendency to get steely and cut off. We will use dreams-within-conflict and come back to building fondness and admiration.

In the meantime, the success that has occurred has not been as much with Mike and Alice (although they have had successes and have been very brave) but rather with me as a therapist. The Gottman approach has continued to provide me with many paths. The multifaceted, multileveled SRH has been and continues to be a rich teacher and a source of steadiness in the high intensity of couples therapy. Even when I decided that Mike and Alice needed me to be actively engaged, I never felt that debilitating sense of helplessness that couples can engender. I kept my equilibrium, and best of all, I've enjoyed my work with them.

REFERENCES

Bowen, M. (1978). *Family therapy in clinical practice.* New York: Aronson.

Cecchin, G. (1987). Hypothesizing, circularity, and neutrality revisited: An invitation to curiosity. *Family Process, 26,* 405–413.

Guerin, P. J., Fay, L., Burden, S. L., & Kauggo, J. G. (1987). *The evaluation and treatment of marital conflict.* New York: Basic.

Haley, J. (1991). *Problem-solving therapy.* San Francisco: Jossey-Bass.

Minuchin, S., & Fishman, H. C. (1981). *Family therapy techniques.* Cambridge, MA: Harvard University Press.

White, M., & Epston, D. (1989). *Literate means to therapeutic ends.* Adelaide, Australia: Dulwich Centre Publications.

Wile, D. B. (1993). *After the fight: Using your disagreements to build a stronger relationship.* New York: Guilford Press.

Chapter 3 ❋

Treatment of a Couple With Trauma-Related Domestic Violence

Regina Delmastro

One of the greatest challenges in couples therapy with traumatized individuals is balancing the focus between the presenting issues in the relationship and the enduring vulnerability of childhood abuse. Navigating the psychoemotional and neurological posttrauma landscapes of two individuals in an intimate dyadic process is much like trying to walk two tightropes at the same time.

The psychoemotional and neuroendocrine artifacts of childhood abuse disrupt intimate attachment, creating turning away and, even more disruptive to the relationship, turning against. Psychic numbing prevents the person from experiencing emotion and at times body sensation, creating disengagement and an inability to feel emotional or physical stimuli. Psychic flooding states overwhelm the neurological and emotional system with sensory flashbacks. These states may also involve profound feelings of fear, aggression, hopelessness, and despair, and the alteration between these states creates extremes in relationship interaction. In addition, partners may be passive and overly accommodating or hypercritical and controlling. Bids for connection may be misinterpreted as seduction, creating suspicion, disengagement, and vilification of the partners. The ability to create fondness and admiration, accept influence, resolve conflict, and experience intimacy are profoundly disrupted, creating severe negative sentiment override.

With traumatized couples the negative sentiment override is more rigidly held. Not only does it become a psychoemotional reenactment of the childhood abusive relationship, but it also establishes a neurological reinforcement of the posttraumatic stress disorder (PTSD) abuse/humiliation/shame paradigm of childhood trauma. Escalation of contemptuous interactions may result in violence, as each member of the couple experiences diffuse physiological arousal (DPA), flashbacks, and dissociation. Thus, the dyadic process and the couples therapy itself may become the subject of posttrauma avoidance.

Treatment of the traumatized couple involves healing disrupted functions on all levels of the SRH and, in turn, healing the disruption of childhood abuse. Support to create or improve fondness, friendship, and intimacy involves mediating the DPA during the sessions as well as in everyday life. The Gottman interventions of DPA monitoring, soothing, turning, and repair provide a structure for creating a safe therapeutic context for healing the traumatized couple.

This chapter's focus is twofold: First, it illustrates an example of interdynamic childhood trauma with a couple whose reenactment creates DPA, PTSD symptoms and violent behavior. Second, it demonstrates the application of the GMCT and interventions to mediate DPA and create secure, positive sentiment override and intimacy in the couple. The Gottman interventions employed include use of wrist pulse monitors, self-soothing, dreams within conflict, aftermath of a fight, repair, and the Gottman Couples Workshop.

MARINA AND DEREK

This case spans a time frame of several years during which couples therapy and individual therapy were blended for a traumatized couple, Marina and Derek. Marina had been in individual therapy with me for many years for alcoholism and trauma recovery prior to meeting Derek. After 6 months in their relationship, Marina and Derek requested couples therapy with me to deal with Marina's inability to have sex and Derek's anger about the "the relationship not moving forward." Marina had begun to have nightmares, flashbacks, and angry outbursts as the pressure around sex had increased. Derek had begun weekly individual therapy with a different therapist shortly after starting the relationship with Marina due to stress in the relationship.

My decision to proceed with couples therapy in addition to my individual therapy with Marina was based on three clinical considerations: First, Marina expressed that she would not trust a new therapist with intimate sexual information and feared experiencing PTSD symptoms "in front of a stranger." This statement represented one of the most common fears and processes of sexual abuse recovery: the reexperience of overexposure, humiliation, and shame. Marina expressed that having an unfamiliar couples therapist would "feel like being stripped naked in front of two people, the therapist and Derek," because both would be hearing information for the first time. Because of the voyeuristic qualities of Marina's childhood sexual abuse, the possibility of her inadvertently being retraumatized in couples therapy with a different therapist was significant. Second, both Marina and Derek felt it would be expedient to work with me because Marina trusted me and I knew her family history. And third, after many years of referring sexually abused women clients to couples therapy, I have found that the majority have either suffered a retraumatic experience or have felt too vulnerable to access the depth of their trauma.

This was a concern for Marina as well. However, after processing the potential benefits and pitfalls of this therapeutic paradigm, we decided to proceed into couples therapy with a plan to evaluate periodically if progress was being made. Marina continued in individual therapy with me, and Derek continued in individual therapy with his therapist, with whom I coordinated during the couples work.

Three episodes of couples therapy with Marina and Derek are presented here: premarriage, followed by a 6-month break in couples therapy; postmarriage/prenatal, followed by a 3-year break in couples therapy; and later, during the adjustment to parenthood.

Case History

Marina was a 34-year-old successful business woman and had been in individual therapy for several years. She was initially referred by her medical doctor, who was concerned about her alcohol intake, angry outbursts, insomnia, and history of childhood abuse. Marina completed outpatient treatment for alcohol abuse early in her therapy and had been clean and sober for many years. She had continued in individual therapy with a specific focus on PTSD symptoms related to sexual abuse and violence in her childhood alcoholic home.

Marina was an only child with a history of verbal and physical violence and sexual abuse by her alcoholic father against her mother and against her, starting at age 9. Marina's father had made crude sexualized comments and engaged in name calling with Marina's mother and women in general. Marina had an early sexual development and by age 12 was the focus of her father's sexualized behavior. Marina's father would plan "special dates" for him and Marina. He would buy Marina sexy clothing to wear, take her out for dinner, and drink heavily. These "special dates" often ended with Marina and her father returning home late at night and dancing in the living room to romantic music. Marina recalled feeling nauseated and "hazy" during these dancing episodes and remembered that her father sometimes had an erection and would slobber kisses on her neck and face. On several occasions her mother came into the living room and furiously provoked a violent episode with the father. At times these fights would endure through the night, with the mother sometimes calling Marina a "selfish little slut."

Marina began using alcohol at age 12. By ninth grade Marina was drinking regularly at weekend family parties at the family cabin. These parties often involved open sexual behavior between her parents and their friends and at times verbal and physical violence. When Marina was 17, during a weekend stay at the cabin with her friend and her father, Marina's father coerced Marina into having sex while her friend was out hiking. Marina took full responsibility for this because she "made the choice to drink with him, knowing it might lead to that."

During college Marina's drinking escalated when she developed a relationship with a musician. Due to flashbacks of her father's violence and sexual abuse, Marina was unable to engage in sex with him unless intoxicated. Despite a gentle and mutual breakup with this boyfriend following a violent outburst by Marina, she suffered intense humiliation and grief over the loss of this relationship. Following the breakup, Marina was unable to engage in any long-term relationship. She was disturbed by repetitive nightmares and flashbacks of her father's violence and recurrent dreams of a particular incident when her father raped and beat her mother.

Marina's parents divorced while she was in college after her mother discovered her father having an affair, which Marina had known about for months. Within 3 months of the divorce, Marina's father remarried a women with whom he was also violent. Upon receiving an ultimatum from this woman, Marina's father stopped using alcohol by "going cold turkey"—"proof," he professed, that he was not alcoholic. Meanwhile, Marina's mother remained single and never dated.

In the course of her individual therapy, Marina processed much of her childhood trauma, which allowed her to enter into a relationship with Derek. She met him at a friend's party. What drew her to Derek was his calm demeanor and his gentle way of asserting his opinions and ethics related to work situations being discussed at the party. She found him attractive and humorous. Soon afterward, they began dating.

Derek was a 39-year-old marketing director at a large corporation. He was the youngest of five boys. His father was an untreated maintenance alcoholic who was emotionally absent as a father except as the disciplinarian. Derek described his father as "a bulldog that I avoided as much as possible." Derek also openly voiced hatred for his mother, whom he described as "evil and nasty" and who had "angry outbursts of vicious profanity." He noted that his brothers beat him up and that the children were to remain quiet at all times so as not to disturb their father, who drank beer every evening alone in his bedroom. Once disturbed, his father would be violent, and the children would be blamed and punished.

Derek began using marijuana with one of his brothers when he was 14. At age 15, while being chastised by his father for smoking marijuana in the basement, Derek provoked a physical altercation to "let him know once and for all that he wasn't going to bully me ever again." Following this altercation, Derek's mother began offering him a beer each time she served his father one, which he gladly drank down. He spent his remaining high school and college years drinking and smoking marijuana, primarily in isolation.

Derek discontinued using all drugs including alcohol without treatment when he attended graduate school. He expressed pride that he was "disciplined enough to decide to quit and just do it." His only long-term intimate relationship with a college girlfriend ended when she gave him an ultimatum to marry her or she would leave the relationship. He again spoke with pride that "I certainly wasn't going to let her bully me into marrying her."

Derek remained single with little dating prior to meeting Marina at their mutual friend's party. What attracted him to Marina was her kind way of socializing and her sense of humor. He noticed that she was the only person at the party who was not drinking alcohol.

Premarriage Couples Therapy

After 6 months of dating, Marina moved into Derek's house, as the couple wanted to "check out if we're a good match." In the next months, Marina and Derek experienced challenges in "staying connected," which prompted their request for couples therapy. They described having arguments in which they would "get out of control" and "say things we don't really mean."

This initial therapy period laid the groundwork for the later therapy, which would be more rigorous and intensive. During this phase of therapy we met weekly for about 6 months. Marina and Derek also attended the Gottman Couples Workshop to facilitate their understanding of the Gottman concepts and interventions that were to be used throughout their couples therapy.

Several issues were focused on during this initial phase of couples therapy: First, Derek frequently withdrew from Marina, feeling like she was "a time bomb ready to go off at any minute." Instead of being with her, he spent his free time involved in isolating activities, playing computer games, hiking, or reupholstering furniture, which were his favorite pastimes. Second, Derek expressed that Marina's occasional angry outbursts and name calling had made him "gun shy" to approach her. The extreme difficulty they were having sexually concerned him about the feasibility of a long-term commitment. He acknowledged that he did not know what to do but keep his distance and let her make the overtures for any contact they might have. Third, Marina had begun to experience regular PTSD flashbacks, nightmares, and other symptoms since moving in with Derek. She felt great pressure to function romantically and sexually and became acutely aware of her inability to do so. She described that in the past, she was able "to fake it well enough" but that loving Derek and hoping for marriage and children made her feel despair and an "almost constant feeling that my head and chest are going to explode." At this point Marina was rarely able to have sex, began having panic anxiety and numbness in her body, and began thinking about drinking again. Occasionally she would wake up at night, frantically screaming. Her angry outbursts occurred during psychic flooding states that disrupted the engagement she felt from Derek. She accused him of being self-centered and selfish.

Assessment

Building a therapeutic trust with Derek was quite challenging. He was skeptical about therapy and therapists, and he felt that he and Marina should be able to resolve their own problems, like he had recovered from substance abuse. He openly stated his belief that therapists foster dependency with their clients, convincing them that they need the therapist to make decisions that they should make on their own. Derek refused to complete the Gottman assessment, although he attended an individual assessment interview. He said that he would agree to participate in couples therapy only to help figure out why Marina couldn't seem to handle sexual intimacy.

TREATMENT

During these initial months of couples therapy, the focus was on the enduring vulnerability brought on by childhood trauma. Marina shared with Derek her history of sexual abuse, verbal belligerence, and violence by her father. Derek also shared his childhood history, stating that his experiences were "nothing out of the ordinary and definitely not as bad as Marina's." We explored sexual inter-actions between Marina and Derek that were triggering a traumatic reaction for Marina. She was able to identify that having her neck or face kissed, certain sexual positions, and viewing or hearing sexually explicit material or movies triggered flashbacks and panic anxiety in her. She also shared that initiation of even play-ful contact with Derek created PTSD anxiety states, during which she relived her father's calling her mother and other women "sluts." In addition, discussing flir-tation or seduction with Derek created either intrusive flashbacks of sexual abuse or "that familiar hazy feeling like when I danced with my dad."

This exploration was quite challenging for both Marina and Derek. Marina was easily triggered by sexual discussions and experienced dissociation states dur-ing the couples sessions. Derek also found this exploration uncomfortably personal and shared his fear of being exposed as a poor lover and the cause of Marina's difficulty.

Their early sharing of intimate information was a compelling segue to es-tablishing rituals of connection. Marina and Derek agreed to spend 20 minutes a day talking about their thoughts and feelings in order to stay connected. Derek created a "20 questions" game that incorporated love maps on his computer for Marina and him to play. Both Marina and Derek found the SRH construct a helpful roadmap that showed them "where we are and where we are going in this therapy."

Education about PTSD and its etiology, symptoms, and interplay in re-lationships reassured both Marina and Derek that working together in heal-ing its ravages would strengthen their relationship. Discussing the psychoemo-tional and neurological enduring vulnerabilities from childhood abuse helped Marina feel less shame about her sexual difficulties. The focus on DPA as a signal that past abuse was being triggered helped Marina and Derek under-stand that physiology was quite involved in the difficulties they were having, especially during arguments and sexual intimacy. This was a relief as they ex-pressed that they had each found a special person in the other and hoped they could commit to marriage in the near future. Derek expressed a dedi-cated commitment to participate in the couples therapy and an extreme sad-ness about the "scars" from Marina's childhood that affected her and them so profoundly.

Derek, however, had difficulty accepting that his own childhood and coping mechanisms overlapped with Marina's to create trauma triggers in their relation-ship. An example we discussed was how Derek's childhood behavior of withdraw-ing into isolated activities as a refuge from the distress of his parents' profanity during family fights, was not unlike his current withdrawal from Marina. He would withdraw from Marina, which would remind her of the "calm before the storm" phase that preceded her father's violence. She would attempt to pursue connection with Derek to feel that all was okay between them. When her bids for connection failed, Marina's anxiety escalated to aggression and contempt, re-sulting in abusive behavior much like her father's. This created a double bind for Marina: She could either not pursue Derek and feel lonely, anxious, and disen-gaged, or she could pursue Derek, risk the failure of connection, and have PTSD symptoms related to her childhood abuse.

For Derek, Marina's PTSD symptoms became a reenactment of Derek's mother's behavior, which he described as "mean, nasty, and evil." In remembering his mother's behavior, he recalled being particularly fearful of his mother when he was a child and preteen. When she became angry he would quickly climb out his bedroom window and run to his uncle's furniture refinishing shop a block from his house. Often he would help his uncle with the furniture repair and stay for dinner or the night. In sum, Marina's behavior triggered Derek's childhood trauma, resulting in fear, DPA, and withdrawal. As the disagreements escalated further or were specifically centered on Marina's family wealth and gifts, Derek would tell her she was a "selfish brat." This reminded Marina of her mother's screaming at her when she and her father returned home from their "special dates."

In time, Marina and Derek realized that when "things just kept getting uglier" between them, they had both been in DPA. Thus, a circular interaction loop of PTSD and DPA wove reenactment of their childhood abuse into the fabric of their present relationship.

At this juncture in treatment, there was no violence between Marina and Derek, but Derek shared that he was afraid when he saw Marina "go into that state." In an effort to make Marina "come to her senses," Derek would confront and provoke her when she began to escalate, which made the situation even more volatile. His response was a reenactment of his provocative behavior with his father at age 15. Only when Derek realized that his interaction with Marina was a reenactment and was making things worse did he agree to extended couples therapy.

This initial couples work became the groundwork for what I anticipated could be a lengthy process of learning and deep therapy for both Marina and Derek. During this therapy episode Derek still rejected the idea that his childhood history had any bearing on the problems he and Marina were having and felt that stress had been the precipitant for his individual therapy. However, he acknowledged that his childhood home life had been "stressful" and that he "got out of there as soon as he could." He also acknowledged that "it isn't common for a person to hate their parents" but he felt that he had vowed never to be like them, and he asserted that "when I put my mind to something I always accomplish it," meaning that he'd succeeded in not being like them. Thus, his presence in couples therapy from his point of view was mostly for Marina's benefit and was a way to work on the problems they were having regarding her inability to have intercourse.

I noticed that in these initial sessions, Derek showed an interesting pattern of behavior. Whenever he was listening to Marina speak, he repeatedly stroked a lock of hair on the right side of his head like an overly fatigued toddler. This appeared to be a "soothing" technique, as Derek seemed to enter a trance when he did it. This led me to believe that Derek, too, had probably suffered from early childhood abuse. Yet he was still unable to accept that his parents' behavior could be considered abusive.

The Gottman construct of enduring vulnerabilities, in this case childhood abuse, was very helpful for Marina and Derek. Once the enduring vulnerability from the childhood trauma was clearly understood, Marina and Derek could approach, even playfully at times, how each of them was responsible for a part in the reenactment interactions that triggered their past trauma. They agreed to support each other in taking a break when in DPA. Also, Marina agreed to refrain from the use of profanity, especially when she was angry at Derek, and they mutually agreed to refrain from all name calling.

Marina and Derek developed a "stop action" signal of raising their right hand like a traffic cop, which they used when they began to experience DPA symptoms. Both agreed that when either of them gave this stop action signal, the other would immediately respect the signal and a 20-minute break would be taken. They agreed to check in after 20 minutes to see if continuing the discussion was possible. If it wasn't, they extended the break and made an appointment to attempt another discussion later. It became clear at this point that Marina, once triggered, had great difficulty calming her physiology. She expressed fear that she had the temperament of her violent father, and was committed to changing this.

Marina and Derek identified that their common dream was to have a child someday and be healed enough from their own scars to offer a child a happier life. Learning the skills to interrupt DPA was straightforward and Marina and Derek assumed that once they learned these skills they would have no difficulty implementing them. This was not the case. Each of them struggled with disengaging from the trauma reenactment dynamics. By using the aftermath of a marital argument questionnaire, they each learned to identify and share feelings, something neither of them had experienced before in an intimate relationship. They also found it a relief to share the responsibility for what happened in the interaction rather than feel blamed and rejected by the other, as they had in childhood by their parents.

Disrupting DPA was the initial step in creating a safe personal relationship as well as a safe therapeutic environment in which the traumatized couple could heal. The 20-minute stop action break allowed them to calm their hyperaroused neuroendocrine responses to the perceived threats in their interactions. The resolution of their DPA progressed most efficiently when it was supported by psychological soothing methods. It was essential to explore with each partner which methods of soothing would be most helpful to employ during the stop action break.

Soothing methods can include formalized relaxation techniques, physical exercise, music, yoga, tai chi, or something more individualized. Any of the five senses or sensory pathways can be the key to effective soothing. For Marina, going for an hour-long run was most effective in calming her. For Derek, the smell of his furniture refinishing workshop calmed him almost immediately. The smell of the shop transported him to his uncle's shop where he had retreated as a child when he feared his parents' rage. He associated this smell with safety.

In addition to the stop action break and soothing methods, special emphasis was needed to disrupt Marina's tendency to ruminate about the interaction. Like other traumatized individuals, Marina often felt a need to be prepared and in control, so rumination was difficult to change. This, too, she accomplished in time.

Once Marina and Derek learned how to manage reenactment interactions, DPA, and self-soothing, they felt secure in sharing feelings and taking responsibility for their own respective behaviors in their interactions. They particularly enjoyed the repair checklist. They decided to post it on their refrigerator as a reminder to take a stop action break when needed, and they made a practice of using it at times when they had been critical or contemptuous. Marina also agreed to use softened start-up in letting Derek know when she felt distant from him, which would be his cue that she wanted contact. Derek agreed to arrange his computer-game time so it would not interfere with their 20-minute daily connection time. In addition, they used the aftermath of a marital argument exercise to help them share feelings and explore how they each had contributed to their interaction in helpful and unhelpful ways. As the reenactment interactions diminished, the couple experienced increased trust and fondness, which facilitated a transition from negative to positive sentiment override in their relationship. In turn, their positive sentiment override allowed them to develop deeper trust, friendship, and shared meaning.

Meanwhile, sexual contact was, at this point, a separate and scheduled encounter, which minimized triggering Marina's sexual abuse trauma. The couple negotiated that Saturday would be the night when sex would most likely occur. It was important to introduce the topic of presex relaxation methods to increase Marina's sense of safety during sex.

Marina and Derek discussed in detail how their sexual intimacy would proceed. This included identifying positions and ways of talking and touching that would be safe at each stage of healing. The couple also agreed that staying emotionally present throughout their sexual intimacy would be something they both would attend to. If either one experienced a sense of disengagement, they would supportively create a pause to slow the process down or stop and reconnect emotionally. Marina learned to express herself clearly when she began to experience posttrauma symptoms. They agreed to stop the sexual interaction if Marina experienced anxiety, a hazy, unreal, or panicky feeling, flashbacks, or numbness in her body.

During this phase of couples therapy, the sexual relationship took on a rigidity that was difficult for Derek. But gradually they worked together on presex relaxation, including hot baths, essential oils, massage, heat, a darkened room, and specific positions, types of touch, and so on to accomplish sexual intimacy that included intercourse and was satisfying for both of them. Marina was unable to experience orgasm, though she expressed that having closeness without the severe PTSD symptoms she had had in the past was enough for her at this point. They both felt hopeful that their sexual relationship would continue to improve with time as deeper trust developed between them. Marina felt less vigilant, and they both expressed a growing trust and love for each other.

At this point Marina and Derek began to plan their wedding. This involved increased contact with Marina's parents, as they each offered to pay for an extravagant wedding celebration, which was the family tradition. But this reinstated the triadic conditions of Marina's childhood trauma—that is, contact with and between her parents, who were still angry at each other. Subsequently, Marina experienced a resurgence of trauma memories and PTSD. She increased her individual therapy with me in order to process the trauma memories, reactions to contact with her parents, and developments in her sexual relationship with Derek.

Despite these stresses, Marina and Derek progressed well. They consistently used the Gottman strategies learned in therapy and at the workshop. Finally, the special day arrived and Marina and Derek married. We agreed that doing couples therapy on an "as needed" basis rather than weekly was appropriate at this point.

I continued individual therapy with Marina, and Derek terminated his individual therapy, having felt it had "reached its maximum benefit."

A Six-Month Break After the Initial Therapy Episode

During the next months Marina was free of PTSD symptoms and was gradually able to have sexual intercourse without difficulty, though she did not experience orgasm. Marina and Derek felt confident in the improvement in their relationship and decided to discontinue birth control and attempt to get pregnant. During the next 6 months of trying to conceive, however, Marina noticed a dramatic change in Derek's behavior. He withdrew into spending more time playing computer games, and he began to watch violent movies. He spent late hours in his shop, worked overtime needlessly, and withdrew when Marina made overtures for connection and sex. Marina feared that Derek did not want to have a baby, which he denied; nonetheless, he continued to withdraw from her.

During this period, Marina's father sent her a picture of himself and her dancing at her wedding with a caption that read "just like old times." Marina began to have a recurrence of flashbacks, panic attacks, nightmares, and anger outbursts. She requested that Derek return to couples therapy with her, but he refused, as "this was Marina's problem." Derek continued to isolate in his shop, and he began drinking beer occasionally, especially when Marina was angry. Marina's PTSD symptoms escalated, but she continued to try to contain her anger and to avoid DPA by practicing self-soothing methods daily, including running, hot baths, classical music, acupuncture, and essential oil massage. We discussed the possibility of antidepressant medication, which she refused.

The second episode of couples therapy was initiated following a violent interchange between Marina and Derek while on a date. They had gone to see a movie in which there was a rape scene. Marina wanted to leave but decided not to because Derek wanted to stay until the end of the movie. She covered her ears and closed her eyes, which she had done as a child during the family parties at the cabin and when her father beat and raped her mother. Becoming extremely distressed, Marina left the theater and set out to walk home. Derek followed her by car in the parking lot, trying to convince her to get into the car so they could go for coffee. Marina went into a rage, yelling profanities at Derek. Then Derek forced Marina into the car, concerned that others in the lot would hear her and call the police. As Derek climbed into his side of the car, Marina took the ice scraper from the floor and hit him, cutting his arm. She screamed that she never wanted to see him again and left. Derek drove around the block and returned for Marina, finding her still in the theater parking lot, bent over, retching and crying. I received an emergency call that night from both Marina and Derek. That night they slept separately and saw me the following day, which began our second episode of couples therapy.

Postmarriage and Prenatal Couples Therapy

In this second phase of therapy, we met weekly for 90 minutes each session. Marina continued in individual therapy with me. Despite my recommendation, Derek refused to resume individual therapy, but during the couples therapy sessions he was more open to sharing his childhood history and how it was involved in the relationship. The couple's main focus was on getting control of their negative behaviors, reinstating trust in the marriage, and deciding whether or not to move forward with getting pregnant. More specifically, the issues they addressed were: (1) A decline in intimacy, with Marina having increased contempt toward Derek and PTSD symptoms, and Derek withdrawing more from Marina; (2) the violent episode in the parking lot with a review of DPA, PTSD, and the enduring vulnerabilities from trauma, including more confrontation of Derek's role due to his childhood trauma; and (3) whether or not to become pregnant.

When we resumed couples therapy, both Marina and Derek were very fearful about their behavior and the fact that it had led to violence. Derek described that he felt they were both "in shock" that they had "let it go that far," and that he had actually thrown Marina into the car for fear that others would hear her screaming. At this point he poignantly described how his mother "threw me into my room while my father beat up my brother. I could hear him screaming. Then my mother went and closed all the windows in the house so the neighbors could not hear. She was embarrassed, but she never stopped the beating. That's when I snuck out my window and fled to my uncle's shop. I would spend hours there. He taught me a lot about antiques and refinishing furniture. He taught me how to whittle a stick and make a whistle. My parents never missed me. I just came back whenever. I would call if I was going to stay the night there. They never cared what I was doing or where I went. Whenever I came home, everyone acted like nothing was any different."

This was a breakthrough for Derek, as it was the first time he acknowledged that his own trauma related to the explosiveness between him and Marina. He was quite agitated and guilt-ridden that the reenactment of his past trauma had hurt Marina. He also apologized for blaming the relationship explosiveness on Marina. At this point Derek wanted to learn more about his own part in this interplay of trauma. I suggested that Derek resume individual therapy, but again he refused to do so.

During the next months of couples therapy, we reviewed the Gottman principles and tools that had been introduced in the initial episode of couples therapy. Derek shared his belief that relationships should be easy and took responsibility for refusing to use the Gottman tools that they had learned. Derek became aware that when Marina disagreed with him, he assumed it was her way of bullying him. He realized that the immediate anxiety he felt made him want to disappear or run away and that he had "become entrenched in a fear pattern like when I was a kid." He described that he had replayed in his mind Marina's words of profanity during the recent violent episode between them; he was unable to release them. "That is what I did when I went to my uncle's shop. I sure could sand that furniture though. No wonder I was such a good sander; I was scared to death." Derek shared his frequent thought that his marriage to Marina had been a mistake. He realized that when he ruminated on this thought, he withdrew from Marina and began to isolate and drink, while at the same time creating festering anger, distrust, and fear of Marina.

Derek's increased willingness to deal with his trauma this time in therapy made Marina feel less alone and blamed and more hopeful. Marina dealt appropriately with her anger that Derek had refused to continue the Gottman techniques and had earlier refused to resume couples therapy. Several Gottman interventions were used effectively, including love maps and turning toward to build connection and friendship; review of the four horsemen, DPA, and enduring vulnerabilities; soothing techniques; dreams within conflict; and the aftermath of a marital argument questionnaire. Despite the positive effects of these interventions, Derek remained skeptical that "a good relationship" should need such focused attention despite the enduring vulnerability from childhood trauma. He did, however, note that when he and Marina regularly used the exercises at home, things went smoothly and he felt more secure and trustful that there would be no violence.

Both Marina and Derek felt a deepening of their relationship, more open sadness about their past abuse, an increase in humor, increased closeness and passion in their sexual relationship (though Marina was still nonorgasmic with intercourse), and more reassurance about getting pregnant. We discussed that a likely effect of having a child would be increased stress on the marriage. They agreed that they would return for a "tune-up" if needed. With the strengthening of the relationship, increased insight into the enduring vulnerabilities, and commitment to resume couples therapy if needed, Marina and Derek decided to discontinue marital therapy and resume attempting to conceive. Marina decided to decrease the frequency of her individual therapy with me to two times a month.

A month after discontinuing couples therapy, Marina became pregnant. I had a brief congratulatory phone conversation with Derek in which he thanked me for the couples therapy and for having faith in them. He expressed support for Marina's continuing individual therapy and requested to come in himself if needed, to which I agreed.

Three-Year Break Between the Second and Third Episodes of Couples Therapy

Marina's pregnancy was very difficult. She suffered extensive morning sickness throughout the pregnancy, which her doctor could not remedy. During these months Marina had a resurgence of flashbacks triggered by a memory she had not recalled until pregnancy. This memory involved the 2-month period of time following the sexual abuse experience with her father when she was 17 and drunk. She shared that for 2 months following this abuse, Marina had no menstrual period and thought she had been impregnated by her father. She attributed her current lengthy "morning sickness" and frequent vomiting to the recovery of this memory. She shared her abuse history with her obstetrician, who monitored her closely for electrolyte imbalance and weight loss, and she went on a bland diet throughout her pregnancy. Marina experienced deep grief and rage that her childhood abuse was interfering with a positive pregnancy experience.

Derek was able to respond supportively to Marina's emotional and physical needs during the pregnancy, but Marina felt that he was beginning to withdraw from her again. Marina lost interest in sex during this time but Derek didn't seem to mind. Marina feared that her disclosure about the sexual abuse had "turned Derek off for good." Following her emotionally and physically difficult pregnancy, Marina had an uncomplicated labor and delivery of a healthy baby girl, whom they named Mellita. Derek called me when Marina went into labor and informed me of the birth. At this point he thanked me for my "diligent work and support, which helped to make this dream come true for both of us."

Despite severe sleep deprivation in the next months of adjusting to parenthood, Marina and Derek did well staying connected. They easily worked together to establish new family routines and rituals to accommodate the new demands of parenthood. They were proud and happy, though Marina felt a growing distance because she and Derek had not resumed a regular sexual relationship. Marina resumed individual therapy weekly and brought baby Mellita. The focus of the therapy during these early months centered on the adjustment to parenthood, infant care, breast feeding, and care of the marriage. She described that having Mellita had created a deep closeness between her and Derek that they had never experienced before. They were adjusting easily to parenthood, but she still felt concerned about their lack of sexual intimacy.

As might be expected in a postpartum period, Marina focused on her own mother's role in not protecting her from her violent abuse in childhood. She became keenly aware of the vulnerability of children as she experienced Mellita's complete dependence. Her intense feelings of love and protection for Mellita left her profoundly shocked at how remiss her mother had been as a parent. During this phase, Marina had many insights, but with quite modulated emotional reaction to them. She remained steadfast in her enchantment of nursing Mellita and learning all she could about infant development. Derek shared in this quest for up-to-date knowledge about child rearing, and called me occasionally with questions about his role in supporting Marina and fathering baby Mellita.

When Mellita was about 10 months old, Marina reported that Derek was experiencing a major reorganization at his company. He was called upon to "clean house" in his department, which involved confronting colleagues and coworker friends. There were betrayals he became aware of that resulted in his having to fire people he had trusted. One situation involved a woman whom he described as "just like my mother." Marina felt unable to respond to Derek's increasing anxiety and agitated reactions. Derek began to make regular comments about his mother's "nasty and evil" behavior, including the fact that his parents made no acknowledgment of Mellita's being born. He regularly stated that he hated his mother, noting in contrast the love he witnessed between Marina and Mellita. He shared with Marina that he now could see what love and care looked like and that he had never experienced love in his childhood. Marina shared concern with me that Derek was becoming depressed. She decided to suggest to Derek that he join us for a session to "check in." Derek refused. He felt confident that he had control of all that was stressing him.

Marina continued in therapy weekly, bringing Mellita to most sessions. We discussed research regarding the adjustment to parenthood and what she could do to balance parenting with supporting the marriage, as she had reported that Derek was "reverting back to old ways," such as spending extensive hours on his computer. She also reported that despite her initiations, Derek was disinterested in sex. Marina decided to hire a part-time nanny so she and Derek could arrange a weekly date and get reconnected emotionally. She discussed with Derek her desire to have intimate contact with him; she wanted them to get back to incorporating Gottman interventions, as she was feeling disconnected from him.

Despite Marina's efforts, Derek continued to withdraw from her. He seemed most happy when he had exclusive time with Mellita, but seemed disinterested in Marina. He had lost interest in spending time in his shop. She began to feel overwhelmed with parenting and his withdrawal from her. Interactions between Marina and Derek began to escalate over several months. Derek continued to refuse to reenter couples therapy, despite Marina's request, my suggestion, and my offer to refer them to another couples therapist if he preferred that.

The third episode of couples therapy was initiated following a violent interchange a few days before Mellita's 2-year birthday. Derek had planned an outing where he and Mellita would go to a toy store and pick out a birthday toy. Marina had just finished dressing Mellita and expressed a desire to go along. Derek asserted firmly that he wanted to go with Mellita alone. Marina became angry and, as Derek firmly told Mellita to come to him so they could go shopping, Mellita began to cry and ran to Marina. As Marina consoled her, Derek demanded that Marina give Mellita to him. Marina refused. Derek became furious and accused Marina of purposely disrupting his plans because she was jealous of his love for Mellita. He then accused her of being "evil" and turning Mellita against him. He began to repeat in a chanting voice, "admit it, you're evil." Marina turned her back to him and huddled against the wall with Mellita in her arms. Derek then forced Marina to turn around, sneered "I'm not your dad," threw his jacket in Marina's face and retreated to his computer room. Marina was very upset and had great difficulty calming herself down enough to soothe Mellita. After an hour, Marina was finally able to calm down and Mellita was able to nap.

Later that day, Derek called me requesting to resume couples therapy.

Final Couples Therapy Episode

Marina and Derek discussed this recent interaction. Both described being unable to stop their behaviors during the incident, and they couldn't stop ruminating about it since it had occurred. They recounted the incident similarly but perceived the causes and motivations for it quite differently. Both felt fearful and guilty that their behavior had negatively affected Mellita.

Derek accused Marina of trying to control his relationship with Mellita, a dynamic that he felt was manipulative and destructive to the family. He was clear that the motivation for his behavior was based on a theory he learned from his father. This theory was that if you provoke the other's unacceptable behavior to its fullest ridiculousness, the person will come to their senses and behave appropriately. He admitted to provoking Marina. He felt she was purposely attempting to damage the bond between him and Mellita with a "heartless and evil motivation," and he would not abide it.

I saw Derek individually to learn more about his perception that Marina had evil intentions. Derek asserted that he believed that "the DPA stuff is just a way to excuse bad behavior. What does John Gottman think about that idea, I wonder? Does he excuse bad behavior because of this DPA?" It seemed clear that Derek had incorporated John Gottman and me as parental objects and that we were now embarking on a deepened level of healing. This was a transition in trust for Derek. I was hopeful that Derek would come to understand that Marina's behavior in the recent violent interaction had a positive motivation. But he seemed convinced that she had a desire to disrupt his bond with Mellita. Derek's suspicious and rigid thought process made me concerned about a severe comorbidity. I decided to venture further to propose that his supposition about Marina's motivations and his reactive violent behavior could possibly be a result of a triggered PTSD state related to his "evil and nasty" mother's disrupting his bond with his father.

In my past experience dealing with trauma resolution with psychotic patients, the distinction between the paranoid content that was posttraumatic villification and the paranoid content that was a psychotic process was often obscure. I was concerned with the possibility that Derek was psychotic. However, during my exploration of the meaning of Derek's accusation of "evil intention," I could see that Derek was transported into past memory as he stared out my office window. He shifted in his chair, looked at the floor and began to speak.

"I remember when I was 2, or maybe 3. I was crying at the dinner table. Everyone was silent except me. My mother yelled at me to shut up. Soon after she picked me up and carried me through the house, dragging my highchair behind us. Things were moving very fast by me and there was a lot of banging. That must have been the highchair banging behind us. I remember that banging. I remember seeing a toy of mine on the floor and calling for it. But she wouldn't stop. We ended up in a room at the far end of the house. I began to cry harder and louder. I think I was angry. They always said I was an angry little kid. She tied me in my highchair and closed the door. I heard the doors slamming shut. I remember feeling that I was getting smaller and smaller with each door slam. I was hysterical. I don't remember what happened after that. Maybe I fell asleep there, I don't remember. This was my mother's favorite punishment if we made noise and disturbed dinner silence."

After a few moments, Derek finally looked up and with quiet, halting amazement said, "Wow, I haven't remembered that before. I had heard that story, but had never actually remembered it, the banging and slamming, all of it." Despite this recall and my suggestion that the triggering of his past trauma, like Marina's, might be involved in their relationship difficulties, and despite again reviewing the enduring vulnerabilities concept, Derek held that his assumption of Marina's motivation was probably correct. We again discussed his resuming individual therapy and again he refused. He shared that though he had disclosed some of his childhood history with his individual therapist in the past, he had now lost trust in him, as the therapist had minimized these events.

I decided to use wrist pulse monitors to evaluate the propensity of DPA in Marina and Derek, to which they agreed. They purchased the monitors to wear at home when discussing difficult issues. They reinstated their previous relationship agreement to use their stop action signal when in DPA, take a break, and use soothing techniques that worked for each of them. It soon became clear that having monitored DPA with Marina and Derek in earlier episodes of treatment would have been very beneficial. From this point on Marina and Derek wore wrist monitors in every session. This especially allowed Derek to be aware of entering into DPA sooner, something he was unable to do prior to use of the monitors. Marina wore a monitor in her individual sessions, also.

In the first session of this final therapy episode, we processed the violence and the interactions preceding it. We focused on the presumptions they each made and the trauma triggers that escalated to violence. Using the aftermath of a marital argument exercise, Marina and Derek were able to share their experience with each other. They were each able to identify that their negative assumptions about the other's motives were directly related to reenactment of abuse with their parents. Marina's wrist monitor beeped 170 times in the first session, whereas Derek's beeped 20 times. Derek stroked his hair throughout the session whenever he was not speaking. Clearly there was more work to be done, so we decided to meet every other week for 90 minutes.

Marina and Derek expressed fear in attempting to discuss issues at home and requested that difficult discussions be limited to my office. Many such discussions followed. At these times, however, when Derek's monitor beeped, he attended to its notification that he was in DPA and focused on soothing himself.

As Marina and Derek progressed, their monitors beeped less often. Derek moved into DPA when he talked about his mother on past betrayals and abuses by siblings, friends, and so on, as well as when the marital conflict interrupted his self-soothing. Marina's monitor beeped 10–20 times per session, usually when discussing the hurt she felt when Derek referred to her "evil intentions" regarding his relationship with Mellita. But as time went on, Derek was able to understand that these accusations related to the past trauma of his mother's abuse; he no longer believed that Marina's motivations were "evil and nasty." There was a return of humor, tenderness, physical closeness that included sex, and an increase in trust between them. Derek realized that his resistance to resuming therapy was out of fear that remembering his trauma could make him "lose control of my faculties." He agreed to consider individual therapy again in the future if needed.

Due to Marina and Derek's pattern of turning against and Marina's hypersensitive and chronic DPA response, we discussed the possibility of psychotropic medication. Marina agreed to have a complete physical exam and to see a naturopath, who determined that she had severe mineral deficiencies and a thyroid imbalance postpregnancy. She began to take supplements and thyroid hormone and slept well for the first time since pregnancy. In addition she used homeopathic remedies to mediate sympathetic nervous system reactivity and to balance her adrenal function. Marina continued to refuse psychopharmacological intervention but was willing to consider it should the natural remedies prove ineffective.

Gradually Marina and Derek restabilized their relationship and developed a deeper friendship and trust than they had ever had. Derek disclosed more about his past abuses and took full responsibility for his part in the violence in their relationship, and due to their increasing closeness, Marina experienced orgasm with intercourse for the first time. They also worked on balancing family time, relationship time, and individual time with Mellita, as well as alone time for each of them. They slowly became allies for each other in situations where they were with either of their families of origin, especially their past abuse perpetrators. Derek began to talk openly with his brothers about the abusive nature of their childhood, and his brothers helped him to recall other abuse memories as well.

Derek's trust in me deepened as well. As we discussed rituals of connection to further develop love maps and fondness and admiration, I suggested that the couple reinstate the Gottman 20-minutes-a-day ritual. Derek forcefully refused. As I supportively and curiously nodded at his firm refusal, there was a silent pause as we sat sharing our anticipatory gazes. Suddenly he began to laugh and said, "Ok, I can see that you are concocting a diagnosis about why I'm refusing to follow your suggestion. Why don't you just level with me? Tell me, Doc, what's the diagnosis?"

I smiled, suspecting that Derek's playfulness signaled a new level of trust. Gently, I said, "I'm happy to level with you. I'm even known for leveling with clients quite directly at times. What is it you would like to know?"

Derek paused and became half serious. "I want to know if you think I am crazy and what you think my main problem is." I realized that Derek had finally arrived at a place of trust with me.

I answered, "I do not think you are crazy. As for your main problem . . . I think you have had many reasons why you never learned how to trust easily—many experiences early in your life that made it impossible for you to learn trust. I think trust is the main issue for you."

Derek said, "I think you are right. Do you know how to help me with learning to trust?" He turned to Marina and tearfully asked if she would be patient so he could learn to trust more, and then help teach Mellita to do the same. They freely embraced, something they had never done in my office before.

CONCLUSION

Derek and Marina terminated therapy a year later, with no subsequent episodes of violence. In a subsequent check-in 6 months later they reported continuing to do well. It was crucial to their therapy that their episodes of violence not be interpreted as untreatable and intractable, but rather as reenactment of earlier trauma history that was, in fact, a third and potent partner in their marriage. With careful trust building over time and learning new tools for deepening their friendship, regulating their DPA, and deescalating conflict, the couple worked through very difficult and painful issues. This work served not only to heal the marriage but also to help them to recover from their own traumatic beginnings.

It is important to realize that not all marital violence is treatable in a couples context. In relationships where the perpetrator consistently refuses to accept any responsibility for the violence, denies feeling guilt for it, and repeatedly uses violence as a means of intimidation and control, couples therapy is not recommended. It is critical in these situations to help the victim through individual therapy to establish safety for herself and her children (most victims of serious violence are female), and to refer the perpetrator to an individual treatment program.

In the case of Derek and Marina, however, incidents of violence were rare and mortifying for both partners, and they both felt intensely motivated to change, for their own sake and for their daughter's. Thus, couples therapy combined with individual therapy was deemed appropriate for them. Fortunately, due to their fortitude, their work proved successful. I expect that their marriage will never be perfect, as none are. Yet with their well-practiced skills and commitment to building a loving life together, their marriage has the hope of providing their daughter with something they each never had, a childhood free from trauma and abuse and rich with love.

Chapter 4 ❖

Extramarital Affairs: The Pearl in the Oyster

Julie Schwartz Gottman

Affairs hurt marriages. A marriage begins by drawing a shell of commitment around a couple that separates their relationship from other relationships. The couple receives support and nurturance from the surrounding environment but remains a separate entity. Storms may batter the relationship, but, if built well, the marriage stays healthy and whole despite them.

If a grain of sand enters that shell of commitment, there is irritation. If a rock cracks its way in, damage ensues. Another intimate relationship intrudes into the interior chamber of the marriage. Tissue is torn, the soft underbelly is lacerated, and the marriage is all but destroyed from the inside out. The affair shreds the trust that earlier formed the heart of the relationship. As couples therapists, it is our duty and privilege to witness the devastation wrought by an affair and attempt to help heal it. But how?

First, who are we most likely to treat for an extramarital affair? Atkins and colleagues (2001) reported that men aged 55–65 and women aged 40–45 were most likely to have affairs. The younger they married, the more likely they were to have them. The age of the women correlated with those women who had entered the workforce, were making more money, and had more access to available men. Individuals of either gender who earned more than $30,000 a year were also more likely to have had affairs, as they enjoyed higher status, traveled more, and were home less often. The greatest incidence of affairs occurred when one partner worked and had access to others while the other partner remained at home. In addition, partners who reported themselves as "not too happy" were four times as likely to have had affairs than those who were "very happy," and couples who said they were "pretty happy" were twice as likely to have had affairs as the "very happy" ones. Apparently, an "OK" marriage doesn't buffer couples from affairs. In other words, the association between marital satisfaction and affairs exists on a continuum and doesn't only occur at the extremes. In the "pretty happy" or "not happy" marriages, religion didn't affect affair rates either; if relatively unhappy, religious couples also have affairs.

The statistics are mixed regarding the rate of affairs in the United States. When the National Opinion Research Center at the University of Chicago interviewed couples from 1991 to 1996, 25% of couples presenting for treatment had as an issue an extramarital affair. Greene (1984) also found that another 30% of couples who did not present with an affair would disclose one further along in treatment. Christensen (1962) found that 10% of the population had affairs, whereas Glass and Wright (1997) in their clinical sample found the rate closer to 80%. However, Glass was well known for specializing in the treatment of affairs, so her statistic may have reflected that fact.

Most researchers agree, however, that extramarital affairs are one of the most difficult issues to treat. In the random sample survey sponsored by *Reader's Digest* (John Gottman served on the advisory panel for the survey; Reader's Digest & Gallup, 2004) couples who were scarred by an untreated affair scored as more damaged on multiple dimensions of marital health than any other group. Glass and Wright (1997) found that betrayed partners often suffered from the symptoms of PTSD, including intrusive thoughts, flashbacks, emotional constriction, psychic numbing, hypervigilance, physiological arousal, and nightmares. These symptoms complicate treatment.

Let's analyze what an affair does to a marriage using the perspective of the SRH theory. In brief, an affair shatters every level of the house. On the ground floor of love maps, one partner no longer knows the other. Let's imagine that "he" has had an affair. "She" thought he was religious, hated liars, and was never that interested in sex. Now she learns that he flouted his religious values, lied to her continuously for a year, and had extramarital sex all those nights that he allegedly "worked late." She's even more traumatized when she remembers that he treated her romantically, made love to her passionately, and seemed totally in love with her—in short, when he compartmentalized his affair and simultaneously maintained a loving relationship with her. She has a glazed look of shock in her eyes when she asks him, "Who are you?" If she has suspected an affair all along and finds the receipts for flowers in the car glove compartment, she's relieved that her suspicions have been validated, but she's hurt and furious nonetheless.

Her fondness and admiration for him, of course, are in shambles. She feels betrayed, disrespects him, and holds him in contempt for his immoral behavior. She doesn't dare feel her love for him because that hurts more and makes her more vulnerable to his attempts to win her back. Nor does she trust any attempt he makes to turn toward her. How can she trust him to be sincere in his efforts? Furthermore, her PTSD symptoms constrict her affect, leave her depressed, and render it impossible for her to turn toward him once again. Instead, she turns against him, blaming him with hostility and anger, and refusing to get near him. How can she respond to him when she feels robbed of innocence, trust, safety, and love? Needless to say, between these three levels of the SRH, negative sentiment override is everywhere. Every gesture he makes is viewed through her fear, anguish, and suspicion. Criticism and contempt flow from her, only to be met by his defensiveness and stonewalling. Connection on any level becomes impossible.

The upper levels of the SRH are also devastated by the earthquake beneath them. With no friendship system buttressing the relationship, plus a bankrupt emotional bank account, simple problem solving becomes insurmountable. Softened start-up translates into her dragging out the ammunition about his affair, and in no way will she accept influence from him, as accepting influence would mean giving up core ideas she holds about herself. Repairs misfire, and compromise remains unreachable. And with easy problems impossible to solve, perpetual problems become worse. How can there be dialogue and exploration of dream-within-conflict when there is no trust that either partner's dreams will be validated and respected? The trust on which to build emotional intimacy is gone; thus, nothing is safe to share. Last but not least, shared meanings have also dissolved. A marriage should reach upward toward shared beliefs and common values. When an affair has occurred, these values and beliefs are blown into the stratosphere—he has countermanded them, and because beliefs and values form the heart and soul of each partner, she is left asking him, "Who are you?" Sometimes, neither of them knows. How, then, do we help this couple rebuild a sound relationship house when the old one is destroyed?

The following case presentation combines several cases into one and highlights the most important aspects of treatment.

FRANK AND JUDY

Judy left a message on my voicemail. "My husband, Frank, has been having an affair for a year. I've kicked him out and filed for divorce, but now I'm rethinking things. I want us to come in. Can you see us?" Her voice sounded low, monotonal, and depressed. When I called her back, Judy recounted that 3 months earlier she had been checking e-mail on their home computer, and had discovered a message to Frank from a mysterious "Anna." It was full of sexual innuendos, suggesting a rendezvous in San Francisco, where Frank was traveling the next week. Judy had confronted Frank, who at first denied knowing Anna. Over the next 2 days of pounding conversations, Frank finally admitted having an intimate "friendship" with Anna, who worked in his San Francisco office. Judy screamed at Frank to leave the house and not come back. He moved in with a male friend across town. In phone conversations that followed, there was more screaming and more of "his blatant lies." She then hired a detective, who searched both their home e-mail and a secret e-mail line Frank had set up, as well as hotel check-ins in San Francisco. A bigger and more devastating story emerged of monthly sexual liaisons, multiple phone calls, and continuous e-mail containing sexual content for more than a year. Armed with this information, Judy consulted an attorney and filed divorce papers.

Frank begged her to reconsider. She initially refused but then began to think it through. Given their long-standing relationship of 21 years and a daughter in college who would be devastated by their breakup, Judy decided to seek couples therapy to give the relationship one final try. Nervously, Frank agreed to participate.

Assessment

A week after Judy called me, the couple entered the office. Frank was short, powerfully built, and balding. He moved quickly and decisively to the far corner of my couch. Judy was red-haired and very thin and peered at me from behind her bifocals. She sat squeezed up against the opposite corner of the couch like a beaten puppy. I asked them to tell me their story.

> Judy: This creep lied to me for a year. He's been seeing a piece of meat in San Francisco. I've got pictures of her. She's ugly— I don't know why he'd go for her. I've worked my tail off organizing his life for 20 years, raising his daughter, cleaning his house, paying his bills, and this is how he repays me! Goddamn bastard.
> Gottman: You're so furious and hurt that words aren't big enough to convey it. (*Frank shifts uncomfortably on the couch.*) Frank, this must be terribly difficult to hear.
> Frank: No kidding.
> Gottman: I'd like to hear about the beginning of your relationship, before all this started. How did the two of you meet?
> Judy: At school, where I mistakenly thought he was smart.

I noted the contempt in Judy's comment but chose to not confront it until I'd established some trust with her. Frank shot Judy "a look" and added that they had been in school together in Connecticut, where he studied law and Judy completed her B.A. They had met through friends, discovered that they both loved long-distance running, and began training together, spending long afternoons running across the open fields outside their small college town. When asked what attracted them to each other, Frank replied that he loved Judy's elfish red hair, spunkiness, spontaneity, and enthusiasm for life. Judy reluctantly admitted that Frank was cute, intellectually challenging, and had the "right" political views. They started dating later that summer.

As the oral history interview continued, Judy seemed to soften slightly. She recounted how swept away she was by Frank. He romanced her with big sweeping gestures, like filling her dorm room with flowers on her birthday, hiring Italian singers to serenade her, and saving for months for the beautiful diamond ring he'd given her when he proposed the next year. She couldn't resist. For the first time in the session, Judy glanced out the corner of her eye at Frank and caught him smiling at her. She quickly turned away and scowled.

Frank described the sheer bliss he felt when their daughter, Stephanie, was born 2 years later. Frank had taken a job in Seattle with a law firm that demanded 12-hour days and weekend work. As an associate lawyer, he eyed a junior partnership position with the glint of determination. He wanted to work hard, and

Judy seemed not to need him at home. She even laughed and teased him about his awkwardness in diapering the baby while taking over the job for him. He good-naturedly agreed he was no good at it and retreated into work. More and more hours were spent at the office.

After several months, Frank noticed that Judy seemed down and blue. "The spunk disappeared," he said. A cloud descended over the house. "I just chalked it up to her being tired. Stephanie was a poor sleeper and Judy was always the one getting up with her at night." But as the months dragged on, Judy's "down" feelings did not subside. Even when Stephanie began to sleep well, Judy remained irritable, moody, despairing, and tearful. Once, when she dropped a cup in the kitchen that shattered on the floor, she screamed out invectives and ran crying from the room. Ill-equipped to understand Judy's feelings, Frank figured it was just temporary and vowed to work harder, thinking a promotion at the law firm would make her feel better. When the hard-won promotion finally came through, however, Judy just shrugged, said "way to go," and went upstairs. Frank felt increasingly alienated from Judy. It seemed like she and Stephanie had their own little world from which he was excluded. At the end of their day, Judy didn't want to share with him, and he chose not to burden her with office worries.

After 6 months, Judy began to feel a little better and met with three neighboring mothers and their young children for play and tea. The mothers traded recipes, household tips, and family stories. Eventually, as the women drew closer, they discussed the upcoming presidential election, realized they preferred the same candidate, and chose together to volunteer for him. The women wrote letters, stuffed envelopes, and canvassed shopping malls while the children played in the mall courtyards. Meanwhile, Frank lingered at the office even later. Being a junior partner was good, but he felt that being a senior partner would really show that he'd succeeded.

Over the years, Frank's and Judy's worlds floated apart. They sometimes attended Stephanie's swim meets together, as well as Frank's annual holiday law firm parties, but no other occasions drew them together. Judy and Stephanie ate dinner at 6 P.M; Frank came home and ate 3 hours later. Frank went into the office on the weekends, while Judy ran household errands and chauffeured Stephanie to lessons and to friends' homes. Judy went running with one of her women friends in the mornings, and Frank worked out at the office building gym in the evenings. They watched videos to relax, their eyes fixed on the screen.

Finally, Frank's coveted promotion came through. He moved up to senior partnership and was asked to help open a law firm office in San Francisco. It was there that he met Anna, a young attorney who was joining the San Francisco office. Business meetings evolved into coffee together, dinners, and, finally, romance.

At the end of the first session, I asked Frank and Judy to discuss a problem for 15 minutes so I could get a sense of how they resolved conflict.

Frank: Judy, I want to move back in.
Judy: Why?
Frank: Because I miss you.
Judy: Now that you're here and not in San Francisco?

Frank: Come on, Judy, give me a break.

Judy: Why the hell should I? Did you give me one ounce of consideration? One bit of care in all these years? All you've cared about is yourself, your office, your promotions, your ambition. You don't give a damn about me. You're a selfish, heartless phoney.

Frank: I don't think that's called for. I know I was wrong. But I deserve a little forbearance. After all, you haven't been exactly available all these years. In fact, you've been an absentee wife, hanging out with your friends all the time. Talk about selfish.

The conversation deteriorated from there into more vicious contempt, name calling, and sarcasm. Finally, the talk ended. Judy and Frank sat icily staring out the window in silence. Frank angrily said to me, "Is this what you want to see?"

I replied, "It looks like the two of you are in so much pain that all you know how to do is sling insults at each other. You don't know how to bridge over the betrayal that's occurred. That's a terrible place to be. And yet, I wonder if you're also wanting some way to connect with one another, to reach each other. Judy, maybe you're needing to tell Frank about the nightmare you're living in now, and how completely devastated you feel. Frank, perhaps you're simply bewildered by how you've gotten here and how all this could've happened. I doubt that you set out to betray Judy when you first fell in love with her. But given that you're both here, there must be some ember of hope left, despite how bleak it feels. We'll have to see what happens when we breathe on it."

At Frank's individual session, he described his childhood home life as privileged but lonely. Frank's father ran a corporation and was gone most of the time. There were rumors that he had women elsewhere. Meanwhile, Frank's mother quietly drank, while maintaining a facade of perfect gentility. As Frank was the eldest of the four children, Frank's father expected the best from him and railed at him when he brought home mediocre grades. It seemed like nothing he did was good enough for his father.

When Frank turned 12, his mother developed breast cancer and had to have a double mastectomy. Frank was terrified, but no one discussed it, so neither did he. His mother simply left for the hospital one day and a week later returned, disfigured. Frank felt shock and grief and for months suffered nightmares of decapitated bodies. But there was no one to talk to. Frank figured it was manly to keep quiet. Besides, he had no words for how he felt, so why try?

As his mother continued to drink and his father traveled more and more, Frank felt increasingly isolated. He threw himself into schoolwork to at least please his mother. When his grades improved, he thought his father might want to spend more time with him, but this wasn't the case. Frank began to spend time away, studying at libraries, museums, anyplace unreachable by phone. Books became a refuge, especially those focusing on stories of partnership. Later, when Frank decided to study law, he chose the legalities of intercompany contracts as his focus.

Frank had fallen deeply in love with Judy upon first meeting her. She brought sunlight into his life. He began to open up to life in her presence. But after

Stephanie's birth, something changed. It was Judy. She seemed so depressed, shut down, and unreachable. It never occurred to him that she might be suffering from postpartum depression, especially as the months dragged on. In many ways it felt like being home again as a kid. No one talked; people just did what they were supposed to do, and so did he.

Did he want this marriage? Yes. Was he willing to cut off the relationship with Anna entirely? Yes, but he wasn't sure how he'd continue to supervise the San Francisco office. Could he ask her to leave? Doubtful, but he'd think about it.

I explained to him the following: "Here's an idea that comes from the research of the late Shirley Glass. If you imagine your marriage like a house, you've erected a wall between you and Judy, and you've opened a window to Anna. That means that Anna has received your confidences, your care, and your love and knows all about your life. But Judy has been shut out. She knows nothing of your feelings, your worries, your hopes … or your secrets. To heal this marriage, the walls and windows have to be reversed. A wall has to come between you and Anna with a window opening up between you and Judy. In order to do this, you will have to remove Anna from your life altogether and answer all of Judy's questions about your affair and your life as best you can. You'll also have to hear her rage, her anguish, and her fears about you. This may happen repeatedly, but should diminish if you hear her well. I'll also work to support both you and her through this so no one is destroyed in the process. We'll then need to rebuild a different marriage from the ground up, one that will hopefully include more connection and intimacy for both of you. Are you willing?" He said he was.

When Judy sat down for her individual session, it took only seconds for the tears to begin. Collapsing in despair, she covered her face with her hands and repeatedly cried out, "I thought he was so good, so loyal! Why did I try so hard?" She went on to describe how her working class childhood family life as the eldest of nine had prepared her for a homemaker's job. At 8 years old, Judy learned how to cook breakfast for the family while her mother finished the laundry she took in to help make ends meet. At 10, Judy bottle-fed the little ones in turn. At 12, she had full responsibility for Amy, the 1-year-old. School was important but household work was more important. Her father worked long hours at a gas station, and her mother, often exhausted, responded irritably and critically to Judy when Judy tried to confide in her.

Much to Judy's surprise, she was given a scholarship to attend a nearby university, and with her family's blessings she took a part-time job and a studio apartment and started school. Then she met Frank.

Frank walked in from her dreams. He was smart, charming, and seemed protective of her. He even did the dishes when she had him over for dinner. And he loved to run like she did. What didn't she see back then? There must have been warning signs she missed, clues that he would turn out to be a cheater. Too much charm perhaps?

Judy also noted that in the month since learning about the affair, she'd had frequent nightmares. She couldn't get thoughts of Anna and Frank together out of her mind. They intruded in the middle of her most mundane chores, such as scrubbing floors. She added ruefully that her floors were very clean now. She also mentioned that she felt jumpy in a strange way. Any unusual sounds startled her. She was also having trouble concentrating and repeatedly caught herself reading and rereading a page of her novel without absorbing it. Judy didn't understand these feelings.

It was clear that Judy was suffering from PTSD. I described the symptoms of PTSD and explained that this was a normal response to the trauma of learning about her husband's affair. Judy was encouraged to hear that these symptoms would probably diminish over time as the affair was discussed in therapy and she was given the chance to voice her feelings about it, including the more vulnerable ones like the terror that Frank would betray her again. Given therapeutic support, was she willing to try to speak about those feelings as honestly as possible? Yes. Would she also be willing, in time, to hear Frank's feelings about the marriage? It was hard to imagine, but she knew that would be necessary to rebuild things. She hadn't been perfect either. I quickly reassured her that no one had to be perfect for a marriage to work. But both parties had to be willing to talk to each other when things weren't working well, and it looked like neither she nor Frank had ever really learned how to do that. She nodded.

The questionnaires that Judy and Frank filled out showed what I expected: Both their Weiss-Cerrettos showed scores indicating thoughts of separation, and Judy's high score reflected her legal consultations regarding divorce. Both Locke-Wallace measures of marital satisfaction were low, with Judy's being the lowest. The SRH questionnaires revealed the mess their marriage was in. The friendship system was marked with poor love maps, little fondness and admiration, and much evidence of turning away from each other. Conflict skills were poor, with all four horsemen present, flooding was common for both, and emotional distance was a rock weighing them down. However, their shared meaning system held some light—they shared the same beliefs about religion, work ethics, holiday rituals, and parenting. Overall, they were a couple in much pain but who still desired to try and had some fundamental values in common.

At the third assessment session, I laid out the strengths I saw: In the oral history interview, there was a sense of "we-ness" as they described their early history together, indicating that at one time there had been romance, admiration, and caring for one another. Similarly, they both felt passionate about parenting and shared spiritual values and physical self-care. They also preferred to work hard, which would come in handy during treatment. Above all, they still valued the marriage despite the damage done and wished to attempt to repair it.

The challenge they faced was that all seven levels of the SRH had been blown out by the implosion of the affair. But as is common with many affairs, there may have been weaknesses in their marital structure to begin with. It looked like Judy had suffered some postpartum depression after Stephanie's birth. Both Frank and Judy's inability to get help for Judy may have resulted in Judy's feeling isolated, despairing, and alone at home. Frank had mistakenly gotten the message that neither Judy nor Stephanie needed him, and, thinking of his early childhood training, he figured that hard work at the office would fix things at home. Thus, he and Judy grew distant. Judy turned to women friends for support, found it, and began to develop a life for herself apart from Frank. All of this would have been fine had Frank and Judy continued to talk to each other throughout their changing lives. Unfortunately, neither of them had grown up learning how to share feelings or thoughts or how to state their needs. Thus, they grew apart and stayed apart. When conflicts arose, they were avoided. Every now and then when Judy became irritated at Frank's perpetual habit of leaving his clothes on the floor, she would explode at Frank in a rash of criticism. Frank would snap back at her, reform for a while, and then resume his old habits. Conflicts were not discussed and negotiated through to resolution.

Now, with the affair exposed, the four horsemen had descended and were trampling the relationship with raging fights full of criticism, contempt, defensiveness, and stonewalling. On this ground no listening was possible. The conflicts added insult to injury and made things worse.

It was also clear that both Judy and Frank were flooding physiologically during these conflicts. They needed to learn the art of self-soothing. That would be an early step in the treatment.

I explained to Frank that Judy was suffering from PTD as a result of their marital troubles. It would take time for her to recover from it. In the process, Frank would need to answer his wife's questions about the affair, listen to her feelings, and reveal any further contact Anna made with him *before* Judy asked. He would also need to tolerate Judy's distancing from him until she decided what she wanted regarding his moving back in. Judy would need to learn how to state her feelings without criticism and contempt and figure out what questions she wanted to ask. She would also need to be aware that specific answers, especially regarding sexual details, could further traumatize her, so she would need to think carefully about which questions to ask. Later, they would need to both honestly examine the marital difficulties that might have contributed to the crisis and be willing to recreate their marriage by both making changes. Judy and Frank agreed to continue with treatment.

THE THERAPY

In the first post-assessment session of therapy, Frank reported that he had written a letter to put an end to the affair. He'd also talked to Anna on the phone when she'd called him to ask that he reconsider. Following a suggestion I'd made in his individual session, Frank called Judy into the room to make sure that she was there when he spoke with Anna.

Judy dryly said that there was still no trust. I encouraged her to begin to ask questions, but cautioned her to limit them to what, where, and when questions to begin with.

Judy: So why did you do it?
Frank: I don't know.
Gottman: Judy, it's going to take some time to really answer that well. I know that's the most pressing question, but can you ask Frank a different one for now?

Judy: So when did you first meet that cow?

Gottman: I'm going to have to stop you here, Judy, as everyone needs to be spoken of with respect here.

Judy: So when?

Frank: About a year ago, during that first trip to meet the San Francisco staff.

Judy: When did it get sexual?

Frank: A couple of months later, after the office open house party.

Judy: You decided to cheat on me that fast? Bastard.

Gottman: I'm going to have to stop you again, Judy. I know you're furious, and it's horrible to hear the details, but we can't do name calling here — it's contemptuous, abusive, and sabotages your feelings' getting heard. Your anger deserves to be heard, but it can't be in that way.

Judy: What attracted you to her?

Frank: (*pausing*) She was a good listener. She was kind, gentle, compassionate...

Judy: And you think I'm not? How dare you! I've done nothing but take care of you for 20 years, and this is all I get for it? I can't take this! Judy stood up and walked to the door, then stopped.

Gottman: Judy, that must have really hurt you. All your efforts must seem invisible to Frank; in fact, you must feel invisible to him. Crying, Judy returned but sat as far from Frank as she could.

Judy: I hate you!

Frank: (*to me*) Can she say that? Isn't that contempt?

Gottman: No, it's a statement of feeling, and unfortunately that is how Judy is feeling right now, especially when she hears the things you admired in Anna.

Frank: It doesn't mean I don't love you, Judy. I do. I just felt so alone. It didn't seem like you liked me very much.

Judy: How the hell could I like you? I hardly ever saw you. You were always gone, the office was always more important, everything was more important than me. How was I supposed to listen to you when you were never here? All you cared about was that fat cow.

Gottman: Judy...

Judy: OK...the point is, it's hard to have a relationship with a phantom.

Gottman: Right. Maybe you both were missing each other.

In subsequent sessions, Judy continued her questioning. She learned what Anna and Frank talked about, when Frank telephoned her surreptitiously, and how they disguised their illicit meetings. For 10 sessions, Frank answered as honestly as he could and managed to listen to some of Judy's feelings. Finally, in the 11th session, Frank admitted that he felt suicidal.

Frank: I don't know how long I can do this. Every day I end up feeling battered. I appreciate that Judy is doing less criticism and contempt, but sometimes I feel so worthless I don't want to get up. I want to disappear, just escape somehow.

Gottman: It sounds like life is hard to take right now. Do you ever think about suicide?

Frank: Yes, but I'd never do it to Stephanie.

Judy: What about to me?

Frank: What difference do I make to you?

Judy: (pausing) I don't know yet, but I just know you make some kind of difference because I keep coming every week and I don't want to talk to my attorney.

Gottman: Judy, do you remember what you used to love about Frank?

Judy: I remember that he was good to me—took good care of me when I broke my ankle running down a steep hill once. He was passionate, sexy, intelligent, and warm. I don't know what he is now.

Gottman: That's part of what we're here to discover—who you are to each other as well as to yourselves. Frank, can you make me a promise that you'll do nothing to harm yourself and you'll call me if you're feeling suicidal again?

Frank: Yes.

In these sessions, it was clear that Judy and Frank had no love maps of one another. Their worlds had run parallel without intersection for so long that neither one knew the thoughts, feelings, and dreams of the other. It was crucial early on to support Judy in her anger but also help her curtail her criticism and contempt. This was difficult for her to do, but slowly she learned that her anger was just as powerful without name calling as it was with it, and it reached Frank more deeply when it was pure.

If we were to begin building back a fondness and admiration level, it was important for Frank to repeat his love for Judy with sincerity whenever he could access it internally. For Judy, this task was much more difficult. It was impossible for her to risk the vulnerability of voicing her love for Frank either to him or to herself. Both would move her closer to him and make her feel unsafe. She had to tread water first with a hand on the dock of ambivalence before letting go to swim. However, she could state her memory of love with the safety of knowing that it committed her to nothing in the present. At the same time, it was quietly reassuring to Frank to hear that Judy at least remembered loving him; his betrayal had not blotted out that memory.

Frank, meanwhile, wrestled with the decision about whether or not to ask Anna to leave the San Francisco office. She was too competent, he complained—too much loss to the firm. I wondered whether it was too much loss to him, whether he still had ambivalence about leaving Anna. Judy insisted that Anna go, which brought therapy to a standstill. I decided to meet with Frank individually to talk through his decision.

Frank: She really is good, one of the top earners of the firm.

Gottman: And is she still near the top in your mind?

Frank: No, of course not.

Gottman: Are you sure? You've said that you were in love with her. It must be very hard to think of her disappearing forever from your life, especially when you don't know what will happen with Judy.

Frank: But I really want this to work out.

Gottman: Then you may have to make your marriage a priority over work. Rebuilding trust with Judy will be much more difficult if Anna is still a part of the firm and you have contact with her, even if it's just for business. It's like quitting cigarettes. How could Judy be sure you were really quitting if you still kept a carton in your desk because some of your clients liked cigarettes? It's too hard a habit to break, and Judy knows it. She knows how much Anna meant to you. It will be tough for her to imagine that on business trips to San Francisco, you won't have anything to do with Anna. You'll have to decide, Frank, which comes first, rebuilding trust with Judy, or keeping a good earner in the San Francisco office.

Two days later, Judy exploded at Frank for coming home late. When he angrily protested her criticism of him, she flooded and screamed, "Go to your piece of meat!" Dazed and confused, Frank left the house for a hotel and stayed away that night. The next day an emergency session was called.

Frank: What you said was crazy. What's the matter with you?

Gottman: Frank, you're obviously very upset by what happened, but it's coming out as criticism. Instead, why don't you try to tell Judy what that fight was like for you? Here's a questionnaire to help you. (I give them each a copy of the aftermath of a marital argument questionnaire). Start with the first question, Frank. Judy, just listen, and then you share with Frank your answers to that same question.

As the questionnaire was followed and their two subjective realities were revealed, Frank mumbled his surprise, hurt, and fear at Judy's "attack" on him. In his "reality," he was trying hard to meet Judy's needs now and felt he deserved appreciation of that fact. He still had to work late, despite his marital difficulties. Judy disclosed her fear that because Frank hadn't asked Anna to leave the S.F. office yet, he must still have an interest in her. In her "reality," his staying at work late meant he might still be pursuing her romantically. She felt enraged at him and doubted his full commitment to her. She did appreciate Frank's efforts but didn't know how to shed the burden of rage she felt.

We talked about how flooding had thrown her back into old, contemptuous behaviors. I briefly described DPA and consequent flooding. I told Judy that the contempt during her explosion made sense, as it was likely that her pulse had elevated way above the 95 beats per minute threshold, and at that level, no one had the cognitive energy to think clearly. It was crucial that they both become aware of initial signs of flooding and, when feeling them, ask to take a break for at least 20 minutes in order to calm themselves down. Then they could return to the conversation with quieted bodies and minds and think more clearly. We practiced deep, diaphragmatic breathing, muscle relaxation, and guided visual imagery to strengthen their ability to soothe themselves. Judy noticed that when she began to feel upset, her jaw tightened, her stomach felt slightly sick, and she wanted to draw her knees up toward her chest. Frank felt his fists clench and his breath become more shallow and rapid when he grew angry. With these warning signs made conscious, Frank and Judy could both stop the action before their conflicts escalated and the four horsemen took over. They decided on a hand signal that would indicate that they needed to take a break and on a 30-minute time interval for their break, after which they'd return to talk.

The following week, Judy and Frank proudly shared that again a heated conflict had occurred but this time they had taken a break, continued the conversation later, and reached a resolution. Judy had made it absolutely clear that she could not rebuild her trust in Frank unless Anna was completely out of the picture—gone from the San Francisco office. Frank finally agreed to ask her to leave. That evening he called Anna with Judy again present, and this time Anna dismally agreed that it was for the best and that she'd begin looking for another job immediately.

In the session, Judy reported that she had felt a shift in herself take place. She knew how important the success of this office branch was to Frank and that he was putting it at risk by asking Anna to leave.

> Frank: It wasn't easy to do this. I'm completely invested in this marriage now, but I'm afraid the San Francisco office may go down the toilet without Anna.
> Judy: Why did you do it?
> Frank: Because, faced with losing you, it just wasn't worth it. Better the office closing down than our family breaking up.
> Judy: What will happen to you if it does?
> Frank: I don't know.... The other partners won't be too pleased, I'm sure.
> Judy: Frank, I need you to know something.... No matter what happens, if you lose your job even, this has proven to me that you're back, that you want *us,* so we'll figure it out somehow. We can always find jobs. But I don't want to find somebody else. I want you.

With Frank's finally turning toward Judy and making her a priority, Judy could now more fully turn toward Frank and allow herself greater vulnerability to him and to their life together.

The therapeutic work shifted to helping Frank and Judy turn more toward one another in everyday ways. It was difficult for Judy to voice her needs.

> Frank: So in what ways can I be there for you, Judy?
> Judy: Well, you can write more letters to Stephanie... help her figure out when she's coming home, for Thanksgiving or Christmas....
> Gottman: Judy, it's easy for you to ask for needs to be met on Stephanie's behalf, but what about your needs?
> Judy: (*laughing*) Do I have any?
> Gottman: You'd be the first person I've met who didn't. What makes it hard for you to voice them?

Judy: Maybe I'll get shamed for them, like "come on, Judy, you can do that yourself, can't you?" when I ask for help with the computer.

Gottman: And who said that?

Frank: Her mother.

Judy: She was so busy with the other kids, it would be too hard for her to attend to my problems—she had everybody else's to worry about.

Gottman: You sound as if it was OK for her to ignore yours, like as long as there were other kids around, you didn't matter. You sound like you were speaking again more on her behalf than on your own. I'd imagine her explaining her ignoring your needs the way you just have. But how about you? In sympathy for your mom, you must have felt pretty alone and overwhelmed always having to take care of yourself. And now you've got someone who wants to take care of you, who wants to give to you, but you're having a heck of a time letting him in. Connection goes both ways. One person can give, but the other person needs to be willing to receive. Frank, what's it like for you to give to Judy?

Frank: Like trying to give to a brick wall. It just bounces back. I tried years ago to help you, Judy, when Stephanie was born, but my efforts seemed foolish to you, so I stopped trying. But I want to give to you. It feels so good to be needed — it makes me feel important, strong, protective, like a man. I know I won't be able to always do what you ask, but I really want to try. I want you to ask. It's not an imposition. It's more like an honor, like you're honoring me with your trust and reaching out to me because you value what I can give.

Judy: Oh....

Judy had a puzzled, dawning-awareness look on her face. She'd never imagined that asking someone to meet her needs could also be a gift to the other person.

I gave Frank a clipboard, and while Judy hesitantly named a number of ways Frank could turn toward her, Frank jotted down her requests. Then the roles were reversed, and Judy noted in what ways Frank wished her to turn toward him. They agreed that in the following week they would respond to at least two of the needs they'd each listed.

Several sessions later, a bomb was dropped.

Frank: Judy, I have to admit I'm not as attracted to you as I used to be. You're too thin.

Judy: That's the craziest thing I've ever heard. I have the only husband in America who'd complain about my being too thin. What are you talking about?

Frank: I don't know.... There's something about how thin you are that turns me off.

Judy: Oh, thanks very much. You asshole. Who do you think you are, criticizing me?

Gottman: Judy, take a couple of deep breaths. Do you want to try to rephrase that?

Judy: How dare you tell me I'm ugly? That cow you dated was a lot worse than me. Why don't you go find her again? Then you'll have plenty of meat to cuddle up with!

Frank: Judy, please stop. She's not a cow and I resent you calling her that.

Judy: Oh, fine, just take her side. (*silence*)

Judy was outraged that Frank was criticizing her looks. She was also terrified that Frank was telling her she was unacceptable to him. Again, the affair lifted its hoary head.

Frank seemed to be uncomfortable with something about Judy and it precluded his drawing closer to her.

Gottman: Judy, in order to understand this better, I'd like to ask Frank some questions. Is that all right with you?

Judy: Go ahead.

Gottman: Frank, what exactly is it about Judy's thinness that bothers you?

Frank: I don't know. I feel weird talking about her like this. But I feel anxious when I look at her nude. There's no curves—I want to feel attracted to her, but I just don't.

Gottman: Her lack of curves—and that anxiety you feel? Have you ever felt something like that before?

Frank: Maybe when I was young.

Gottman: With whom?

Frank: With Mom. I remember that she used to be warm, a large woman, I used to love to sit on her lap. After her cancer, it was different. She lost a lot of weight. After she had the mastectomy, her attitude was different. She stopped wanting to hold me. She'd sort of sidle away when I got close to her, like she didn't want me near her.

Gottman: Hmm, sounds painful.

Frank: It was.

Gottman: Any chance that Judy's thinness might be reminding you of her?

Frank: I suppose so. I feel anxious when I hug Judy sometimes. Like how is she? Will I crush her? Will I hurt her if I hold her? I think my mom's mastectomy was really painful, and she couldn't be held for a long time because of the wounds needing to heal.

Judy: You mean I remind you of her?

Frank: Yes, sort of. I mean you're nothing like her, you're kinder and warmer and much more gentle. But something about how you look must trigger those old memories, because I feel that same anxiety when I hug you as when I hugged her, or tried to.

Judy: Honey, I need to tell you you're not going to crush me. I love it when you hug me. And I'm strong. All those years of running and working out—I'm nothing like her. A good hard hug feels wonderful to me, because I love to feel your strength. It's sexy.

Frank: Really?

Judy: Really.

With this exploration of Frank's internal working model, the link he was making between Judy's body type and his memory of his mom after cancer caused an old trauma to surface for him. Cancer had altered not only his mother's body but also her emotional connection to her son. Frank was pushed away and rejected. As any child would, Frank blamed himself for the distance between his mother and him, and he tried hard to be what she needed: a more distant, less needy, and less affectionate child. It didn't work. He gamely went on, buried himself in books, and "forgot" about his needs. Now as his closeness to Judy and dependence on her was deepening, an old trauma was resurfacing. Closeness meant rejection. Frank needed to uproot his feelings, link them to their source in childhood, and separate them out from his connection with Judy. Then he could be free to embrace her in every way.

A month later, Frank was invited to attend a law conference in Denver. Anna would be there. Judy vacillated between anger at his desire to go and her wish to show her trust in him by supporting his going. A year had passed since therapy had begun. The couple had drawn closer, shared many meaningful moments together, and become more passionate in their sexual connection. Why shouldn't Judy let him go? Trust was still an issue.

Judy: Why do you want to go?
Frank: Because I want to learn from this professor—I hear he's one of the top experts in the country on contract law, and I always need to learn more. This isn't a static profession, you know.
Judy: Can't you hear him somewhere else?
Frank: Only if I enroll in law school again in Boston. I don't think you'd like that.
Judy: Well, I don't know what to say. I'm scared about your going. She'll be there. You'll see her. Then, what will you do?
Frank: I'll say hi and move on. I don't want to have a conversation with her or anything else. I'm yours.
Judy: It feels good to hear you say that, but I'm still scared.
Gottman: Judy, what would it take for you to not be scared?
Judy: Riding in his back pocket?
Gottman: Maybe there is a way to do just that. When other couples who have suffered from affairs encounter a situation like this, they will often stay very closely in touch with each other, even calling in once an hour just to make sure everything is OK. Why don't the two of you have a discussion about what you can both do to help you feel safer, Judy, and for the two of you to maintain your connection?
Frank: Judy, I'll do whatever it takes. I don't want you to be scared.
Judy: OK...can I call you every hour, or will you call me?
Frank: It's gonna look a little weird, but I can do it.
Judy: What if you told everybody you had a sick family member and needed to check in on them? That's me, of course, neurotic as hell.
Gottman: Judy, there's nothing neurotic about your fears. They're very normal for someone who's gone through what you have. After an affair,

it's very tough to build back trust. This is the first trip Frank has taken without you. And especially with Anna there, you're entitled to be afraid. I don't think Frank will betray you again, but nonetheless, you don't know that until you've gone through this first trip and you've seen what happens.

Judy: OK. Then call me hourly. Day and night.

Frank: Day and night?

Judy: Yup. I want to know where you are at 3 A.M.

Frank: How about if you have the freedom to call me anytime during the night, to check on me? Your choice of time? I'm just concerned that if I'm calling you hourly for two nights, I'll be a basket case and won't be able to attend to anything at the conference.

Judy: That sounds all right. But anytime, right?

Frank: Right.

Frank went to Denver. Dutifully he called Judy every hour the first day. She called him at 1 and 3 A.M. that night. The second day, after four calls, Judy told him to call again at 6 and 8 P.M. She in turn called him at midnight and 3 A.M. Upon their reunion, Frank told her that he'd seen Anna but not spoken to her. He'd enjoyed the conference but missed her. He was happy to be home.

The next step in therapy involved a perpetual issue that was gridlocked. Judy hated how much Frank worked. She felt deserted and deprioritized. Frank insisted that without his working so hard, they'd have nothing. Stephanie would have to transfer to a cheaper college, they'd have to sell their house, and Judy would no longer be able to buy clothes with impunity. Judy felt insulted by Frank's last comment.

Judy: You think all I value in life is my wardrobe?

Frank: Well, if it wasn't for my money you wouldn't have two full closets, would you?

Judy: And what about the gifts you get from me? And what about what I contribute? You act as if you do it all and my contributing means nothing.

Frank: Look, I'm the provider. I bring home the bucks.

Judy: So I'm worth nothing. I get it.

Frank: I'm not saying that.

Judy: Yes, you are. You're saying that you're the big man who does everything, has built everything, has raised our daughter, has taken care of this house, has done the cooking, cleaning, laundry, has driven Stephanie everywhere. . . . Without you there'd be no life, no marriage, nothing.

Frank: You're just being unreasonable. Why don't you calm down?

Gottman: Is this typical of how this discussion goes at home?

Judy: A little worse, maybe.

Gottman: It looks like it's pretty uncomfortable for both of you. How about an alternative way of discussing this?

Frank: Good. She needs one.

Gottman: Frank, like any discussion, it takes two, and it looks like you both could use some help, right?

Frank: OK.

Gottman: So I'd like to suggest a different structure for this conversation, called "the dream-within-the conflict." Judy, it sounds like you're hurt and angry that Frank works so much and doesn't spend more time with you. Frank, working hard is the way you provide for your family. Perhaps it would be helpful to explore the meaning of each of your views on a deeper level. Here's how you can do it: One of you be the interviewer while the other is the speaker. Interviewer, your job is to listen and just ask questions that can deepen your understanding of your partner's position—questions like "What is the meaning of that for you? Is there a story or some history you've experienced that relates to your view? What are your feelings? Is there a dream you have that relates to your issue, a dream about the future, or maybe a fear from the past?" It's very important that you not present your opinion at this time or try to influence your partner one way or the other. After 15 minutes, the roles are reversed and you get your turn to present your view. I'll coach you to help you ask these questions. Speaker, your job is to be as open and self-disclosing as you can in order to help your partner really understand your position on the issue. Try to keep the four horsemen out of the picture, and to speak as personally as you can about your own feelings and what's meaningful to you. Ready? Who wants to start?

Judy: I will. Frank, here's what I want you to know. I love you and I miss you. I don't like it when you work so much because we don't have a life together. Even when you come home, you're so tired you have nothing to say to me. You just want to hibernate.

Frank: So you don't like that I work so much?

Judy: Right. I want you home more.

Frank: That feels controlling.

Gottman: Frank, your own view seems to be sneaking in. Let me help you here. Why don't you ask Judy what's important to her about spending time with you? That may seem obvious, but maybe it isn't.

Frank: OK, so what's important about me being home more?

Judy: I guess I'm afraid that if you're not, then we'll drift apart and wind up where we were before... before Anna came on the scene. Distant, isolated, lonely.

Frank: (to me) What do I say here?

Gottman: Try asking her if there's some history behind this for her, other than in her relationship with you... in her earlier life maybe.

Frank: Is there a story behind this for you?

Judy: I just know that growing up I was super lonely. That might seem crazy given there were so many siblings around, but I really was. Everything was about doing—the laundry, the meals, the bottle-feeding, the schoolwork. Nobody had time to just sit down and talk. I hated that. I couldn't talk to anyone in our family. It seemed like we were always in overdrive, running like crazy to catch up and never doing so. The washing machine was always piled high with lights and darks, somebody was always crying, somebody was always hitting somebody else, and somebody needed calming down. There was no room for me, just me. All I could be was an automaton, doing everyone's bidding. And it feels like I've been that in this marriage, too. Doing your bidding, Stephanie's bidding, what the house needed, what the bills needed, what the cleaning needed. I've felt like a slave. And it's lonely. I don't want that life anymore. I want a life with you.

Frank: I didn't know you felt that way.

Judy: I know you didn't. And I was too busy being the good little wife to tell you. But I've felt that way for years.

Gottman: Frank, that "good little wife" part—why don't you ask her about that?

Frank: Why is being a "good little wife," as you put it, so important to you?

Judy: Because that's what I was trained to be. That was the only way I got recognition in my family and could feel close to Mom, by being the good helper. She didn't have time to recognize me for anything else, or for that matter, to be close to me. She was too busy. It was like doing laundry together was a connection between us, but unfortunately the only one. So in this marriage, I try to be the good little helper to you, thinking that will bring us closer together. But it hasn't, really. Because neither one of us has had time for the other. And now I want that to change.

Frank: What kind of closeness do you want to have?

Judy: The kind where you sit across the dinner table and spend an hour talking together. Where you choose to not watch TV but instead go out to some art galleries and talk about what you see. Or maybe just go out for a glass of wine and share dreams together, not the nighttime ones, but the ones about us, and about Stephanie, and about growing old together. We're almost there, you know. You're turning gray.

Frank: (*laughing*) Don't tell me that!

Gottman: OK. Let's switch the roles now. Judy, you become the interviewer and Frank, you tell Judy your side.

Frank: I've always believed that hard work was the answer. If I just worked hard, everything would work out. I'd have a good life, a good marriage, be a good husband and dad, lead a happy life.

Judy: How did you come to believe that?

Frank: Well, I don't know. I guess my dad taught me that. He always worked extra hard, and he was my role model. He seemed to have it all—power, prestige, a beautiful wife, the kids, the works. I saw him as a big success and I wanted that, too. Also, doing anything less wasn't acceptable.

Judy: What do you mean?

Frank: I mean if I did only average, he was furious with me. I wasn't good enough. You know how you said that being your mom's helper brought you closer to her? Somehow, being accomplished and productive brought me closer to my dad, or at least I thought it would. I guess it didn't really. But I always figured if I just did a little more, a little better, he'd really appreciate me and love me and think I was great. That's still how I think. I've always imagined that if I worked harder, then you'd think I was great, the best husband ever.

Judy: And then?

Frank: Then we'd have the best sex in the world.

Judy: Oh, great.

Frank: No, really, I thought you'd feel better about me and value me. I need that from you.

Judy: You do?

Frank: Of course I do.

Judy: Why?

Frank: Because you really do matter to me. Your opinion matters more to me than anybody's, yours and Stephanie's. You may think I don't value you, but the truth is that I value you so much that all I want is for you to love me, like me even, and to respect me.

Gottman: Did you know that, Judy?

Judy: No, actually. I'm stunned. I didn't know I mattered so much. Is that true, Frank?

Frank: Yes.

Judy: You need to know something. It's not your work or your status or your promotions that I value so much. It's you—your warmth, your laugh, your wit, your ideas, even that old bathrobe of yours. I just want you. I don't want your work—at least, not as much as you do of it. And sex, of course, sex is always good.

Frank: Anytime.

With this dialogue, Frank and Judy added another brick to their foundation. The conversation was especially healing for Frank, who learned that Judy loved him for qualities other than his ability to work. The couple relaxed more and began to laugh and enjoy each other more.

The time had come to examine what had gone wrong before and what had led to Anna. Neither Frank nor Judy had known how to express their needs. As Stephanie grew and Frank's career took off, the couple spent less and less time together. In addition, they had a conflict style full of the four horsemen. Their criticism, contempt, and defensiveness had created more distance between them and the need to withdraw. Frank had grown lonely. Along came Anna. Frank longed for excitement and romance, but above all he sought a sense of closeness and warmth that he didn't know how to resurrect in his marriage, for which he felt he could do nothing right. Anna had idealized and adored him. It was just the boost in self-esteem he needed. But when Frank grew more distant from Judy, Judy felt angry and abandoned and responded with more criticism of Frank. The cycle between them spiraled downward further until they both ended up in separate galaxies, completely disconnected from one another. They had no idea how to turn toward each other. Judy didn't know how to influence Frank to come closer, and Frank didn't know how to influence Judy to accept him. The tragedy here was that for both of them, their emotional needs had been deeply important, but neither one was equipped with the skills to express them.

Discussion followed about each of their vulnerabilities and needs. They both had experienced loneliness and low self-esteem and needed reassurance from the other that they were cherished. Both had felt rejected by the other and needed signs that they were wanted. Both had difficulty voicing their needs and needed practice in doing so. Also, both had a tendency to numb their feelings and needed support to stay in touch with themselves and feel that their emotions were valid. They agreed that their relationship should give them plenty of practice in all of the above.

Summer arrived. Frank and Judy planned a 6-week trip to Ireland, their ancestral homeland. Excitedly they decided to schedule one more visit upon their return to check in on their relationship. If all was well, we would stop there.

Upon their return, they recounted with delight missing plane flights, scheduled train stops, and good coffee. They'd had a wonderful time. We decided to terminate the therapy, with the door open if they wished to return. A year later, a postcard from Prague indicated that they were still doing well and still missing their trains on occasion.

CONCLUSION

Frank and Judy illustrate the dynamics of applying the Gottman method of couples therapy to a relationship all but destroyed by an affair. When a partner has had an affair, every level of the SRH is shredded to dust by distrust. The difficulties are compounded by the wounded partner's bearing the weight of PTSD. There is also the unreality of not knowing who one's partner really is, morally and spiritually. A new marriage must be built.

The work begins with questions and answers, the opening of windows to the world of the affair, and the building of walls to the extramarital partner. A complex dance begins when the wounded spouse learns about the affair and the partner's methods of betrayal. This is the beginning of the formation of new love maps. As details are revealed, emotions must surface, be aired, and be validated. Gradually, their intensity diminishes, although they can be set afire at any time and often are.

Slowly new methods of turning toward each other are introduced. New rituals of connection are tried. Sometimes they are discarded if they are too much at once. Reconnection must begin very tentatively with tests of love and respect passed by the partner who's committed the betrayal. Words of fondness and admiration must also be shared to rebuild faith that any love remains. Slowly a new, hesitant friendship can develop.

Conflict skills must also be honed. The four horsemen are almost always present, especially at first. Couples cannot be admonished for them. Instead, the feelings behind them must be revealed and listened to, with gentle awareness that the horsemen only corrode connection rather than rebuild it. Solvable problems can help teach the value of softened start-up, repairs, and accepting influence. Gridlocked problems can help reveal underlying dreams, values, and histories.

They can also help to establish deeper love maps and faith that there are still ties of meaning that bind the couple together.

Finally, the setting in which the affair occurred can be explored—how the distance grew and allowed a third party to enter in, how betrayal could happen within the pathos of the marriage, how one partner could possibly forgive another. Much can be discovered. In this final work comes the most rewarding aspect of working with couples struggling with an affair. There is probably little that is more destructive to marriage than an affair. Yet somehow couples manage to rise again and to love. In doing so, couples perform their small part of an old Hebrew "mitzvah," or good deed: "tikkun olam," the healing of the world.

REFERENCES

Atkins, D. C, et al. (2001). Why do people have affairs? Recent research and future directions about attributions for extramarital involvement. In V. Manusov & J. H. Harvey (Eds.), *Attribution, communication behavior, & close relationships: Advances in personal relations.* (pp. 305–319). New York: Cambridge University Press.

Christensen, H. T. (1962). A cross-cultural comparison of attitudes toward marital infidelity. *International Journal of Comparative Sociology, 3,* 124–137.

Glass, S. P., & Wright, T. L. (1997). Reconstructing marriages after the trauma of infidelity. In W. K. Halford & H. J. Markman (Eds.), *Clinical handbook of marriage and couples interventions* (pp. 471–508). New York: Wiley.

Greene, G. (1984). *The effect of a relationship enhancement program on marital communication and self-esteem. Dissertation Abstracts International.* July 45(1–A), p. 302.

Reader's Digest & Gallup. (2004). *Reader's Digest Family Index and Survey.* Pleasantville, NJ: Reader's Digest.

Chapter 5 ❧

Working With a Couple With Depression

Terry Sterrenberg

This chapter is about treating a troubled marriage in which one member of the couple suffers from recurring depression. Depression is a very common disorder. Twenty-five percent of women and 12% of men experience at least one episode of major depression, as defined in *DSM-IV* by the American Psychiatric Association, over the course of their lifetime. Typically episodes last 6 months if untreated. Also, major depression is a highly recurrent disorder; 50% of those who have one episode can expect to have at least one more. Major depression is only one kind of depression. Other types include bipolar illness, dysthymic disorder, and post-partum depression. Depression is a common component of medical, psychiatric, and social problems. In short, the commonness of this disorder means that every therapist dealing with couples is dealing with depression in their practice.

Depression can have serious consequences. Assessment for medication and suicide disorders needs to be done at the beginning of the therapy. Also, if the client has a personal therapist it is helpful to talk to that therapist in order to coordinate treatment. If the client is suicidal or has other mental health issues, couples therapy may be contraindicated unless the client is also getting help with the individual problem.

Depression can never be ignored. It needs to be identified and labeled as soon as therapeutically possible. All effective therapies for depression need to be considered in treating a couple where depression is present. It is a devastating and pervasive illness that affects an individual's emotional life, physical health, and ability to think productively. It colors a person's being like dye colors water.

Research reveals that the most effective courses of therapy for depression utilize medication and psychotherapy, separately or in combination (Elkins, Shea, Watkns, et al. 1989). Psychotherapy that has been effective in treating depression is usually structured, and it works to eradicate beliefs and behaviors that reinforce repetitive negative thoughts and low self-esteem. Specific goals are identified and techniques such as self-monitoring, identification of automatic negative thinking, relaxation, assertiveness training, and arranging pleasant activities are taught (Beck, Rush, Shaw, & Emery, 1979).

To some extent every kind of depression affects the couple in similar ways. Depression in a relationship leads to emotional disengagement, decreasing couple interaction, and a general feeling by both partners that their spouse doesn't seem to like them very much. This may in fact not be true. Friendship skills are usually weak, but the couple may genuinely like and care about each other. However, they tend to use the four horsemen in their communication and, as a result, they develop an overall negative perspective of their relationship. General isolation and loneliness for both partners soon follows.

In many relationships depression also manifests as a feeling of being powerless to make a difference with the partner. The usual ways a depressed person has learned to get his or her needs met do not work. These ways may have worked at one time or they may have never worked. Powerlessness easily can develop into resentfulness, despair, feelings of being completely alone, and resignation. Depressed individuals give up trying because they feel trying makes no difference. They end up feeling like none of their needs are getting met, and that they cannot meet any of their partner's needs, and they keep all of this to themselves.

For the partner of a depressed person, the turning away of the partner can be quite puzzling and confusing. Normal behaviors such as talking to the depressed partner, asking him or her to do activities together, and giving compliments and praise often do not work to reengage the depressed individual.

Depression also clouds a person's perception of life and of his or her partner's behavior. What partners need most from each other is appreciation and a sense of being valued, but they often do not trust any appreciation that is given because of low self-esteem and past experience with the partner. They point to many instances where the partner has not been trustworthy in order to justify their untrusting feelings. They reason that it would be foolish to trust a person who did what their partner has done.

Research supports the conclusion that depression is helped by improving the individual's primary relationship (Beach & O'Leary, 1989; Kung, 2000; Teichman, et Bar-El, Shor, Sirota, & Elievr, 1995). Gottman method therapists work to improve relationships by helping couples strengthen their friendship, manage their conflict, and find deeper levels of meaning with one another. In the Gottman method, when depression is a factor, several components are key: the internal working model, physiological self-soothing, and the amount of residual pain they have collected over the years, which has affected the couple's commitment to each other and their belief that change is possible.

"The internal working model" is what drives an individual's behavior, thoughts, and feelings. It basically refers to how a person views the world and interprets what happens. Affecting the internal working model of clients creates new experiences, thoughts, and beliefs, which in turn affect the depression.

The internal working model includes negative thinking about oneself, one's partner, and about the future of the relationship. It is based on the negative thinking of the past. Having depression "on the table" as a topic of discussion for the couple is a primary way a depressed person's negative thinking can be addressed. In talking about the depression itself and the effect of the depression on other family members, the arbitrariness of the negative feelings and thoughts becomes clear and the underlying meaning of them surfaces, allowing new decisions to be made. At this point the therapist can reframe and redirect the negative beliefs. Both the depressed person and the partner are able to recognize that there is more than one way to view problems and that depression becomes worse with demoralizing discussion and negative thinking. The depressed person is empowered by their partner's understanding and acceptance and learns new ways of thinking through open discussion. When partners have the opportunity and freedom to express how the depression affects them, they are more likely to be able to be accepting and understanding.

Relaxation and self-soothing as a response to heightened physiological arousal is often taught by therapists trained by the Gottman Institute. They point toward the research that reveals that thinking and problem solving are impaired when individuals are physiologically aroused. Self-soothing not only helps depression by facilitating and enhancing expressions of caring and deepening of love maps, but also is a necessary skill in dealing with conflict for couples.

Clearly the commitment the couple has to their marriage makes a huge difference in the effectiveness of therapy. If the couple is so filled with contempt, rage, and hopelessness that they are not willing or able to experience love and affection for their partner therapy may not be effective or may take much longer than expressed in this case presentation. Investment and caring for the partner are two of the most powerful motivations for success in couples where depression is present. In many cases the problem is not lack of caring. It is the feeling and belief that their caring makes no difference to their partner. In these cases a major function of therapy is to facilitate expressing and receiving of the love that is already present.

JAN AND JACK

When Jan called me to make the first appointment, she said that she was fed up with the marriage and with her husband, Jack, and that she was at the end of her rope. When I inquired about that she told me that Jack was clinically depressed and would do nothing about it. She said that she loved him but that she could no longer tolerate his emotional unavailability. She said that they often would not say one word to each other in the evening.

When I went to the waiting room to introduce myself and invite the couple into my office for the first session, Jan was waiting quietly with her purse on her lap and sitting upright with her back away from the back of the chair.

Jack was sitting in a chair at a 90-degree angle to Jan's chair, leaning forward with his elbows resting on his knees and hands clasped and holding up his chin. Both looked distressed. I invited them into my office. They chose to sit in separate chairs even though I have a small couch on which two people fit comfortably.

Assessment

After completing the paperwork I told Jan and Jack that I would like them both to have a chance to tell me what in their relationship was going wrong and what had compelled them to come for therapy today. I also wanted them to tell me the story of their relationship. (As I conduct the oral history interview, I look at how the couple tells the story together and separately. What is their sense of "we-ness"? Is there pain and blame? What were the points of transition and how did they affect the relationship? Is the couple respectful of each other? Do they touch each other? Do they laugh? Do they focus only on the negative or the positive? How do they remember differently? Often, remembering the early years of the relationship puts the couple back in touch with positive elements they have forgotten or minimized.) I told Jan and Jack that I understood they probably had different memories and feelings about their relationship history, and that I didn't expect them to agree on every detail. I told them I would like to hear from both of them.

Jan spoke first. "He won't communicate with me. He's so morose. All he does is sit and watch television."

"I guess she's right," Jack admitted, "but I don't know what to say to her."

"I can't stand it! Anything! Just say anything to me!"

"But you . . . ." Jack's voice trailed off and he sighed. "I don't know," he finally mumbled.

"So you see what it is like," Jan said, turning to me. "I have to do everything. I can't count on him to do anything. He probably will do what he says but he might not. Don't you see why I have so little hope about our marriage?" Her eyes became tearful. "All these years we've been together. Have they made no difference to him?" She paused for a moment before continuing. "He never talks to me anymore. When we talk it's almost always about the children, and this has been going on for years."

Jack sat quietly looking at the floor. I asked Jack if he could tell me why he had come to therapy. "She's right," he said, as Jan rolled her eyes. "I . . . I don't know what to say. She's always doing something. I can't respond to her. I just, I don't know . . . get confused."

I asked him how much of his paralysis was a result of his depression. He said "a lot." I asked if this was always true in the relationship and they both agreed that the depression had always been there but that some times had been harder than others.

Jack was well aware of his depression. If he had not been, which is the case with many clients, I would have explored depression with him in his individual session. If his wife had been "accusing" him of being depressed, I would have asked him how he felt about his wife's comments and continued to make my own assessment of it by keying into the oral history and checking out his scores on the SL-90, which has a depression indicator.

I said that I would like Jan and Jack to more intentionally focus on the story of their relationships, and I asked them to go back to the very beginning and tell me how they met. Jan said that they had met in graduate school in the late 1970s. At that time they shared a lot of common interests and common values. Jan reported that she felt pushed into marriage by their parents, and that she still felt angry about letting her parents have so much control. I asked how she was pushed and she replied that both parents made it known that they would feel much more comfortable if she and Jack got married and did not just "live together." Then she looked expectantly at Jack.

Jack looked back at Jan, pressed his lips together, and said he really didn't remember "being pushed" and that he certainly wasn't against getting married. He reported not remembering very much about how the decision to get married took place and that it was a kind of formality for him.

I listened intently as they discussed the birth of their first child, which they both described as a "great experience." I asked if having a child changed their relationship in any way. Jack said that he didn't remember its changing their relationship. Jan said that having children seemed to make Jack happier and that their attention seemed to focus more on the children than on each other.

I wondered how Jack's inability to remember and share his feelings about these important events affected Jan's feelings toward him. Jack's feelings seemed to be absent as he reported these events, whereas Jan's were very present and intense. Perhaps his feelings had been worn down by years of depression or perhaps they were never present.

The couple had raised two children. Both were now adults and had moved out of the family home. This meant that Jan and Jack had more time together and could no longer use the children as a buffer in their interactions with each other. This had been true for several years.

Jan described the marriage as being very stressful for her and reported that it had not been good for a long time. She indicated that she had been staying with Jack for the sake of the children and now that they had both moved away from home the stress of the marriage was coming to the forefront. She reported feeling sad that she was not important to Jack anymore. She said she had thought he was just antisocial and she usually made excuses for his not wanting to attend parties and family events.

She described Jack's bouts with clinical depression as an intolerable destructive force on the relationship. She talked about learning how to cope with periods of her own deep sadness and anger, of which Jack was probably not even aware. She learned to keep incredibly busy at work, admittedly to distract herself from having to deal with the pain she experienced in her marriage. Jan seemed depressed as she spoke and I made a mental note to discuss this with her in the individual session.

Jack reported that he had never been hospitalized for depression. He had been prescribed Prozac in the past but was not presently taking it because he had run out of the medication about a year ago and had not asked the doctor for another prescription. When he became depressed he felt awful about himself. Anything he tried he couldn't do well enough, so he often ended up doing nothing. He said that he did not feel this way as much at work because his work was fairly routine and repetitive. His work was meaningless, but he had no trouble doing it. He mumbled that he felt no purpose for his life, that he only produced problems for his family, and that they might be better off without him. I asked him if the medication had been helpful.

Jan interrupted, "I need him to take his medication. We do the best when he is taking it. The hardest thing is that I never know when that cycle of depression will start. For him not to take his medication when he knows it will help us makes me feel like I'm being abused."

I wondered when Jan used the word *cycle* if Jack's depression was part of a bipolar illness. I dismissed this idea as I learned more about Jack's depression and agreed with the diagnosis of episodic major depression given by his doctor. I asked Jack if he knew Jan felt this way.

"No," he said softly. He looked longingly at Jan and said to me, "I don't want her to feel that way. I just don't know what to do to make her happy."

"Don't do that!" Jan said emphatically. "Don't try to make me happy! Make yourself happy! That's what I want you to do. Make yourself happy. Weren't you happier when you were taking your medication?"

"Well, I guess I was, but . . . " Jack's voice trailed off.

"Then why don't you want to take it?"

"OK, I guess I'll try it again," Jack offered, "but I don't like the idea of always being on medication. I shouldn't have to take it to feel all right."

"Well, maybe you need to sacrifice a little," Jan snapped back. I felt myself wince a little at this expression of anger. Personally I thought that it would be important for Jack to agree to take his medication again. I have found that antidepressants can help many people with depression and for most clients with clinical depression it is an essential part of the treatment. I routinely attempt to reframe a client's hesitancy and equate taking antidepressants for a person who is clinically depressed to taking insulin for a diabetic. I did this later during his individual session.

It was also clear that this couple needed to talk about how depression had affected their marriage. As they talked about how their marriage progressed through the years they both expressed a great deal of sadness, regret, anger, and resignation. Jack seemed less resigned than Jan. I wondered if this meant he was truly more hopeful or if he merely was not in touch with how much pain this depression had caused Jan over the years.

As the initial meeting drew to a close I asked them to tell me briefly how they would like their relationship to be. I said that one way to do that was to think of people in their lives who they thought had a good marriage and to describe what they liked about those marriages. They both sat quietly for a minute. Jack spoke first, saying that he really had not thought much about it. He looked at Jan in a way that seemed like fondness to me but perhaps was my own projection. "I want a good friend and companion. I want us to enjoy each other. I don't know if that is possible."

Jan turned to me and said, "I think we're here on earth for a reason and in this relationship for a reason. Marriage is to assist each other through life, to grow together. Relationships help personal growth; it is about sharing when things are hard, being supportive, communicating, sharing, and mutual respect. . . . I haven't felt very accepting or supportive for probably the last 6 to 8 years. In fact, I have felt there have been periods of emotional abuse."

"There is a lot of anger in both of us," Jack added.

In my individual session with Jack, he shared about how his family never expressed emotion and placed great importance on being civil, in control of oneself, and nice to one another. Jan's family, on the other hand, expressed their emotions freely and even screamed and yelled at each other on occasion.

Jack's parents had been married for over 50 years. He reported that his mother tended to "shed" his father emotionally (that is, ostracize). He characterized his parents' relationship as unaffectionate and his dad as "wimpy." He had a twin sister and had always felt like he had been overshadowed by her. "I've always felt like an outsider, even at school." He reported not having friends.

Jack was very clear about wanting to maintain the marriage and seemed optimistic about the couple's ability to work through their current estrangement. When asked about what needed to happen for this to take place he replied, "For me to express more emotion, and for us to establish trust. I need to be able to assert my view. I want to establish a plan for establishing trust, build communication skills, be an equal partner, and deal well with my depression."

I was impressed at his clarity about what he needed to do. I wondered what he understood about why Jan felt as she did. He said he understood that it had been very hard for her and that when he was depressed he did things that hurt her.

"What things?" I asked.

"Well, I'm not entirely sure, but I know she was hurt. I can see it in her face and it hurts me to see it. But I don't know what I can do now to help her. I do love her, I think, and I want to continue to be married to her."

When I met with Jan individually, she said that she was the oldest of six children. She tended to take on a great deal of responsibility from an early age. Her mother was ill frequently and required a lot of help doing housework as well as looking after the other children. Her father tended to be a workaholic and remained distant from the children. He died when Jan was a teenager. Jan's mother was therefore the primary parent but was not really able to be very effective. Jan reported that she "raised herself" and became very independent as a teenager. At a fairly early age she became interested in horses and she used riding as a way to stay away from home and avoid home responsibilities. She rode in various equestrian events as a teenager.

Jan also described feeling numb and detached much of the time and at other times feeling very sad and angry. She described long periods of just bearing it, becoming busy and not relating to Jack because it was too painful to do so. She said that she did not really know whom she would be talking to when she talked to Jack and therefore it was just better not to talk to him. She said that Jack seemed to go through periods or cycles of depression and that she got tired of it. She was tired of making excuses for him at parties and family gatherings. She felt that she was not important to Jack anymore and felt very sad.

I asked her if she had considered that she could have been depressed, too. She said that she had indeed been depressed in the past year and had taken Paxil for a couple of months. She found it very helpful and felt that now she did not need it because she was being more direct and assertive with Jack about her feelings. This had been a change for her.

When asked about her commitment to the marriage, Jan responded that nothing had changed to make her want to stay. "I'm not very hopeful. He would have to make a strong commitment to manage his depression consistently. I really do not want this marriage to end, but I just can't deal with it the way it is now. I need Jack to acknowledge the effects of his depression over the years. When we disagree there is no listening to each other. We talk to each other in angry ways; he becomes self-demeaning and self-defeating. I hate it. He is a good man. I wish he could accept that, but because he has such low self-esteem, when I confront him he just caves in and nothing gets handled or resolved."

During our fourth session, I gave Jan and Jack feedback about my assessment of their relationship and developed an informal contract for the course of therapy. This session was a time to make the issues clear. I gave the couple a diagram of the SRH and reviewed the model with them to help them identify how they were doing in each of the seven skill areas.

Jan and Jack were in agreement that Jack's depression was the main problem in the relationship. But there were also other issues. Jan felt that Jack had no idea of the effect of his depression on the rest of the family, but Jack felt guilty because of what he did perceive as his effect on the family. Jan carried a great deal of sadness and anger because she felt Jack was not able to accept the issues that she felt were important. This belief made her feel hopeless about the future. They also agreed that lack of communication, lack of emotional expression, and infrequent sex had been major issues.

Jan felt trapped and not entitled to her feelings of anger toward Jack. He was, after all, ill with depression. Jack felt cut off and shut out of the family. This resulted in gross emotional disengagement, with each partner feeling emotionally deprived and living parallel lives. With the children leaving home Jan and Jack were forced to deal with what it meant for them to continue to stay together. For the first time in many years they were feeling that their marriage was a choice and not just an obligation.

They identified difficulty in expressing their friendship skills and care for one another. I pointed out that their friendship was blocked and I referred to their questionnaires which indicated they had trouble with love maps, fondness and admiration, and turning toward. All needed work.

I asked them how well they knew each other. Jan said that they had grown apart recently but that she felt she fundamentally knew Jack. Jack said that he felt he knew Jan fairly well but they really hadn't talked about anything important in years. I explained that love maps were about knowing what is going on daily with your partner, not just activities but also the joys and trials and stresses—what they were doing that they enjoyed and what they were currently worried about. I said that love maps need to be updated on a regular basis because lives change. After thinking about this both Jan and Jack indicated that they really were not doing very well in that area.

I asked them about their fondness and admiration for each other. Jan said that she had lost a great deal of respect for Jack because he did not seem to be interested in doing what was best for the family: getting control of his depression. She indicated that what she used to admire about him was now obscured by her anger and reactivity. Jack, on the other hand, indicated that he was quite fond of Jan but he didn't think she liked him very much. I explained that admiration is not always constant in a relationship, but that couples who were able to stay in touch with their partner's admirable qualities and communicate these positive feelings tended to do better at working things out. I told them that the key is to have a mechanism in the relationship that keeps the path of communication open for these positive remarks. They must be said aloud and not just thought.

I asked them what they thought about what I had just said. Jan's countenance was sad, as she said again that she knew Jack had positive qualities but she had a difficult time getting past her anger and pain. She looked at him and said that she really did want to care but that it seemed too risky. Jack hesitated, seemingly to gather his thoughts. Then he responded by saying that he liked her very much, but it was hard for him to tell her so.

I asked Jack if he understood what Jan meant by "risk." He said that he thought he did. Next, I described the "negative perspective" to them. I acknowledged that noticing the positive qualities of each other and mentioning them can be very difficult when there is so much negativity in the relationship. I said, "Couples can get in the mindset and habit of seeing and talking about only the negative. This negative habit can feel safe because it is familiar and is a way of emotionally distancing yourself from what you may feel is impossible, such as reengaging with each other emotionally. An umbrella of negativity is created over your relationship that produces a negative tint to what you say and think about each other. This is the negative perspective. When there is a negative perspective even positive comments are interpreted negatively. What we want to do in therapy is to develop a positive perspective so that negative interactions do not destroy your relationship."

Both Jack and Jan indicated that they were willing to work at trying to discover and vocalize positive qualities and behaviors of each other. I then discussed with them how the friendship skill of turning toward was based on the research finding that relationships are built and sustained in the mundane everyday interactions of the couple. I explained that a bid for connection is a gesture or comment that creates an opportunity for the couple to connect emotionally. These are not necessarily profound opportunities; they may be as simple as a smile or a comment about a passing car. What makes the connection happen is the response to the bid. If the response acknowledges the content or feeling of the bidder, a turning toward moment has occured and connection is possible. If the bid is ignored (intentionally or unintentionally), a turning away moment has occured. An aggressive response, that is defensive or attacking is a turning against.

Jack's depression had clouded his ability to recognize Jan's bids for connection. Jan, in turn, felt Jack turning away and began bidding less and less until she became angry even at the thought of bidding. This lack of turning toward resulted in both of them feeling unacknowledged, lonely, and invalidated. In the context of their negative perspective they felt very vulnerable when they showed each other that they cared. When they allowed themselves to feel their love, they experienced loss, disappointment, sadness, and anger.

I reasoned that when people are depressed they might believe that their partner does not value them. A history of depression is compounded by the belief that the world does not support them. They bring to the relationship the thought that their partner is unsupportive and will not respond to their needs. In turn this communicates that the depressed individual does not trust his or her partner and will not accept support. Both partners end up feeling uncared for, unknown, and invalidated. They are on the path of disengagement, vilification and resentment of each other, isolation, and loneliness. Disengagement feels safer than sharing their lives. A pattern of isolation is set up and becomes perpetual. The couple then uses this pattern of avoiding painful interaction in the relationship itself as ample evidence that the partner does not care. They reason that if their partner cared they would not avoid them. This pattern of avoiding interaction needs to be modified if the couple is to experience the benefits of staying together.

I asked Jack if he intended on following through in getting medication. He said that he did intend to go back to his doctor and restart medication. I asked him if he also had a counselor. He said that he was not seeing his counselor at the present time and that he felt he did not need to. I said that I often suggest that individuals in couple therapy get individual counseling to work on individual issues.

I then explained that I thought a major problem with regard to the depression was that it was not "on the table" as a topic for marital discussion. The topic needed to be available and visible to both individuals in the relationship. Both partners needed to be able to ask questions and express their feelings, beliefs, assumptions, and so on about it at any time. In contrast, a topic that was "under the table" resided only in one partner's "gut" and could not be seen by the other. Therapy would help Jan be able to plan with Jack for what he needed and wanted when he got depressed and also be able to tell him what she needed and wanted.

I realized that the key to getting the topic of Jack's depression on the table was having both Jan and Jack feel safe enough to put it there. This safety had to do with the expectation of how the topic would be handled. If it was raised in a way that hurt, then it probably would not be put on the table. Each partner's feelings had to be respected and honored. In short, Jack and Jan needed to learn the problem solving skills described in the Gottman model: softened start-up, repair, and accepting influence.

I suggested that Jan and Jack try not to talk about any major issues at home and if they somehow fell into such a discussion they should stop even if it meant not talking at all to each other. I told them that they had no new skills yet so their discussions would probably follow the same path as in the past and be unsatisfying.

I asked them to be more mindful of what they perceived as going right rather than wrong. I observed that they treated each other with fondness and tenderness, and I told them that I thought they really did care for each other but were acting as if they did not and also were failing to tell each other that they did, in fact, care. I asked them to pay attention to their fondness and appreciation system and to look for positive behaviors, comments, and efforts from their partner this week. I said, "We'll talk about what you have discovered at your next appointment."

Learning to treat one's partner respectfully and in a supportive manner is central to the Gottman model. I wanted Jack and Jan to become more mindful of their treatment of each other and of the positives in their relationship. Before the session ended I asked Jack: "If you weren't depressed, how would you be acting differently toward Jan, and how do you think she would be acting differently toward you?" I asked Jan: "If you felt you could count on Jack, how would you treat him differently and how would he treat you differently?" I asked them to ponder these questions until our next appointment and said we would discuss them at that time.

THE COURSE OF THERAPY

If a couple is to shift from a negative perspective to a positive perspective, both partners must be able to identify the positive intentions of the other. When couples first come to therapy they usually each have only one point of view of their marriage—their own. Their primary goal has been to persuade their partner that their point of view is right. This of course fails because the partner is trying to do the same thing. A major turning point happens in therapy when a partner stops trying to persuade the other that he or she is right and begins to try to understand the other partner's subjective reality.

During the assessment sessions, I had introduced Jan and Jack to the four horsemen— criticism, defensiveness, contempt, and stonewalling—as well as their antidotes, which to help the couple stay out of attack-defend interactions. I reasoned that if Jack and Jan were able to stop the four horsemen, blaming would lessen, making requests would increase, and openings for turning toward and supportive connection would surface. Merely becoming more mindful and reducing the use of the four horsemen could change their relationship dramatically. Jan and Jack recognized all the horsemen in their interactions with each other and they were able to begin limiting their use of them almost immediately. Jan recognized her style of being critical of Jack, and Jack recognized his rampant stonewalling. Using Gottman interventions I helped Jan and Jack develop their friendship skills and limit their use of the four horsemen. They needed to reengage in positive ways.

At the next session Jan and Jack reported that their relationship seemed to be better. They had done the earlier exercise and Jan reported that Jack was more attentive to her. I asked them to face each other and share what they had discovered during the week about what was going right in their relationship. They both were able to verbalize their appreciation of the effort they saw. They talked about this for 20 to 30 minutes. I asked them how it felt to talk like this. Jan appeared calm and said "great." Jack was clearly excited. He looked at me with a kind of stifled smile and said, "Yeh, this is Okay." I asked them if they had ever talked to each other like this in the past. Both said almost in unison, "Not in a long time." I affirmed their ability to be appreciative of each other and their ability to connect emotionally as they had demonstrated throughout the week. I encouraged them to continue talking throughout the week and again suggested to not discuss painful issues if they could put them off.

For Jan and Jack my initial intervention of putting the depression "on the table" made a difference. Over the next sessions their relationship changed dramatically. Jack had begun turning toward Jan in a significant way. I asked him what had happened and he said that he realized that he really did have a choice about his behavior. He talked about getting stuck in his thoughts and not being able to motivate himself, and explained that his medication helped him get through his stuckness. He reported that when he thought about how he would act if he were not so depressed, he just starting doing those things. He said he was very surprised by Jan's positive response and this made him want to continue. "This is how turning toward is suppose to work," I said to myself. "The more you do, the more you want to do."

Jan said that Jack had been doing and saying things that he never did before. They were having "wonderful and significant" talks. Jack even bought Jan roses. Jan told me all this with a bit of disbelief and caution. "I think we're on the right track," she said, "but we do have other issues. Getting Jack to talk to me is great. I love it. Jack actually is expressing interest in me." Jan was delighted but also felt she could not trust this flight into health. Jack agreed that it was sudden and that there were other issues that affected the marriage.

I suggested that they institute the "stress-reducing conversation" they learned in the Gottman workshop. In this exercise one person talks for 15 minutes about his or her stresses of the day while the other listens and makes supportive remarks or asks supportive clarifying questions. The stresses need to be outside of the couple relationship and not involve the partner. I thought this could be a way for Jack and Jan to continue to update their love maps, reengage in a structured way, and practice supportive listening.

Toward the end of the session I talked about the importance of "greetings and meetings" and explained how some couples ritualize a way of leaving each other in the morning and greeting each other in the evening. Such rituals are daily built-in turning toward moments. I explained that rituals can take the guesswork out of making connections, connections just happen because the couple has agreed to it ahead of time and the ritual happens regardless of how the day has gone.

Jan suggested that they try hugging each other in the morning when they parted company and again when they saw each other in the evening. Jack agreed.

A couple of weeks later Jan came in ready to discuss Jack's depression. This session was a major turning point in the therapy. She reported that their relationship was going so well that she was a bit scared. How could this be happening when Jack had been so depressed just a month earlier? Her basic question was: "What if Jack's depression gets bad again?"

There was silence. I asked Jack what he thought about what Jan had said. Jack murmured that his depression would probably follow the same pattern it always had, which meant that it would go up and down, appearing and receding.

"So," said Jan, "what happens then?"

Jack shrugged. "I don't know."

Jan looked around nervously. I thought she might be getting flooded. I asked her to tell Jack what she was feeling. She said that she was very worried about Jack's becoming depressed. It was the primary reason she had come to counseling.

"What can we do about it? How can we make it so he doesn't get depressed?" she asked me.

I replied that I didn't think Jack or anyone could guarantee that he never get severely depressed again. Jan needed to accept the fact that in choosing to stay with Jack she had chosen to live with a partner who suffered from depression. Jack's depression was not a solvable problem that would go away. Jan needed to accept that fact. However, making a plan to manage the depression and its effects could be considered a solvable problem. I encouraged them to share their feelings, try to discover some common ground with regard to Jack's depression, and find an agreeable strategy for dealing with it.

Jan bit her lip and looked at Jack. "I don't know if I can handle it if you get depressed like you were."

I said to myself, "C'mon, Jack, give her something to hold onto."

Jack looked at her sadly and said, "I'm always depressed. It's just that sometimes I can handle it better than other times. I think I'm handling it pretty well right now. Do you?"

"Yes, you—we—are. Maybe that is what I'm saying. How can *we*, not just you, handle it better."

I asked Jan to tell Jack what it is like for her when Jack is depressed. She said, "It is very lonely. The last couple of weeks have been great but I really don't think it will last. I don't want to be in that lonely spot again."

"What else?" I asked.

Jan then proceeded to tell Jack the painful experience of feeling as if she had raised the children on her own and feeling that she really could not count on him. She had hated making family decisions without him but felt she had to. She told him she had given up her dream of what she wanted the family to be. Jack interrupted her a couple of times, but I asked him not to respond but to try to listen and understand what Jan was saying. When she was finished, I asked Jack if he was aware that Jan believed she had raised the family on her own and felt responsible for everything. Jack said that he had not heard that specifically but that he was not surprised. Hearing this from Jan made him sad. He turned to Jan and said, "I'm sorry. I didn't mean to have it be that way."

"What way?" I said.

"I didn't mean that you would have to be so responsible and alone. That was not my dream for our family either. I have always felt we should be more of a team. I just haven't known how to do that. My depression caused all of this."

I asked Jack to tell Jan what it was like for him when he was depressed.

Jack said that he felt lonely most of the time. He got depressed when he couldn't see his way through— when he felt blocked. He talked about being in a fog and feeling slowed down in almost every way.

"Can we do something about that?" Jan asked.

"I don't know. Maybe. I hope so," Jack replied.

I asked Jan and Jack if there were any other feelings that they wanted to share right now. "I'm just . . . afraid," replied Jan. "I want to believe that Jack has changed, but I really can't. . . . I need something else."

I asked them if they could make a plan for when Jack might get severely depressed again as a precaution and a preparation. I asked them to talk about the first signs of depression. It happened that Jan was actually the first to recognize a possible problem. Jack admitted that he was not always aware of the first signs. Jan said the warning sign was Jack's tendency to get more introspective and solitary. He also became less assertive and more invisible. Jack objected to this characterization, saying that he sometimes wanted to be alone even when he was not depressed. "How can I tell the difference?" asked Jan.

"Well, you could ask me," said Jack.

"I could? I really don't think that would be OK with you. I've frequently asked you if you are depressed and you just get mad or roll your eyes."

"That's because you've already decided you know the answer before you ask me the question. It is not really a question you want me to answer."

"But it is! I want to know if I need to start being worried because you are getting depressed. You never do anything about it. I need to be on guard and prepared. If you're not going to do anything about it, then I have to!"

I interrupted them. "I'm going to stop you because you are getting into an attack-defend process. Jan, I'm going to ask you to see if you can talk about Jack's depression as if it were a problem between you—that is, a relational problem— rather than a personal problem Jack has. You were doing that when you were talking about Jack's behavior, how it affected you and what you need. You get into trouble when you talk from the position that Jack's depression is a faulty part of his personality that he has to change in order for the relationship to move on."

"OK, I'll try, but it is Jack's problem, isn't it? He does need to do something about it."

"Yes, Jack needs to attend to his own health and take care of himself just as you need to take care of yourself. However, this is a problem that is between the two of you as well, and that is the problem that you can influence and affect. Think of the depression as a 'thing' between you that affects you both and that you both influence by your behavior."

Jack took the ball. "OK, here's what I propose. I would like you to tell me when you think I'm getting depressed. What I mean is, ask me if what you see is what I'm feeling. I am willing to consider your comments."

"OK, I'm willing to try that. However, if you get depressed I need to be able to do whatever I need to do. That means take you to the emergency room, the doctor for medication, or even to the hospital if need be."

"When have you ever needed to do any of those things?" replied Jack.

"Well, I would have liked to feel the freedom to get you some medication a while back when you refused to go to the doctor . . . I need to know you're not going to fight me if I feel I need to take control."

"When have I ever fought you? I don't fight you. I usually agree with you totally. I know I need your help. I know you see signs before I do. I really am willing to let you have that control. However, there have been times when you think I'm worse off than I am and I'm concerned you will take control when you don't need to. What can we do about that? I need you to be able to trust my judgment as well."

"I do trust your judgment, except when you get depressed. I get nervous when I see you withdrawing. If I see you withdrawing can you tell me if you are getting depressed?"

"Yes, I think I can always tell if I'm depressed. I know you think I just lose it or something, but that's because you never ask me. But if I say I'm not depressed I need you to listen to me."

"I can listen to you, but I need something else. . . . I need to know if you are really in touch with yourself. I need you to somehow make yourself more available to me."

"Well, if I tell you I'm not depressed, I'm not."

"Would you care if I asked you again if my perception continued to be that you were depressed?"

"Sure, ask me as often as you want."

"Really? I think if I could ask you and maybe we could talk about what I'm seeing, you could tell me what is really going on."

"I can try that."

This strategy of Jan's being able to check out her perceptions worked very well for her. When she felt unsure of Jack's feelings she began asking him rather than merely acting on her assumption that he was upset and wanted to be left alone. Jack reported in the following weeks that he actually liked the attention. This was a discussion that Jan and Jack had not been able to have up to now. They had been making decisions about each other based on assumptions that they had been too apprehensive to check out. Jack's depression and the effect it had on the family had been too painful to talk about. This discussion was a breakthrough that made Jack's depression a part of the relationship that could be dealt with directly. Thus both Jan and Jack felt more power and influence with each other.

In a later session I defined perpetual problems and solvable problems. We identified Jack's tendency to avoid conflict and abdicate to Jan as a perpetual problem. Jan, in turn, tended to "take care of" Jack in a motherly kind of way, which most of the time lead her to not take him very seriously. This dynamic created a great deal of loss for both of them, with Jan feeling unentitled to her anger and Jack feeling resentful.

Jan and Jack had opened the door to their marriage again by removing the barriers to their communication, especially about Jack's depression. They clearly loved each other but felt that the dream they had shared for their lives together was no longer possible. Jack's initial epiphany concerning the need to be in relationship with Jan resulted from his ability to turn his attention toward his wife and away from his failures and feelings of depression. No doubt his medication was a major factor in that.

We used the dream-within-conflict intervention several times to help them understand and be supportive of each other. The following transcript is an example of the kind of dialogue they were now able to have. This discussion went from what looked like a solvable problem having to do with doing chores to the perpetual problem of Jan's mothering tendency, which triggered Jack's rebellion against authority.

I had asked them to choose an issue that they seemed to be having difficulty resolving and I handed them a list of possible issues to choose from. Together they chose the issue of doing chores. I told them that I would sit back and listen to their discussion and only interrupt if I felt they needed some direction. I asked them to take turns talking and listening and to ask clarifying questions rather than take issue with each other if they disagreed. We also videotaped the session and I said we might take some time to watch it. (We watched a portion of the tape during the following session.) Jack started the discussion about chores.

> Jack: ·What are your feelings about this?
> Jan: You seem to have reluctance to tackle the maintenance kind of
> thing . . . so it causes conflict if I bring it up. You need to know that I
> have a mental list of chores all the time.
> Jack: What?
> Jan: Things that need to be done. If I bring them up then there is conflict; if I
> don't they don't get done. I don't know if you have a list.
> Jack: (*laughing*), No, I don't.
> Jan: (*smiling*) What can we do about that?

I thought that this dynamic of jumping toward a solution was a common theme for them, which left them void of knowing each other's inner feelings. I wanted Jack to develop the practice of sharing and I wanted Jan to have the experience of hearing Jack share his feelings. I thought that if, indeed, the discussions they were having at home were truly "significant" they would not have trouble doing this. So I interrupted and suggested that, instead of jumping to a solution so quickly, Jack might talk about his feelings about doing chores.

> Jack: You're right, I don't have a list. Things I don't like to do . . . the big
> things . . . I avoid. The smaller ones? I don't really think about them. But
> I think what you are really talking about is getting a negative reaction
> from me.
> Jan: Yeah, that's true. And if I don't bring them up, they don't get
> done . . . unless I initiate them. Then I abandon you sometimes to get
> them going myself.
> Jack: One thing—I'm not even aware of them.
> Jan: I think having a to-do list is good. It's not me nagging anymore; it's just
> on the list.
> Jack: Yeah, that sounds good. I know things need to get done. They usually
> get done eventually. I think having a list on the refrigerator or
> somewhere is a good idea.

This might have ended the discussion if the real issue had been getting the chores done. This part of the discussion was resolvable. Jan and Jack had learned, however, that a resolvable problem often encases a perpetual problem. Jan felt that there was more to this issue and continued the discussion.

Jan: I think it is interesting to talk about why is it so negative for you. What is that about?

Jack: I don't like to make any "big" decisions . . . like drilling a hole in the wall and that kind of thing.

Jan: I feel like I shouldn't bring things up because it causes conflict and by the time I do I feel really negative and angry. I shouldn't get that response from you.

Jack: It is . . . part of it is that I just don't like to be told. Like my mom telling me I'm a bad boy.

Jan: (*getting frustrated*.) I'm really trying . . . I'm being really conscious of choosing my wording very carefully."

Jack sensed her frustration and feelings of invalidation and tried a repair.

Jack: You're not really rude or anything. It's just that there are times when your suggestions have a particular flavor to them. (*They both laugh*.) They are not really suggestions. I know you are not my mom but it feels that way.

Jan: (*grinning*) You're right, that's right. They are not suggestions and I'm not your mom.

Jack: I think having a list is great. It takes the responsibility away from you. What are we going to do with this list?

Jan: If it is on the list I will generally pick things off of it to do.

Jan shared why fixing things was so important to her and discribed her understanding of what was generating this perpetual problem.

Jan: I grew up in a family where people fixed things—the Christmas tree lights, garbage disposals, light fixtures . . . You came from a family that either hires someone to fix it or throws things away. We have a difference in family culture. Remember what they talked about in the workshop? How there is a history behind the conflict?

Jack: I know. I hate fixing. I need to do something. However, it is not really the doing of the task as it is being told to do it. I have the same kind of reaction at work.

Jan: Well, I hate telling you to do things. It goes both ways.

Jack: Yes, I know.

Jan: This all plays into our history of its being really hard for you to make decisions and choices. I feel I've had to make decisions because they were hard for you.

Jack: (*defensively*) What do you mean?

Jan: Family decisions throughout the years. Someone had to take responsibility.

They were in danger of degenerating into an attack-defend argument. At this point I had a choice as a therapist. I could have pointed this out that they were moving into an attack-defend cycle and try to direct them back to the dream-within-conflict discussion. I felt that Jan was touching on her anger of being the responsible parent and blaming Jack for not being there. Reestablishing the dream-within-conflict discussion would have given us an opportunity to process some of Jan's pain and feelings of abandonment by Jack as a parent. These feelings were not unknown to Jack. He, in fact, had apologized for them and he felt burdened by that history. The other option was to stay in the present process of building something new. I felt both opportunities were very important and would come up again. Jack had been able to be assertive and available to Jan in this session. I was afraid that if we started processing Jan's pain he would shrink into his victim position. I decided to give Jack the opportunity to take some responsibility right then in the session from his position of strength. I asked to him, "What is your experience of being responsible? Jan feels that she is the one who needs to take initiative and start projects. Her experience is that you are being irresponsible. What is your experience?"

"That I am being slow and stupid," he replied. I felt that I had made the wrong decision. He had already shrunk.

> Jan: I think that initiating all kinds of things is hard for you, particularly if you feel you might have to make a decision. I think you have a cloud of negative anticipation of doing a lot of things.

I wondered what Jack would do with this criticism. To my surprise, he seemed to recover, and even more surprising, Jan followed with a repair attempt.

> Jack: You're probably right. That may mean that you need to initiate sometimes.
> Jan: OK, but I don't want there to be negative repercussions.
> Jack: Make the list! Write down your top ten. Can you do that?
> Jan: (*still not feeling heard*) Yes, I can, but I don't want to be put in the position that you are doing this because I want you to do it. If it needs to be done, either hire someone to do it or do it yourself!
> Jack: I got it. You want me to take responsibility.
> Jan: Absolutely! This all brings up this deeper issue, too. I feel that I am pushed into being dominant, into a mother role and then you feel resentful.
> Jack: You like to run the show.
> Jan: I've never wanted to run the show as much as this, so I don't like being put in that position.

Jack was silent. "What does it feel like to hear her say these things?" I asked. Looking at Jan, he said, "I feel bad, I feel like I've let you down."

Now it was Jan's turn to attempt repair. "I don't feel you let me down. It is an unconscious thing you do. I regret that I've taken so much responsibility. I just don't want to be in a position like your mother and have you react to me that way." Jan's face relaxed. It seemed that she had said what she had wanted to say all session. In a nutshell: "I'm not your mother. Quit making me responsible for your life."

Her repair attempt was only partially successful. Jack had gone to a familiar place. He reported feeling powerless, stupid, and incompetent and looked up at Jan with tears in his eyes. He said he would like the responsibility to be more equal as well. He said that he just felt stupid when Jan took on that parent role. He felt like a little kid being scolded and punished.

Jan acknowledged that she might reinforce that feeling for Jack because she sometimes got impatient with him.

I reframed Jack's experience as being flooded. We had talked about flooding before so Jack knew what he had to do. I asked him to shut his eyes and he took about five deep breaths. This helped him calm his body and mind. While he was calming himself I talked to Jan about how she might be able to help short-circuit Jack's negative self-talk. I told her that certainly it was not her responsibility to do so, and that only Jack could ultimately influence his own inner thoughts. But, I suggested, she may have participated in it in some way.

Jan said that she tended to have little faith in Jack's efforts and that her attitude had become quite negative over the years. She realized that she had not been giving him the benefit of the doubt because it just seemed too risky for her. When she perceived him being depressed she tended to jump to "here we go again" and fall into her preconceived idea that she needed to take over, without discussing her perceptions and the situation with Jack. She realized that this was not fair to him and that it also created a kind of frantic frustration for her. She acknowledged to Jack that she had been shutting him out at those times, believing that nothing would get done unless she did whatever was necessary. She promised Jack that she would try to give him the benefit of the doubt and check out her assumptions with him before she acted. Jack responded by thanking her and promising to tell her if he felt she was shutting him out and taking over a situation inappropriately.

I then talked to Jack about his negative self-talk. I asked him if he really thought that he was stupid. He replied, "Most of the time I feel that I should know more than I do about most things, but I don't think I am stupid. I feel stupid a lot. "

"I would like to help you get control of your negative self-talk and make it more positive," I said. "Are you willing to work with me on that?" Jack said that he was willing.

This discussion continued and ended with me giving Jack a form to help him keep track of his automatic self-talk. He routinely used the form during the following weeks of therapy.

CONCLUSION

Jan and Jack rekindled their friendship through the use of love maps and turning toward and by putting rituals of connection in place. They became more aware of when they succumbed to the four horsemen and used a repair attempt when they slipped. Eventually they grew to a greater understanding and appreciation of each other's underlying dreams and motivations through the use of dream-within-conflict discussions.

The primary energy that allowed them to succeed was their underlying love for each other, which blossomed once they were able to communicate their true feelings. Once the depression was managed even slightly, Jack's love for his wife and family became a motivator instead of a burden to him. If he had been questioning his love or felt he was too hurt to work on the relationship, the process of therapy would have been very different. Learning the skills of friendship and the repair process would have been much slower. Also, Jan's desire to keep the relationship together won out over her frustration with Jack. She clearly wanted the marriage to continue and her frustration turned into hopelessness when she concluded that Jack could not give her the emotional support she felt she needed. When Jack demonstrated that he was able to give her some of what she needed, Jan's hopelessness disappeared and she became highly motivated to work on the relationship. The deeper relationship dynamics were not "cured," but when Jack's depression was being managed the other relationship issues were able to surface and be discussed. Conflict management took the place of disengagement, isolation, and anger.

Depression had had a detrimental effect on Jan and Jack's marriage, causing them to disconnect from one another and feel angry and isolated. Once they were able to put the depression "on the table" as a subject for discussion, their disconnectedness began to heal. Gottman principles and tools are not intended to "cure" depression; however, they can be used by therapists to help couples reestablish communication and intimacy. The therapy helps the couple manage and minimize depression by solidifying their emotional connection. Couples who are able to communicate their needs and validate one another's wishes and requests are able to live with depression more successfully and experience more satisfaction in their relationship.

Over the course of their therapy, Jan and Jack discussed many issues. During that time perhaps the most important insight they had was that the issues were not what kept them disengaged. What kept them apart was how they talked about the issues. They learned that coupling is about relatedness, not about agreement, or absence of conflict, or having the same likes or dislikes. What made them love each other was relating to each other in a loving, respectful manner. The issues we talked about were only the means to a pathway for them to learn how to relate.

REFERENCES

American Psychiatric Association. (1994). Major depressive disorder: Bipolar disorders. In *Diagnostic and statistical manual of mental disorders* (4th ed., pp. 339–363). Washington, DC: Author.

Beach, S. R. H., & O'Leary, K. D. (1989). The treatment of depression occurring in the context of marital discord. *Behavior therapy, 17,* 43–49.

Beck, A. T., Rush, A. J., Shaw, B. F., Emery, G. (1979). *Cognitive therapy of depression.* New York: Guilford Press.

Elkin, I., Shea, M. T., Watkins, J. T., et al. (1989). National Institute of Mental Health Treatment of Depression Collaborative Research Program: General effectiveness of treatments. *Archives of General Psychiatry, 46*(11), 971–982.

Kung, W. (2000). The intertwined relationship between depression and marital distress: Elements of marital therapy conducive to effective outcome. *Journal of Marital and Family Therapy, 26*(1), 51–63.

Teichman, Y., Bar-El, Z., Shor, H., Sirota, P., & Elizur, A. (1995). A comparison of two modalities of cognitive therapy (individual and marital) in treating depression. *Psychiatry, 58,* 136–148.

Chapter 6 ❋

Working With a Couple With Borderline Qualities

Barbara Johnstone

As therapists we need to be weavers, pulling grasses from this hill and that valley, from different perspectives, to weave the baskets in which we hold the struggles of our clients with compassion and respect. For the case I present in this chapter, I wove the SRH model into a flexible therapy for a couple in which each partner had a traumatic history and presented with borderline qualities. The SRH oriented the therapy toward specific skills that altered the couple's relationship.

MYRA AND THOMAS

Myra and Thomas had been together 20 years when, entrenched in contemptuous arguments, they began therapy. Myra complained that the relationship was "a desert." In her view, Thomas was not authentic; he would say what he thought she wanted to hear and then, "like shifting sand," he would change his position. He was passive-aggressive (for example, completing home maintenance jobs poorly and being grouchy on outings he had consented to go on). Also, she felt "put on the shelf" by him; he would shut her out until he wanted to relate. He wasn't fun. And he dominated everything in the relationship. She felt "like a stupid chump" for even trying to make the marriage work.

Thomas complained that Myra called him names, pointed out his inadequacies, made mean-spirited threats to end the relationship, and exploded in anger "if

I don't follow her orders." He experienced her as dominating everything. He felt like she was two different people, one who was very loving and one who pushed him away completely.

I met with Thomas and Myra initially together and then had an individual session with each of them. They filled out the solvable and perpetual problems questionnaire, the SRH questionnaires, and the Weiss-Cerretto and Locke-Wallace questionnaires. (Now I also use the SCL-90 and the conflict tactics and emotional abuse questionnaires. At that time, I addressed those issues in the individual interviews without the added benefit of a written assessment.)

Couple History

In the oral history, Thomas voiced a lot of love and admiration for Myra. Myra was contemptuous of Thomas and expressed that it was "a personal failure of boundaries and assertiveness that I got involved and stay involved." She said she got hives on her wedding day, and that meant to her that her body was saying this marriage was not right. She said she had been seriously considering divorce since she married.

After talking about why they were here, I asked them to tell me what they remembered about when they first met. Thomas had been divorced for a year and a half, and prayed to meet someone. He heard a voice in his head say "there she is" when he first saw Myra, and he told her he loved her the next day. He saw "her golden heart, compassion, and sensitivity," and he felt she was "an innocent, sweet child."

The year before they met, Myra had been brutally date-raped and then publicly humiliated in a highly publicized case that did not go to trial because, the prosecutor told her, she was not a good witness. She was infatuated with an alcoholic when she met Thomas. Thomas did several things the night they met that disgusted her (like suggesting a sexual threesome), but then he showed up at her church the next day and wooed her successfully. She felt she needed someone because she couldn't be safe from another rape on her own, and she decided that Thomas was a healthier alternative to the alcoholic. But, she said, she should have been more cautious. She had talked about divorce ever since their wedding, and she believed it was because of her low self-worth that she hadn't left.

Chaos colored their history together, with no sense of couple efficacy. Thomas's angry, disruptive son from his previous marriage visited them on weekends during the first 10 years and was sent to live with them full-time when he was 13 and out of control. Myra's unemployed uncle simply showed up one day and began living with them also. The couple had serious financial problems as well. Thomas worked one full-time and two part-time jobs while Myra worked and attended school. Myra had lost several jobs and tried different careers. In addition, the IRS had audited them with disastrous results.

After Thomas's son turned 18 and moved out to live independently, Myra and Thomas had a baby (which she had very much wanted). Their baby girl was 16 months old when the couple began therapy. Myra resolved that for the baby's sake she would try to save the marriage and have no more chaos in their life. Thomas seemed to share this intention.

Personal Histories

Myra was the youngest in a family of three children. Her father was a raging alcoholic. Myra remembered his frightening anger as he broke furniture and overturned meals. Yet he was also the one who loved her and had time to play with her (though even then, she said, he would hurt her "accidentally because he had no feeling in his hands for some unexplained reason"). Myra's mother was depressed. She was critical of Myra and verbally abused her when angry. Myra's two older brothers also terrorized her. Myra became a caretaker in the family. She held in her feelings and, consequently, had her first bleeding ulcer at age 4. She also had a history of major depression and night terrors. She suffered from obesity. She failed at several different kinds of jobs. Finally, she established a successful business where she served as a personal assistant to some wealthy women.

Thomas was an only child. His stepfather demanded absolute obedience and regimented and controlled every aspect of Thomas's life. Generally, Thomas took on the role of being "a fixer and a pleaser." He said he could never have any feeling, thought, or behavior of his own; if he did, his stepfather would strip him naked and belt him all over his body. The day he announced he was going to let his hair grow long, he was thrown out of the house and excluded from the family for years. He also had a hearing loss, possibly from blows to his ears. He used compulsive routines to complete many tasks. Not surprisingly, his civilian job with the military involved enforcing compliance with fiscal regulations.

Individual Assessments

Thomas was a hard worker who took his commitments to his work and to his family seriously. He loved Myra and wanted her to be happy. Myra was a thoughtful, resourceful parent who wanted her family to share joy. They were both wholly invested in improving the relationship. However, because of the instability and abuse they endured throughout their childhoods, Myra and Thomas each developed borderline personality traits that contributed to the negative intensity, instability, conflict, and chaos in the marriage despite their deep yearning for a peaceful, loving home. Their borderline traits included unstable affects and self-images, dissociation, impulsivity, chronic feelings of emptiness, splitting, and a pattern of rapidly alternating clinging and distancing behaviors.

Thomas idealized Myra, the "sweet and innocent angel," and then devalued her. Myra was either loving and affectionate or contemptuous; she could not hold onto the good experiences of the relationship when she felt the bad. Thomas made frantic efforts to avoid abandonment, pursuing Myra from room to room rather than letting her take time-outs. At other times, when they grew closer he would flip instantly into shutting her out altogether. Myra would say that she wanted to leave because the relationship had always been bad and almost in the next minute reach out to him with affection and become enraged when he didn't respond. They both experienced intense, uncontrollable outbursts of contempt and rage. They also acted out in other impulsive ways: Myra binged, and Thomas went on spending sprees and drove recklessly. They both had chronic feelings of emptiness and deep self-contempt, as well as moderate dissociative symptoms. Often triggered by their partner, they reexperienced past trauma as if it were happening in the present, or they felt outside their bodies or outside the room.

ASSESSMENT AND CONCEPTUALIZATION OF TREATMENT

I could easily have been overwhelmed by the thought of treating two clients with borderline personality traits at once, and at times I was. But I found that Gottman's SRH theory helped me contain my anxiety and gave me hope that I'd be a "good enough" marital therapist. John Gottman's research showed that there are three aspects to making a marriage successful. The first two involve social skills, for friendship and for regulating conflict; the third involves the existential process of creating shared meaning. The SRH assessment (from questionnaires, interviews, and observations) of Myra and Thomas's relationship revealed significant deficits of every skill and of shared meaning, but the assessment also quickly identified strengths to build on in their friendship (some love maps and turning toward) and in shared meanings (especially related to their daughter). Clarity gained from the SRH theory helped ground me so I could more confidently hold the couple's struggles, weaving the strands of friendship, conflict regulation, and shared meaning, and not be overwhelmed by their individual needs.

In Gottman's model, friendship is based on how much each partner knows, thinks about, and considers the other (love maps). Although Myra and Thomas had a lot of cognitive room for the relationship and they scored well on the love maps questionnaire, what they did not know about themselves and their partner on a deeper level was destroying the friendship. Most importantly, they needed to gain language to identify the feelings and needs behind their rage.

It was impossible for Myra and Thomas to freely express and receive fondness and appreciation when they felt such self-contempt. I knew that throughout the therapy we would have to work to heal their self-contempt and replace it with compassion. Also, they both used the borderline splitting defense, in which the relationship or the other was viewed as all good or all bad. They still loved each other, but if they were to be able to express care, love, or affection when they felt any hurt or disappointment, they each would have to develop the ability to experience both bad and good at the same time.

Despite their individual traumas and interpersonal hurts, Myra and Thomas still made many attempts to turn toward each other. This was a significant strength. They also had ways of staying in touch with each other, including several phone calls a day and dinner and bedtime rituals.

However, they only knew how to react negatively to each other when they felt vulnerable. They needed to learn that hidden beneath their anger were vulnerable feelings such as pain and desire for something they didn't know how to express; the anger was a bid for connection. They both yearned for deeper connection with each other. If they could learn to self-soothe and ask their partner questions instead of reflexively reacting to the other's anger with their own, they could connect instead of escalating.

Work on the three aspects of friendship (love maps, fondness and appreciation, and turning toward) would be woven through Myra and Thomas's therapy along with skills to regulate conflict. Although the couple ultimately needed to work on all the conflict skills, they first needed to self-soothe, because being flooded makes it impossible to process in new ways and try new behaviors. They also needed to eliminate contempt, because contempt inflicts much damage on the recipient and the relationship. In his research, Gottman found that contempt in a marriage is the greatest predictor of divorce. Contempt corrodes love, he said "like throwing battery acid on the relationship." Research also shows that contempt in a marriage predicts illness in the recipient (Gottman, 1994). As a battered woman once told me, contempt "bruises the soul."

Myra and Thomas needed to eliminate contempt and then, gradually, replace it with a culture of respect and appreciation. Compassion in place of contempt would help smooth the way to appreciation. To enable them to be compassionate with themselves and each other, I planned to initially use interventions like those of Dan Wile (1993). Wile helped the couples have the conversation they needed to have by speaking for each partner to the other, carrying on a more vulnerable dialogue in which they express their feelings and needs and admit the ways they are being defensive. In Wile's terms, couples develop a joint platform, where they talk in a collaborative way about the issues they are dealing with. In addition to Dan Wile-type interventions, I would need to set a boundary of "no contempt," as I always do with couples, and I knew I would be setting this boundary over and over again for a long time. Once Myra and Thomas could identify what they needed, they could learn to complain in a "soft" way and ask for what they wanted.

Another key conflict skill for the couple would be self-soothing. As long as Myra and Thomas were in a state of DPA they would be thrown back into their oldest defenses, including dissociation, splitting, contempt, and rage. I knew self-soothing would not be easy. As Marsha Linehan (1993) described, it is often difficult for borderline individuals to comfort, nurture, and be gentle and kind to themselves. Some believe they do not deserve the kindness; they may feel guilty or ashamed when they self-soothe. Others believe they should be soothed only by others; they don't self-soothe as a matter of principle, or they feel angry with others when they self-soothe. I suspected neither Myra nor Thomas would believe they deserved kindness and it also seemed likely that each would feel the other should do the soothing.

In Gottman's model, a sound relationship house is built when a couple has a strong friendship, the social skills to regulate conflict, and the ability to create shared meaning. In comparison to their difficulties, Myra and Thomas had a moderately strong shared meaning system. They deeply wanted to give their new daughter the loving, safe home they never had as children, and, in building it for her, they knew they would be giving it to themselves as well. They had succeeded in creating shared meaning in several rituals and roles, and I was surprised to see that they both marked "true" in response to the question that "if I were to look back, in old age, I think I'd see our paths had meshed well." They indicated that they had similar values and views about home, peacefulness, family, the meaning of being married, education, adventure, having possessions, and nature. But neither of them enjoyed their weekends together, nor did they agree about the meaning of freedom, independence, sharing power, or being a "we." We would need to start by building on the shared meaning they did have.

THE THERAPY

Therapy took place over a period of 2 years. From the beginning, even if the couple came in calmly, in an instant one or both of them turned intensely angry. Myra especially moved quickly into contempt either at Thomas or herself, and then she stonewalled. Several times when she was flooded, my words were meaningless to her and she flailed her arms, repeating, "I can't understand you. I'm stupid." I finally got her to hear "Just breathe." I normalized not being able to think when you are flooded. I worked with them in sessions to take time-outs and to self-soothe, which they weren't able to do on their own effectively for at least a year. They did each eventually self-soothe with my support and validation.

Early in treatment, Thomas dissociated a number of times when Myra raged contemptuously. He felt as if he were physically shrinking, and then he reexperienced his father standing over him with a belt. He would become enraged at Myra and his father; he couldn't separate them. I helped him ground himself in the present, process feelings from the childhood abuse, and differentiate between his response as a child (powerless rage) and his present option of learning to be more powerful. I educated the couple about trauma responses, including flashbacks and dissociation.

I repeated many times to Myra and Thomas that beneath their anger was the desire for connection, and I used the Dan Wile-type interventions to speak for each partner. They began to be able to speak more clearly to each other about what behavior of the other's "hooked" them. Many times it helped to connect these triggers to painful events and relationships in their individual pasts. Despite these efforts, Thomas said that it made "no sense that you could work to get your needs met if you have to be understanding of your partner." After many sessions, the joint platform they arrived at was the idea that, because of their painful histories, neither of them had a strong core self and both were working to develop that and to help their 2-year-old daughter grow strong in herself, also. Over time, Thomas identified that he was reworking the developmental tasks of an 18-month- to 3-year-old, saying "no" and learning to think and feel for himself just as his daughter was learning to do. Myra identified herself as reworking the developmental tasks of a 3- to 6-year-old, asserting her own separate identity and trying out ways of being powerful in relationships. There was a slight opening in Myra's good-bad split thinking when she felt hurt by Thomas and thought about where he was developmentally rather than thinking he was out to get her. They found a safe, nurturing way to turn toward each other throughout the week by giving each other relevant developmental affirmations from Jean Illsley Clark and Connie Dawson's *Growing Up Again* (1998).

We worked in sessions to come up with simple questions Myra and Thomas could ask each other instead of overreacting with contemptuous rage. After about 5 months of work, Myra realized that she got contemptuous when she wanted connection. I suggested that she could instead ask Thomas for time together. And Thomas, instead of reacting to her contempt, could ask her what she wanted right then. Myra was still unable or unwilling to control her contempt, though she began announcing its presence: "I'm getting contemptuous now. [eye roll] You liar. You did not think about anybody but yourself." I worked with Thomas to set a boundary and take time-outs, leaving the room rather than sitting and listening. He could assert a boundary but couldn't leave as yet.

Myra continued to react with contempt, but began to express hurt as well, which was important progress. Yet she felt they were "back at the beginning," with no progress made in therapy. This happened several times throughout the work. To counter her splitting, I repeated the theme that "when you feel this hurt and angry, it's hard to see your progress and remember what felt good."

Myra often restated her initial complaint that Thomas "put her on the shelf." She was finally able to specify that she felt "shelved" when he engaged in his compulsive routines, such as the very precise routine he had for cleaning up after dinner. I interpreted to the couple that Myra was now feeling what Thomas had felt as a child when his bids for connection were responded to with his parents' rules and routines. He identified that he felt that if he could finally get through all the routines, he might have some time for connection. Based on this, they were able to find some ways to turn toward each other after dinner. They would not have been able to process this failed bid in a dyadic conversation, so I interpreted the meaning of their behavior for them.

After a year, Myra and Thomas occasionally had fun but still struggled with fights that hurt them deeply. Myra sometimes saw when she was triggered and ran from the room to self-soothe. I continued to explore with her ways she could more effectively calm herself than by bingeing on food or flipping the TV channels. She had made one room a "sanctuary" and designed a "serene" yard for soothing herself, but she couldn't use them, probably because she felt she didn't deserve them. Many soothing activities, such as music and reading, brought up more pain than she could contain. Yet she was learning to tell herself, "Breathe . . . I am Okay here . . . I can think this through clearly."

Thomas, too, was learning to self-soothe. But he also complained, "Time-outs aren't allowing me to be honest." I normalized that he needed to express his anger to assert himself. The goal of time-outs was not to give up his anger but to stop flooding, which would enable him to focus his anger on expressing what he wanted. He began to use his time-outs to vent his contempt in private and, after that, to calm down and think about what he wanted.

Fourteen months into treatment, Myra almost quit therapy over the issue of "two subjective realities" when I had the couple process a conflict using the aftermath of a fight handout for the first time. They had had this conflict many times: Myra was angry that Thomas wasn't enthusiastic when he agreed to a recreational activity Myra suggested. After they stated what they had felt in the fight, I introduced the concept that in every argument there are two subjective realities, neither of them wrong. Myra's subjective reality was: "I was feeling again the message [from Thomas], 'I don't want a life. I don't want you to have one either. When I want to have fun, I'll take you off the shelf and you better be ready.'" Thomas's reality was: "I didn't get a chance to explain what I wanted to do. If I wasn't positive about [Myra's] suggestions, I'd get the trigger response. I'd better appease, and I didn't do well at that. I'd better go with the program. In that case, I couldn't enjoy myself." When I asked Myra if she could find some part of Thomas's subjective reality that made sense, knowing what she knew about Thomas, Myra dissociated (psychically left the room).

Myra told me I was making her go crazy. She said that if she said something was white and Thomas said it was black, it was a big cover-up of her issue. And that if she gave credence to his experience, it would mean stuffing her emotion, submitting, and giving up a part of herself. "You're saying it's Okay to be treated that way by Thomas and I have to be compassionate and I'm not worth being treated better." I didn't see it at the time, but now I'm sure that Myra was getting triggered back to her experience of feeling crazy after being raped and not being seen as a credible witness. Had I realized it then, I would have said that rape is not a subjective reality. What I did do was work with her on self-soothing and on "being more powerful" in stating "the truth of her experience."

I led them through the aftermath of a marital argument process many more times, soothing them and supporting them both in stating their subjective realities. The aftermath of a marital argument process, conducted triadically rather than dyadically for some months, was helpful in creating some emotional boundaries in several ways. I directed them back to the developmental objective that their work was "to become two separate, whole people, connecting," which, I said, meant that each of them had and would share his or her *own* feelings, perceptions, and needs. Prior to this work, Thomas pursued Myra when she shut down or took a time-out, and he insisted she was contemptuous and escalating at times when she was actually expressing her hurt. Yet Thomas wanted to be a separate person, so it finally made sense to him to let her be separate, too, and have her feelings and take space if she wanted. Also, I worked with him to assert his subjective reality, which he called "What is true for *me*." This helped him to validate Myra. He was able to admit his contribution to a fight without giving up his own needs. In turn, I worked with Myra on validating her own feelings and experience. The couple also struggled with the question of how they each could express a negative feeling, like hurt or disappointment, without the other person feeling "slammed."

After 16 months, the couple experienced some feeling of togetherness. There were some soft start-ups. They were able to utilize their awareness of being triggered and sometimes avoid escalating. Myra admitted that contempt was her big contribution to their fights and she worked hard to not express it.

However, Myra still had a hard time hearing Thomas's truth; she accused him of thinking only of himself when he was not validating her reality. Thomas struggled to figure out whether he was, indeed, being "selfish" when he had perceptions and needs that were separate from Myra's. Also, Myra could not yet accept that Thomas was being truthful when he tried to repair his contempt. When he restated something in a softer way, it felt to her like the "shifting sand" she had initially complained about, where he said what she wanted to hear. Again, I asked him to figure out for himself whether he was repairing the interaction or appeasing Myra.

Nineteen months into therapy, Myra felt unbearably vulnerable and moderately depressed. She recognized that contempt had been her protection. Now that Thomas expressed anger more directly instead of passive-aggressively and she had lowered her shield of contempt, she was afraid she would "get smacked" at any time. John Gottman has said that to work on the meta-emotions of a couple, it is often easiest to work with the couple on what they want to teach their children about emotions. Accordingly, I used the issue of emotion coaching their daughter to help Myra explore beliefs about anger and how to be safe with it.

Myra's contempt also shielded her from feeling how deeply lonely she was; now without it, she felt a vast sorrow. The couple had another fight about her being shut out by Thomas's compulsiveness. This time, they processed the missed bid for connection on their own at home. Myra was able to say what she wanted. Thomas then reached out and tried to soothe her, saying he'd been frustrated by her interruptions when he was trying to get a project done. He tied this in to the belief that if he did his job well enough and fast enough for his parents, *then* he could get back to the relationship. But he also said he really wanted to change and connect with Myra even as he was doing tasks. Myra accepted his soothing.

Myra's negative sentiment override was finally shifting, though she could only acknowledge sorrowfully, "things are different, not better." She spontaneously expressed appreciation to Thomas. Also, in contrast to her negativity when therapy began, she could now tell the story of falling in love with him. When they were anticipating a holiday full of extended family obligations, I had them plan one thing they could do for just the two of them, and as they did this they expressed genuine sweetness, with Myra taking Thomas's hand and saying, "I love you." She often still distrusted Thomas when he expressed what he felt and wanted, but she was accepting what he said more and more. When she seemed open to it, they did the "I appreciate" and "Thanksgiving" exercises, which they genuinely enjoyed.

Then they had a fight about neither partner feeling respected for the job each performed outside the home. The fight seemed rather mild from the outside, but it was crushing for Myra. She shut down and called a divorce attorney ("for information only"). In front of Thomas, Myra and I talked about what she felt before she shut down, which was powerlessness, terror, and shame. When I asked her when she had felt that way before, she became overwhelmed with feelings connected to her rape, particularly shame. Because she was reexperiencing emotions from the rape and was unwilling to expose more of these vulnerable feelings to Thomas, I worked with her in three individual sessions to process the trauma. She made some progress in separating her vulnerability to being raped from the rapist's responsibility for raping her, a key distinction in reducing her shame. I educated the couple about the posttraumatic stress cycle between reexperiencing aspects of trauma and numbing/avoiding, and I explained that what breaks this cycle is finding a "therapeutic window" between reexperiencing and numbing where it is possible to process the feelings and meaning of what happened. Subsequently, Myra reexperienced her powerlessness and terror in yet another fight and, working with the couple, I helped her see that the current fight was clearly different from the rape. This time she had powerfully set boundaries and stated her needs. At her request, Thomas agreed to immediately take a time-out whenever she said she felt powerless.

Shortly after this, Thomas voiced anger that Myra continued to criticize him, and in his anger he made a contemptuous comment about their previous night's sex. After the fights that triggered the rape, and now this, Myra moved back into the negative perspective, saying that the entire 21 years with Thomas had been bad and that she had no love for him. But as hurt as she was, she worked very hard to self-soothe and not flood. They processed the fight without getting back into it. She again felt that by staying in the marriage she was abandoning herself, but this time she decided she would take a break from therapy to figure out what she wanted to do. When they returned 6 weeks later, she had done a lot of thinking about what part she had contributed to the painful patterns of their relationship. She could do this now without expressing any contempt for either of them and without backing down from her complaints. This was the first time she had admitted any responsibility except for her contempt. She particularly took responsibility for withholding affection and approval, and also for having to be right, for fault finding, for not accepting influence and not being able to forgive, for needing to feel safe, for needing directness and concreteness in order to feel safe, and for not knowing any way to soothe Thomas.

Now they were successfully using their own time-out signal: the word *balloon,* as in, "I'm going to pop if we don't stop this instant!" They were staying calmer. Myra wanted some further concrete direction from me. I had them tell me in detail about their commitment to attachment parenting, and then told them they could do "attachment partnering." I reminded them that they knew a lot about being there so their daughter felt safe and respected, as well as about setting boundaries so they also felt safe. I also said that they had lots of practice not reacting to their daughter's acting out but instead focusing on her emotion, thinking about what she might be needing, and helping her put it in words. We summarized therapy in two sentences: "Ask directly for everything you want. Say clear yesses and nos and be as loving when you do it as you try to be with your daughter."

CONCLUSION

Myra and Thomas chose to terminate therapy after 2 years. They were stronger as a couple and they felt they needed to devote their time and resources to caring for one of their parents, who was dying. Unfortunately, I felt that the termination was premature. I would have liked for them to be much more solid in their individual and relationship changes. But I did feel that Myra and Thomas had learned some ways to continue to strengthen their relationship on their own (and to get back on track when they derailed), largely because of the work we had done with the SRH theory and exercises.

We had worked on strengthening their friendship. Love maps were created when Myra and Thomas explored their own personal history in front of each other. They learned about their own, and each other's, enduring vulnerabilities, including their weak sense of self and the ways they were triggered to reexperience past trauma in the relationship. In front of each other, they compassionately connected their intense emotional reactions in the relationship to the horrible abuse they had suffered. As their compassion for themselves and each other grew, their own emerging boundaries against contempt replaced the initial external boundary of no contempt. Then it was possible for the couple to begin to create a family culture of fondness and appreciation by self-consciously expressing appreciations. Also, Myra and Thomas could now make more effective bids for connection because they were more aware of their needs, a result of having those needs interpreted for them. Instead of turning against each other with contempt, or, in Thomas's case, turning away with compulsiveness, they could turn toward each other and ask for what they needed.

We had also worked on skills to regulate conflict. Myra and Thomas created a time-out ritual they liked, and they each found effective ways to self-soothe. They knew that contempt damaged the relationship, and instead of expressing contempt they could now say what they needed using softened start-up. Thanks to the aftermath of a marital argument exercise, they knew how to process a fight without getting back into it. Also, when they suddenly had intense emotion, they could now ask themselves if something was being triggered from their past.

Their learning ways to work together with their enduring vulnerabilities created a shared meaning of healing past trauma. We had also increased the shared meaning they had in their desire to provide a loving, safe home for their daughter and for themselves. They now had some relationship tools to actually build that loving, emotionally safe home. The shared meaning had deepened into having a relationship in which each of them could grow up again in a healthier way and develop a stronger core self.

Not only did both Myra and Thomas know ways they could make the relationship better, but they also each had a bit more sense that they deserved to have the relationship go better. Because they were equipped with these new skills, I felt confident that Myra and Thomas's relationship would continue to grow and deepen, despite its tumultuous beginnings.

REFERENCES

Clark, J. I., & Dawson, C. (1998). *Growing up again: Parenting ourselves, parenting our children.* Center City, MN: Hazelden.

Gottman, J. M. (1994). *What predicts divorce?* Hillsdale, NJ: Erlbaum.

Linehan, M. M. (1993). *Skills training manual for treating borderline personality disorder.* New York: Guilford Press.

Wile, D. B. (1993). *After the fight: Using your disagreements to build a stronger relationship.* New York: Guilford Press.

Chapter 7 ❧

Sexual Dysfunction

Ruth Saks

Frequently couples who come into marital therapy have some level of sexual dissatisfaction. It is difficult to want to make love with someone you fight with all the time or feel distant from. I have often heard clients say, "I just don't feel the same level of attraction; we feel more like brother and sister." Or "All day long you ignore me and tell me everything I'm not doing right. That sure doesn't make me feel like jumping into bed with you." Looking at this from a Gottman perspective, one could conclude that when there is little turning toward (responding to one's partner in small, everyday, positive ways), there is often much less desire to be intimate at night. Sometimes a lack of sexual desire or function is due to medical problems, medication side effects, past trauma, or sexual abuse. Even aging and self-consciousness about body changes commonly affect a couple's satisfaction with their sexual life. The following case, a composite of several couples with similar issues, illustrates how I have used the Gottman approach with couples whose primary presenting problem was sexual dysfunction.

JANET AND STEVE

Janet and Steve were referred to me after they attended a Gottman Couples Workshop. Their presenting problem was a lack of sexual intimacy. In fact, there was almost no physical affection of any kind. Janet and Steve had been married for 14 years. This was the second marriage for both of them. Janet had been divorced after a first marriage of 20 years, and Steve was a widower. His first wife had died in an automobile accident. They had been married for 18 years. Janet had two grown children from her first marriage. Steve had had one daughter in his first marriage; She had died of lymphoma in her early twenties. At the time I met them Janet was 62 and Steve was 69. Janet, who worked part-time as an accountant, was a tall, large women with blond hair that was graying to platinum. She carried her weight well and appeared fit. She was dressed in casual business attire. Steve, a balding portly man about the same height as Janet, was dressed in sweats. Steve had been retired for the last 4 years. He had worked as an engineer.

The four horsemen—criticism, defensiveness, contempt, and stonewalling—were clearly active at our first appointment. Janet could acknowledge that she was very critical but felt it was justified because she was so hurt by Steve's sexual rejection. She also kept slipping in repeated condescending remarks about his sexual inadequacies, inhibitions, and lack of experience. Steve was willing to accept Janet's negative labels. They both described a pattern of loud, angry fighting and critical blaming outbursts followed by long periods where they had very little interaction at all. Steve avoided Janet for long periods of time. He went to bed much later than she did, staying up late to work on his computer. He often had already left to go to the coffee shop or the gym by the time Janet got up in the morning. During the day, Janet worked and Steve rested while Janet was gone. Despite the difficulties they were having, both reported that they were very committed to the marriage.

The oral history interview revealed a fairly positive picture of this couple's relationship despite the presence of the four horsemen. They each frequently looked and smiled at each other and described very positive things about each other as they talked about their dating history. Steve had always found Janet to be a good listener. Both talked about their friendship as the reason they chose each other. They could talk and support each other through various life events, including the death of Steve's daughter. Steve also valued Janet's opinions, advice, and beauty. Janet enjoyed doing many things with Steve. She talked about what a good companion he had been.

When they were dating, the couple had chosen not to engage in a sexual relationship until after they had made a commitment to each other. Janet had found Steve very open sexually during their later dating time. For example, Steve was willing to explore various ways of sexual sharing. A few years into the marriage, however, Steve was less and less comfortable with any sexual exchange other than intercourse in the missionary position with very little foreplay. In describing the ups and downs after they were married, they both acknowledged a gradual decrease in sexual frequency and an increase in the appearance of the four horsemen. Steve shared that he had had difficulty getting and sustaining an erection.

Having attended an earlier Gottman Couples Workshop, they were aware of their pattern of criticism, contempt, and stonewalling. They were trying to use time-outs for flooding and the repair checklist, which is a crib sheet used to help couples with conversations after a difficult interaction. In fact, Steve carried the checklist with him even when they went out. However, it was still very difficult for Steve to express appreciation directly to Janet.

During his individual interview, Steve described his childhood. He was raised as an only child in a very strict, conservative Catholic family in the Midwest. His mother had died in childbirth with him, and his father remarried when he was a young boy. His stepmother took care of him and helped him with his schoolwork. However, she was not an affectionate women. Instead, she was formal and critical. It seemed to Steve that rules and proper behavior were what mattered. Steve described an incident in school when he had been teased and frightened by a group of older boys. This had been very upsetting to him. When he told his stepmother about it, she was critical of him and condescending because he was so upset. Steve felt completely unsupported and invalidated. As he talked about his stepmother, he became quiet and appeared almost timid. Later, while Steve was in college, his stepmother had died of breast cancer. Steve's father died a few years later from a heart attack.

Steve did not have any sexual experience before marrying his first wife. He explained this as "the way things were then." His sex life with his first wife had been old-fashioned, limited to the missionary position. After he was widowed, he had engaged in some limited sexual experimentation before meeting Janet. Steve shared that he often felt guilty about this "indiscriminate" sex. It was only with Janet that he had experienced more varied sexual practices. Although he did not judge these as "bad," he was not fully comfortable with them. Steve was very awkward in his discussion of sex. He used ambiguous terms and sometimes almost stuttered when he talked about his sexual history.

The meta-emotions, meaning and feelings, that Steve associated with love were about grief and loss. Regarding sex, they were guilt and shame. After the death of his first wife and then his daughter he began to feel that anyone he got close to would die. He also connected love with criticism. He often remembered his stepmother's words to him about his inadequacies and mistakes. He also thought that Janet's critical descriptions of him were the truth. Although Steve wanted to stay in the marriage, he did not really expect closeness. In fact, he was able to describe how uncomfortable he felt when Janet tried to be close and loving. He hoped to learn a way to lessen the negative interaction between them so Janet would be less disapproving.

Janet described a very combative first marriage. Although there was no physical violence, the level of open contempt was still so high that it was difficult for her to be in the same room with her ex-husband, even after 20 years of divorce. Janet's parents were also very critical. She was aware that this was now a very strong habit for her. She was committed to changing this response. Janet had taken great joy and pride in her sexuality. She felt enormous sadness and anger at not having sex in this marriage. She felt deceived by Steve, because he had been willing to try different kinds of sexual interaction like oral sex and using vibrators before they were married but had become more and more inhibited in their sexual sharing as the marriage went on. Janet did not want to leave the marriage but felt it might be too big a loss for her over time if there was no improvement in their sex life.

INTERVENTION

I began to think about a treatment plan using the Gottman approach. I knew that regardless of the couple's commitment to stay married, the four horsemen, especially criticism and contempt, were leading to increasing distance and isolation between them. Both were feeling more and more hopeless. Based on this, our work began with a focus on stopping the four horsemen. Because Janet and Steve had attended a couples workshop before beginning our work together they each understood trying to complain rather than criticize. They could accept some responsibility for their individual contribution to their difficulties, and they each were aware of the dangers of stonewalling and of contempt. However, they had trouble stopping these behaviors. Assessment of flooding indicated that Steve became flooded when Janet yelled. It took little provocation before Steve was triggered and yelled, too. During the couples workshop they had chosen a time-out signal to use. I helped them each to try some individualized self-soothing techniques to use when needed. I suggested that they agree to put off sexual contact for a while until Steve was more comfortable with risk taking in this area. Janet revealed a great deal of patience in her acceptance of this. In time, they were able to make considerable progress in decreasing the frequency of contemptuous comments and converting from criticism to complaints.

During this time many of the interventions also focused on the sharing of appreciation. This was fairly easy for Janet. Although she was very quick to criticize she could also express genuine appreciation. I knew it was important to strengthen the fondness and admiration system to reverse the negative sentiment, which was pervasive. Steve found giving appreciation much more difficult. I tried using the adjective checklist, a list of positive characteristics used to help couples acknowledge positive qualities in each other. I encouraged each of them to check the checklist frequently throughout the week to see what appreciations they could share. This was helpful, but Steve had such strong feelings of self-doubt and inadequacy that he was sure he would do it wrong. He eventually tried to use commercial greeting cards to capture some of his positive sentiments. After feeling successful in giving these to Janet, he began to leave her little "Post-its" using ideas from the adjective checklist. Steve took great pride in each of these successes, and Janet acknowledged each effort with much appreciation. In this way they shifted out of the pattern of turning toward followed by turning away and into a pattern of reciprocal turning toward. They were also beginning to be able to give hugs of thanks. Janet showed patience as long as she had hope, and fortunately she felt more hopeful as she felt more appreciated.

During this first stage of treatment we had weekly or bimonthly appointments. After 3 months, Janet and Steve came in looking very upset. They had been away on vacation and had had a very difficult fight. While on vacation they had stayed in a hotel with one bed and went to bed at the same time. This was different from their usual routine, which avoided awake time in bed together. Janet had hoped there would be a little affection or cuddling. She had had a secret expectation that their vacation might lead to at least something physical. She was very disappointed that Steve found ways to avoid coming to bed with her. She felt this was an intentional rejection.

Steve was not aware of any underlying issues that compelled him to avoid bedtime. He was able to hear how difficult this was for Janet and to understand that she was having difficulty remaining patient. He was also willing to make a commitment to try to understand what was making sexual contact so frightening for him. We agreed to have some individual appointments to explore this.

In attempting to help Steve move through this impasse, it was important to understand what he was experiencing when he began to get close to Janet. I used the aftermath of a marital argument exercise, and I asked Steve to go over the fight at the hotel again. When he came to the question "Do these feelings relate to your past?" Steve kept coming back to two issues. One was how critical his stepmother had been and how inadequate he felt in his ability to please her. Second was the lack of affection in the household he grew up in. Steve felt he had no model for affection within a marriage or between loved ones at all. As we explored these messages about love, it became clear, as mentioned earlier, that love not only meant criticism and inadequacy but also loss. Everyone Steve had loved died: his mother, his father, his stepmother, his first wife, and his daughter. If he let himself really love Janet, would she die, too? In Steve's reality, he was keeping Janet alive by not loving her or holding her close.

During the couples session I asked both Janet and Steve to complete the "injury and healing" questionnaire, an exercise in which both husband and wife write about the difficult events they've gone through. The couple agreed to share these with each other when we met in our next session. Janet talked about the years of hostility and humiliation she endured during her first marriage. She needed to be critical and angry with her first husband in order to maintain any power with him. She also shared that her sexual life with this husband had been very unsatisfying. She had not been orgasmic until she was in another relationship after the divorce. In this later relationship she discovered her own sexuality, as well as the notion that a relationship is based on friendship, not domination. She had fears that she would lose the sexual joy that she had learned she could experience in her marriage with Steve. Yet Steve was also a good friend, which was why Janet had married him. Janet wanted all of it with Steve: deep friendship, shared life goals, and satisfying sex. Listening to Janet, Steve heard, for the first time, Janet's fear of losing a dream about the marriage she wanted. Fear of losing a dream was different than an attack on him.

In turn, Janet was able to hear Steve's terror about getting close to her and her dying. Following this exercise, Steve seemed to trust Janet's commitment and love in a stronger way. He let Janet know how much he appreciated the safety that resulted from her giving him time to figure things out without sexual contact. He was also ready to see how hurt and scared Janet felt about his withholding and withdrawing from her. Steve believed he was ready to begin some physical contact again. Janet agreed to let Steve be in charge of what kind, how much, and when. She reassured Steve that hugs, tenderness, and cuddling were what was most important to her and that she would readily accept his advances. Janet hoped to avoid Steve's feeling rejected. I cautioned both of them that it was important that Janet also have a choice in what contact felt comfortable to her. I was concerned that because she wanted sexual intimacy so badly, she would agree to be sexual even when she did not want that kind of intimacy. In the long run this would work against their mutual goals. They talked about ways they could express their sexual desires safely and comfortably. Steve also promised that he would see his doctor to make sure none of his medications would interfere with his desire or performance and to check his testosterone level. He would also talk with his doctor about the possibility of using Viagra.

I encouraged Steve and Janet to take small steps. They had been giving each other kisses hello and good-bye, but hugs at any other time often became triggers for stress. Steve had shared early in our work that he was concerned that hugs would be misread as sexual advances. This was part of the reason he avoided hugs. Trying to set up a structure that would reduce as much anxiety as possible, I asked them not to have intercourse or sexual contact with the goal of orgasm. This was a time for physical affection. I encouraged them to enjoy physical closeness without having to worry about any other intention except affection. When they returned, they were both very happy with the progress they had made. Steve finally felt ready to move toward sexual contact. Again, I encouraged small steps: going to bed at the same time, hugging while in bed with night clothes on, and perhaps some sexual touching. But again I cautioned against moving too fast. I also asked that if they felt uncomfortable at all they should tell the other and then stop. Ideally they could move back to contact that was less anxiety-provoking.

At this point in the treatment Janet understood that Steve's reluctance was not about her; rather, it was related to a long history of loss and pain. Prior to this Janet had felt unattractive to Steve, and she had attributed his rejection to her aging. Now because of all the sharing of appreciation, which had become a much stronger habit, Janet felt more attractive to Steve and better about herself. In turn, Steve felt ready for more overtly sexual contact. He was scared about performance and had some residual old emotions, but he knew how much this meant to Janet and wanted to make her happy. Again I suggested small steps.

When Janet and Steve came to the following appointment they were both very happy. They had had successful sexual intimacy several times over the previous two weeks. Steve had gotten Viagra from his doctor. They had been so comfortable sexually with the Viagra that he had spontaneously made advances without the Viagra, and that went well, too. This success brought up new issues. Janet was afraid that their sexual intimacy would not last. She also was getting tired of feeling that she had little influence. She was so careful to let Steve be in charge of all sexual contact and bids for affection that it seemed that most of what they did in all areas was his choice. Using the dreams-within-conflict intervention, I asked them to have a conversation about each other's dreams within the relationship, dreams for themselves, and dreams for the two of them as a couple. In exploring these dreams, Janet had a picture of being in a relationship where she was not "too much." She saw herself as a powerful women, and she liked this about herself. She also knew that she had used this power in negative ways in the past. Now she feared that she would intimidate Steve if she opened up sexually too much. But if she gave up all her power she might feel angry and resentful.

With some help, Steve was able to ask about these fears during the session. He had difficulty not moving into his own fears but was finally able to talk about how he could relinguish some power and influence to Janet and still remain safe.

However, he acknowledged that it might be hard for him to maintain as much sexual frequency as they had had over the last couple of weeks. He suggested he would make sure he was initiating sexual intimacy often enough so Janet would not get nervous, fearing they were slipping back into their old pattern. He would also try to say "yes" when Janet initiated sexual contact. Still, he was not sure he felt comfortable exploring new ways of sexual sharing yet. He wanted to feel comfortable first with having sexual intercourse in familiar positions. It was a lot to get used to—to not always be the one in charge of their sexual contact. He did say he could see a time in the future when he might be open to conversation about some new ways that they could share intimacy.

In a subsequent session we talked about ways that Steve could accept influence from Janet in nonsexual ways. At one point in the conversation, Steve looked over at Janet and asked, "Is there anything you would like me to do?"

Right away she answered, "I would like to have a birthday party for Joan. Will you help me clean?"

"Sure, that would be easy."

Over the next several appointments Steve and Janet reported how helpful Steve had been on many occasions. At one time and with much pride, Steve shared a story about having plans to drive to a place they had read about in a tour guidebook. Because of delays in leaving and running into unexpected traffic, the outing did not work out as he had planned. He found himself stuck. His old pattern would have been to become frustrated and angry. This time Steve turned to Janet and asked, "Do you have any suggestions?"

"Yes, we could go the lake instead and stop at the store and pick up a picnic lunch," she said.

They did just that. It was not what he had expected, but it worked out well. Even more important, Steve recognized this as "accepting influence" and felt very proud of himself.

At this point it seemed Steve and Janet were ready to plan for termination of treatment. We started decreasing the frequency of our sessions, meeting every 3 weeks, then every 4 weeks, and finally every 3 months and 6 months. At one point they hit a little snag and came in for two weekly appointments to get back on track and identify what was getting triggered for each of them after a particular fight. The fight had been about Janet's birthday. She felt she had made it clear on past birthdays that she wanted Steve to plan the whole day especially for her. This birthday didn't meet her expectations at all. First, the gift did not arrive on time. Then they couldn't go to dinner where she wanted because the restaurant was closed and Steve didn't find another. Janet launched into a very critical, contemptuous attack. Steve went into major stonewalling and was gone "doing errands" or resting for the remainder of the day. In the session the couple did an aftermath of a marital argument exercise and talked about the conversation they didn't have that would have been helpful. We did some relapse prevention by planning for where they might slip up and how to notice when things were going astray. We also planned for how they could begin repair discussions when necessary. Janet and Steve again made a serious commitment to staying in touch with each other and making sure they didn't become distant from each other again.

CONCLUSION

The case of Steve and Janet exemplifies how marital sexual difficulties can be treated using the Gottman method. Although the couple had a fair amount of positive sentiment, the presence of the four horsemen was leading to negative interactions and feelings of hopelessness and loneliness. The exchange of fondness and admiration was limited, and turning toward was frequently followed by turning away. Steve and Janet were caught in gridlock, as core issues of vulnerability were frequently triggered. Both were afraid of losing basic dreams they held for themselves within a marriage. In our work together, we began reducing the presence of the four horsemen and shifting the negative perspective by increasing the sharing of appreciation. In addition, Janet and Steve learned skills for physiological soothing and softened start-up. Steve became more comfortable with accepting influence. As the nature of their fights changed, it became easier for them to approach each other in repair attempts. Janet and Steve were able to hear each other's stories, which helped them to understand each other's personal perspectives in ways they had not been able to do before.

Steve and Janet knew they would probably never have equal levels of sexual desire. But they found ways to talk with each other when this became an issue and to sustain their love, affection, and appreciation for one another.

Chapter 8 ❋

The Emotionally Distant Couple: Creating New Bridges

Connie Feutz

Emotional disengagement is an element of every distressed marriage. The only question is of the *degree* of disengagement. Unlike the situation of other highly-distressed couples, however, the anguish may not be immediately apparent in the emotionally-disengaged marriage. Martial interaction often is *not* characterized by high levels of negativity or strong evidence of the four horseman. One or both members of the couple may even report that things aren't "that bad" between them. This will be reported even as one or both partners are moving toward separation or divorce. This apparent lack of anguish can be perplexing to the therapist. The hallmark of an emotionally disengaged couple is a lack of positive affect—joy, humour, affection. When the therapist looks deeper, he or she will often find that the couple has actually traveled far down the distance and isolation cascade.

Looked at through the lens of the SRH, an emotionally distant couple may at one time have had a strong friendship but now scores low on love maps, demonstrating little interest in each other, and expresses almost no fondness and admiration or turning towards. One or both partners may score well below the 85-point marital satisfaction cutoff on the Locke-Wallace Marital Adjustment Test and well above the 4 cutoff on the Weiss-Cerretto Marital Status Inventory, which indicates their desire to divorce. They may proudly report that they never fight, but they also often have little tolerance for conflict and are lacking the skills needed to dialogue about differences. Each has adapted to their increasing isolation and distance by creating separate, parallel lives. The typical emotionally disengaged couple will turn toward others for emotional support (like an individual therapist), feel great loneliness and distance in their marriage, and work out their problems separately. Surprisingly, they may still show strength in the seventh level of the SRH—shared meaning—but almost nowhere else.

Sitting with these couples, the therapist can palpably feel the emotional disconnection and tension, as if a chasm exists between them. The therapist's first job, then, becomes instilling hope for change while not ignoring the anguish of living in an emotionally disengaged marriage. It is important to find areas of relating where the chasm is the narrowest—areas where bridge building stands the most chance of success. In rebuilding connection, bridges are constructed very slowly, brick by brick. Inch by inch, the estranged couple is trying to find their way back to each other.

The case described in this chapter demonstrates this idea of building bridges between partners in an emotionally estranged couple.

PETER AND ANGIE

It was Angie, the wife, who made the initial call to me. "We've been married for 25 years," she began, in a choked voice. "Peter moved out 5 months ago, saying he wanted out of our marriage, that he just couldn't stand it anymore. None of our friends can make any sense of this. They all think he's having an affair. But he tells me he isn't. Should I believe him? I'm probably being a complete fool, but I want this marriage." In obvious and understandable despair, Angie also gave an impression of fragility and dependency.

"He's a workaholic," she continued, eager to talk about Peter. "His dream has always been to own his own construction business, to be the general, not just one of the hired crew. Well, it's been almost 20 years now since he accomplished that goal but he still works 70 to 80 hours a week. Two years ago, he began to see a therapist. I don't know exactly how often he sees her—Peter won't tell me anything anymore—but I once overheard him tell his brother she thought he was narcissistic. Now that I know what that means, I think she's right."

In that first conversation I learned that Peter had recently filed for divorce, but at the pleading of his wife and 3 adult children, he had acquiesced to try marital counseling "for a few sessions." I asked Angie how she was coping with all of this. After a deep sigh she said, "Oh, I'm doing okay.... I guess. Most of the time, I'm fine. Really, I am."

After listening for a little while, I explained the Gottman assessment process: four sessions to complete an assessment and a direction for treatment. After the assessment, they could decide if they would like to work further with me. Angie agreed and we scheduled the four sessions. I asked her to give her husband my phone number. If he had any questions or concerns before our first session, I'd be happy to talk with him. He didn't call.

The Initial Assessment: The First Three Sessions

Walking into the waiting room to introduce myself, I found the couple sitting apart. Peter, still dressed in his work clothes, was intensely leafing through a magazine while Angie sat with clenched hands, staring out the window. When they walked into my office, they looked like the perfect couple: a very attractive pair in their fifties, tall and tan. All of their comments to one another were polite and congenial. They chose seats in my office that placed them as far apart from one another as possible. It was when the topic turned to more intimate matters that the tension and distance between them surfaced.

When asked about the first time they had met, Angie smiled while Peter looked off to the side blankly. They had met in high school when Angie was a sophomore and Peter a senior. Once Angie graduated from high school, they began to date off and on. After 2 years, Angie told Peter if he wasn't interested in marriage she needed to look elsewhere. He answered that he didn't know if he wanted to marry or not. Their relationship took a turn toward commitment after Angie began seriously dating another young man. Peter explained: "When I saw them together it dawned on me—if I don't act soon, I'm going to lose her. So I did. I proposed." His tone and facial expression were flat as he described his decision.

I then asked the couple what drew them to each other and what qualities attracted them to each other in the very beginning. Angie smiled warmly and could easily describe what it was in Peter that had drawn her to him: his smile, his confidence, his goofy sense of humor, his determination. Peter, on the other hand, struggled with this question. He paused before responding, "She was a good find. She had a good head on her shoulders—and still does—and she's damn attractive. Even now, she could have any man she wanted."

Angie squirmed. Clearly this comment made her uncomfortable. "The only man I want is you!" she said. Peter didn't respond. Throughout the rest of the session, many of Angie's bids to Peter—verbal and nonverbal—went unnoticed by him. Was his disengagement from Angie an indication that he was out of this marriage? Was it possibly a sign of depression?

Peter and Angie had become pregnant 6 months after marrying at ages 21 and 23, and eventually they had three children in 5 years. They adopted traditional roles, with Angie becoming the primary parent, housekeeper, and connector with both of their families, who lived in the same area. Peter set out to prove himself on the job, often working 6 days a week. Their leisure time was spent either with extended family or separately. Peter would go to football and baseball games with friends while Angie attended her monthly book group and volunteer meetings. When their youngest child entered middle school, Angie returned to school herself, earned a teaching certificate, and found a job teaching second grade. After a number of years, she retired from the school district, and for 2 years floundered with where to direct her time and energy. Both partners acknowledged that prior to Peter's moving out, they could not recall the last time they had gone out together alone, without family or friends.

In her individual session, Angie described her own father as absent and aloof and her mother as sweet, timid, and insecure. The oldest of four children, Angie was an obedient and responsible child. When her youngest brother died in a drowning accident at age 6, her mother fell into a deep depression and her father threw himself into his work running a hardware store. Angie was 13 at the time, and even more of the household and childcare duties fell upon her shoulders. On the positive side, Angie reported no sexual, physical, or verbal abuse either in her family of origin or with Peter. She also adamantly denied ever having had an affair. Although there was no family history of drug or alcohol abuse, she admitted that when she and Peter met for dinner after his moving out, she drank more than usual to help her relax.

Whenever possible, Angie turned the conversation to Peter. "He has no friends. His work is his primary source of identity. He is going through a midlife crisis. He focuses obsessively on his body and fitness. He talks about himself incessantly. He doesn't know how to find happiness."

Getting Angie to speak about herself and her own experience took effort. Finally, she sank into her deep fear and sadness and cried. She described her current contact with Peter as a handful of phone calls each week, mostly to take care of business, have "surface conversation," and plan occasional dinners. "He's keeping me on the end of a very long leash," she said.

From Angie's point of view, even before Peter moved out, they had been living separate and parallel lives. Although it wasn't very satisfying to her, she had come to not expect much more from her marriage. She maintained the belief that she and Peter would "find ourselves again" in a few years after he retired.

In my individual session with Peter, he strode over and sat in the large leather overstuffed chair, looking like a CEO. For a brief moment I felt like it was I who was to be interviewed by him.

"So what are we going to talk about?" he began in a commanding style.

"I want to hear about your background, some about your family. But to start, I would like to hear from you about why you chose to move out."

"I know it doesn't make sense to anyone. We've always looked like the perfect couple to everyone." Peter shook his head and stared off to the side. "For a long time, I kept telling myself that things weren't that bad, that other guys had it much worse. But I guess it was brewing inside me for a long time. For years probably. Don't get me wrong—Angie is a great gal and a great mother. It's just . . ." he shook his head as he searched for the words. "It's just . . . well, the simple truth is, I was just going crazy. Her rules, her organization, her perfect little house. Everything has to be *her* way. There just wasn't any room for me to breathe in that house! I know it sounds harsh—it sounds harsh to me! And I wouldn't say it to her face, but I feel our marriage has been dead for a long time."

He hung his head for a while as we sat in silence. I, too, was at a loss for words. Finally, I spoke up. "Do you still love her?"

Peter sighed deeply. "I guess the honest answer is, I just don't know. I wish I knew, but I don't. All I know is I just couldn't live there anymore."

Peter described how he currently felt no spark, no interest, no passion for his wife, and couldn't recall when he had. He went on to explain how immediately after he moved out, he had felt a huge wave of relief. He felt "lighter and like I could suddenly hear the birds sing again." But this relief was short-lived, lasting approximately 4 to 6 weeks, after which he sank back down into a depressed mood. Peter spoke of the importance of his work, of procuring work for his crew, to whom he felt great loyalty. He spoke of searching by taking saxophone lessons and attending lectures at the nearby university, things he had never done before. Yet, for the past 6 months now, he had felt isolated, lonely, and confused about what really mattered to him.

He had been raised in a conservative Catholic family in the upper Midwest. He spoke respectfully of both his parents, yet when he described the interactions of his family, he could recall very little warmth or open affection. His father was "an effective taskmaster." He recalled his mother's "rules" and how important it was that he, her good son, followed the rules: how dishes were to be washed, dried, and put away, how a bed was to be made, how often one attended church, and so on. Peter was the older of two sons. His younger brother learned in college that he suffered from a learning disability and ADHD, "which explained a lot," Peter said. As a child Peter's brother had been rowdy, provocative, and a poor student. In contrast, everything came easy for Peter—grades, sports, girls. Peter had shone.

Although denying he had ever had an affair, Peter did acknowledge that he fantasized about finding a more compatible partner, "where there's some spark," and that he had gone out to lunch with a female coworker. In neither the first conjoint session nor in his individual session had Peter expressed any words of fondness or connection about Angie. His words and tone communicated loyalty, obligation, and guilt: a man stuck in a life he seemed to have fallen into.

Toward the end of the individual session, I mirrored back to Peter what I had heard. "You have always done what was expected of you. You chose Angie because she was smart and beautiful and had a good head on her shoulders. She was a good catch. You are in a very public role in your job, with a lot of people depending upon you and the business you generate. In your role as a father and husband you have always done what was expected. Meanwhile, what happened to the Peter that Angie talked about falling in love with? The witty, carefree jokester?"

Peter snorted and responded sarcastically, "Life kicked him in the butt. He had to grow up and get a job."

As we sat in silence, I wondered, if I was really tracking the source of his pain, which had led him to leave his family, or if I was simply looking for the Peter I would enjoy more than the depressed, sullen man in front of me. I tried again. "It sounds to me like you were dying in your marriage."

Peter peered at me. "I was."

"And that you had been depressed for years and felt trapped."

He nodded.

Toward the end of the individual session, I requested an agreement that if by chance he should find himself interested in another woman, he would stop the marital therapy. "Marital therapy is a farce if one party is secretly involved somewhere else," I said. "I understand those things happen and I trust that if it happens to you, you will do or say whatever you have to to end the counseling here in my office."

Peter rubbed his chin. "I see what you mean. You're right. I'm not involved with anyone now, you know."

"I believe you." I did believe that Peter wasn't actively seeing anyone. But I also thought that if Peter met someone who knocked his socks off, he would probably leave his wife. He saw his depression as residing in the relationship and clearly believed it would dissipate if he left Angie. He didn't know what to do with the fact that he had been living without her for 5 months and that his discontent and unhappiness were as heavy as ever.

After three sessions and the data from the questionnaires, this is what I had: A depressed husband and an anxious wife. A wife interested in putting energy toward a new marriage, but a reluctant, if not recalcitrant, husband. Angie scored 70 on the Locke-Wallace Marital Adjustment Test and 2 on the Weiss-Cerretto Marital Status Inventory. Peter, on the other hand, scored 27 on the former and 8 on the latter, indicating significant marital dissatisfaction.

Although the couple had respect for each other, I didn't sense much fondness between them and little if any friendship. They were low on love maps, and as the distance had increased over time, the bids for connection had diminished. I imagined a long history of missed bids, growing into bids that were turned against. Sentiment override was negative, as it generally is when the friendship is sorely lacking. Regulation of conflict was nonexistent as both avoided conflict. There was emotional disengagement, no passion or romance, and no fun. Although I wasn't completely convinced that Peter wasn't checking out potential mates elsewhere, I would take him at his word that he wasn't involved with anyone now and should that change, he would end the marital therapy. The couple's strengths lay in the areas of working as a team, shared family traditions, similar life goals, and a shared meaning system. At least there was something to build upon, as long as both parties were interested in building. This is what I set out to discover.

The Fourth Assessment Session: Feedback, Goals, and Treatment Plan

We began the fourth session with a metaphor. There are trees, tall and majestic, that die from the inside out, perhaps from termites or rot. Their marriage was like this. It looked beautiful from the outside, but a thousand small losses, a thousand small relationship-destroying exchanges, had, like termites, taken the marriage down. We discussed how building a strong relationship is analogous to building a strong house, something Peter knew about. Certain choices result in a stronger house; others do not. Angie and Peter had built the best house they could and it had functioned well in two areas: working as a team and being united in the discipline, beliefs, and principles of raising their three children. Now with the kids on their own, their house had lost its primary job; it now stood empty with no clear purpose.

"Each of you has been discontent with aspects of the marriage for a long, long time," I said. "You lived together for 25 years without having developed a language or a method for handling your big conflicts. By the time the kids left, you each had quite a stockpile of unhappiness. Peter, your experience of that unhappiness was simply unbearable and you felt you had no choice but to leave. Not because of anything you were doing wrong, Angie," I said, glancing at her and then looking back at Peter, "but because you felt like you were dying inside."

Using the conceptual framework of the the SRH, we then discussed the various "challenges" in their marriage. The three friendship levels—love maps, fondness and admiration, and turning towards—were weak, and they lacked the skills necessary in dialoguing about their perpetual problems. I then listed their strengths (mutual respect, working well as a team, problem solving skills, similar goals, and shared meaning). I asked if there was something I had missed or misunderstood. They somberly shook their heads and said it seemed I had an accurate picture of their marriage.

"I think we could all agree that neither of you wants to return to the marriage you used to have."

Angie looked nervously over at Peter, who was nodding his head in agreement. Angie's motivation to work on their marriage was clear. Her challenge was to manage her anxiety and not lose herself in the marriage in the name of saving it. Peter was the wild card. Was he really interested in putting time and effort toward building a new marriage? Or was he just biding his time until he met someone new? I would need a more direct expression of his needs and wants in this marriage, and I'd have to teach him the skills to connect emotionally to Angie. Both partners avoided conflict, so we would need to work on tolerance of conflict as well as skills for managing perpetual problems and problem solving. Was this too much for Peter? I turned to him.

"I understand that it is too soon for you, Peter, to know if you want to turn toward your marriage with Angie at this time. What I am recommending is that we take a set amount of time—say, 6 months—during which our focus will be on a few goals. The first objective would be to do whatever we can to help you, Peter, make a clear decision one way or another about whether you want to put your energy back into this marriage. Second, we would work on clearing some of the distress and tension between the two of you while rebuilding your friendship. You will be coparents of your three adult children and their children for the rest of your lives. It will serve everyone for the two of you to be friends, whether you are together or divorced."

I like giving timelines when ambivalence for one partner is an issue. Typically, both feel some sense of relief that the "limbo" won't go on forever. Also, a deadline often makes the ambivalent partner feel an increased sense of urgency to reach a decision. But there is an additional factor when a couple is also emotionally disengaged: As therapy heats up, it can stir up affect in what has been an affectless marriage, making things look worse before they feel better. I want people to ride through those rough spots, and the time commitment can assist in that.

I also recommended that each of them seek individual therapy and agree to a release of information between their individual therapists and me. I wanted Peter to explore and clarify his needs and wants in his marriage and to mitigate his depression. Angie needed to learn how to manage her anxiety, and adopt some assertiveness skills, and also have a safe place for herself should Peter decide to leave the marriage.

Because this couple was in a state of crisis, I recommended 2½-hour sessions once a week. I have found longer sessions to be much more productive and satisfying to all parties involved. Research indicates that longer sessions early in marital counseling ($1\frac{1}{2}$ to 3 hours), together with two or three week-long vacations from therapy later on, produce the largest treatment effects and the least relapse (Boegner & Zielenbach-Coenen, 1984).

When both people in a marriage are conflict-avoidant, I assess how much tension the couple can tolerate. I predicted that Angie, because of her strong desire for reconciliation, could probably tolerate long sessions. Longer sessions would work better with her anxiety as well, as they would allow us time to get into difficult areas and have some positive movement before the session concluded. But Peter? Again, I wasn't sure what he could or would tolerate. But I decided that, I should go for a more intensive approach. Longer therapeutic sessions build more therapeutic heat. I also knew that Peter was familiar with being "under a deadline," and whatever skills he must have regarding handling that sort of pressure on his job would, I hoped, carry over into his marriage.

I suggested that treatment continue for a period of 6 months. During this time, we would focus on: (1) moving toward a decision regarding whether or not they wanted to recommit to a new marriage; (2) revitalizing their friendship and increasing positive affect; and (3) teaching skills for handling perpetual and solvable problems. After 3 months we would check in with how the treatment was going and reevaluate at that time.

For many couples in similar situations, having a clear, structured "plan" feels much more reassuring than scheduled weekly sessions without a clear understanding of where the therapist is intending to take them. Angie nodded eagerly at the plan I proposed and looked over at Peter, who shrugged his shoulders and gave his wife a small smile. "Sure. It sounds Okay."

INTERVENTION

During the first assessment session, Peter had refused to be videotaped. He had seemed skeptical of me, so I chose to not push it at that time. Instead, I asked to videotape them during our first treatment session. Peter was hesitant, but he didn't outright refuse. With his agreement, I asked them to talk to one another and try to reach a mutually satisfying resolution to an area of continuing disagreement for them. Then we would watch the tape together. "By watching you do what you normally do, it will help me have a better idea of what conflict skills you may want to learn."

They agreed and I turned on the camera.

Peter smirked and turned to face his wife. They looked at one another shyly.

"What do you want to talk about?" Angie asked.

Peter shrugged. "I don't know. You always seem to know what it is we need to talk about, so why don't you start this time?"

Angie sighed. "I don't want to be the bad guy anymore."

Peter looked exasperated and raised his voice. "Who's saying you're the bad guy?! God, Angie! I really don't know where you get these ridiculous ideas from!"

Angie hung her head, staring at her hands in her lap.

Peter sighed heavily and turned to look out the window. "It's such an uphill battle between us. It's like some giant, or ogre, that keeps changing shape so I never know how I'm supposed to respond or conquer it." He waved his large hands rapidly in the air. "This... this thing between us."

Angie's tone was sharp. "Peter, you're the one who walked out. You're the one who can't tell me why. And I'm not the only one waiting for an answer from you, you know! So are the children. They have no idea what to make of this. And you know that Bobby is furious with you about all this."

Bobby, their oldest son, had announced his engagement just a few months before Peter had moved out. According to Angie, Bobby felt ashamed of his father and believed Peter's choice to move out was putting a damper on his upcoming wedding.

Peter seemed to sink deeper into his chair as he listened to Angie. I imagined Angie's frustration and Peter's guilt. He wasn't living up to anyone's expectations, least of all his own.

Angie's words hung in the air for a few moments. When Peter did respond, I noticed it was a repair attempt.

"That's why I'm here, too, Ang. I just feel so confused sometimes..." he turned his gaze to the trees outside my window, "and I just don't know what I should do."

Unfortunately, it didn't go anywhere. Peter turned his body away, arms crossed over his chest, and both remained quiet. If they weren't in my office, Peter probably would have left the room to escape the tension between them. Both seemed overwhelmed, powerless, and defeated—trapped in the milieu of an emotionally vacuous marriage. We stopped.

Observing couples in their conflict pattern gives one information—both concrete details and a feeling sense of the marital distress. The therapist can glimpse the widest part of the couple's chasm and see which horsemen reign. In this case, Angie and Peter never agreed upon a topic to discuss but rather quickly fell into an attack-defend pattern, beginning with a neutral statement by Angie, which Peter perceived as an attack. Blame and defensiveness were evident; criticism, stonewalling, and contempt were also creeping in.

Honestly looking at the state of one's marriage in the presence of a stranger can spin a couple into feelings of hopelessness—I want to counter that as quickly as I can with an experiential shift in affect. With emotionally disengaged couples, doing the dream-within-conflict intervention in the first treatment session can often get the therapy on track. The connection made by the dream-within-conflict can also begin the slow task of bridge building. Also, helping an emotionally disengaged couple to assert their points of view or dreams counteracts feeling unentitled to one's complaints. This is often an issue with this population; one or both partners may dismiss his or her own, or the partner's, needs and complaints as "not that bad." Meanwhile, a mountain of unmet needs and discontent has slowly and steadily grown. In this case, I also wanted to counteract whatever unresolved feelings might have been lingering from the couple's discussion of their area of continuing disagreement. People often feel demoralized after showing a stranger one of their worse sides, so I used an upbeat voice when I stepped in.

"Thank you. I know that couldn't have been much fun for you, but it was actually very helpful for me. You needn't worry—we won't do this often—but I now have a much better grasp of where it is I want to take you today."

Neither partner seemed at all reassured. I continued. "If you recall from our discussion last week about the SRH, all couples have perpetual problems—it's simply a part of two different individuals trying to live well together. Perpetual problems in and of themselves aren't the problem. The problem is when we leave the domain of dialoguing about them and instead fall into believing our partner could solve this darn problem if only he would try! In other words, over time any perpetual problem can gather a lot of emotional muck around it and become gridlocked. There is an exercise I'd like to do with you right now that assists in moving a gridlocked issue back into the domain of dialogue."

I described the roles of speaker and listener within the dream-within-conflict exercise, explaining that the listener has the harder job. I then asked that they speak about the issue of Peter's choosing to move out. Although it was not a "standard" perpetual problem (like sex, finances, parenting styles, in-laws, and so on), their other perpetual problems had been on the back burner with Peter living elsewhere for the past 5 months. Moreover, this topic seemed to be the proverbial "elephant in the living room"—something both partners found difficult to address. And I was banking on the belief that there were levels they hadn't touched yet on their own.

Angie volunteered to listen first. I gave her the handout of possible questions to ask Peter if she found she was stuck, and then I sat back.

Angie crossed her ankles and smoothed her pants. She smiled anxiously at Peter. "Well, let's see. Okay. I know you've already told me why you've left. Well, at least I think you have. But I still don't understand it." A look passed over Peter's face, and Angie grimaced. "I'm sorry, Peter, but I just don't! So, tell me again—why did you have to move out?"

Peter shifted in his seat, straightening up, and faced Angie as if she were an opponent.

"Yes, I have already told you. I . . . I had no other choice. I was suffocating. I was stir-crazy. I . . ." Peter paused and looked at his hands. "Well, there is one part, I guess, I haven't told you about." After a moment, he raised his head and looked directly at Angie. "You have no idea how many times these past several years driving home I found myself thinking, 'Heck, if this is all there is to my life, it just might be better to be six feet under.' Or maybe I should just stay on the freeway and see how far south I could get. San Francisco! New Mexico! Anywhere! You know how my old man says when you ask him how he's doing, 'Well it's a bit better than the alternative'? Well, far too many times I began thinking the alternative was sounding pretty damn good."

"Honey, I had no idea . . . "

"I know, I know you didn't. At first I thought it was just some crazy thought, but then they just didn't go away."

"What was I doing that was making you feel so stir-crazy?"

I stepped in. "Angie, I don't want to go there in this conversation, to what you may or may not have been doing to make the situation worse. Let's keep the focus on Peter for now. You both are doing great, by the way. You may want to ask him, at this point, if there is a story behind these feelings he's been having."

Angie nodded and asked Peter the question.

"A story? Behind the feelings?" He rubbed his chin. "I don't think so."

"Is this the first time you've ever had thoughts of death? Or running away?"

"Or feeling stir-crazy and suffocated?" I added.

"Well, yeah," said Peter. "I was stir-crazy my last several years at home before I graduated from high school and got out of there as fast as I could. *You* remember."

Angie nodded.

"My younger brother was causing all sorts of problems and Mom practically drooled over the good things I did while behind her back I got away with murder. I felt sorry for the pack of them. Yeah, I couldn't get away from there fast enough."

"So living with me was giving you the same feelings you had then?"

Peter hesitated. "Well, sort of. Well, maybe a lot like then, I guess. I was feeling so trapped, Ang. Work, work, work. Then I'd come home and there'd be the kids and their soccer or basketball games or whatever. Or bills to be paid. Or we'd go to your folks or my folks. And after a while, none of it made any sense anymore. None of it was any fun, that's for sure!"

Angie seemed at a loss. She looked down at the handout. After a brief moment she asked, "What are your aspirations, Peter? Your life dreams? Are they different now?"

Peter sighed and sank back into his chair. "That's the problem, Ang. I don't know what my dreams are anymore. I used to think I'd retire, we'd get an RV and do some traveling like we always said we would do. But then that began to feel like just a new set of bars on the same old trap. I don't know what I'm saying, except...I have realized I have to figure out what I want or I'm a mess. Meanwhile, I'm dragging you and the kids through all this..." Peter slouched deeper into his chair.

"Divorcing you was a way of cutting the line...so that I didn't have to ruin your lives, too."

All of us sat quietly for a few moments. Then Angie spoke up very softly. "Pete. Don't say that. For crying out loud, don't you worry about me right now. What I want is for you to find your dreams. To be happy again." She paused and added, "Even if it means I'm not in them." Peter peered at Angie, with a bit of wariness but also softness on his face.

I sat forward, speaking slowly. "You both are getting it. This is having the dialogue. You are doing really well. As you can see, there is a lot more to be said about this topic. This is the first discussion, not the last. I want Angie to have a turn now." She handed Peter the laminated handout. Again, Peter shifted in his chair and examined the sheet before him. He began, "Okay, now. Let's start with your position about me moving out."

"Well, I hate it!" she responded briskly. Both smiled, if a bit sadly. As small as this gesture seemed, I chalked it up as a positive indicator in the fondness and admiration level—a little bit of teasing, of humor, that was received by the other. It was these sorts of cracks in their armored marriage I was looking for.

Angie continued more seriously. "You know, Peter...yes, I hate it that you're gone and that I have to come up with some explanation for everybody who asks."

"Just tell them I'm a jerk."

"Don't worry—I do." Again, the small, roguish smiles. "Actually, Peter, it isn't that easy. But what I was going to say is, really, the worst part for me is not understanding why you left. It seemed so out of the blue. Granted, things weren't great the last few years, but I did think they were getting better since I retired. I just had no idea you were so unhappy. . . . " Tears began to well up in her eyes. "And all I wanted was to know what I could do to make it better for you. Even if that means you have to divorce me. I just want to know what we're doing!"

Peter looked at a loss as to what to say. I couldn't blame him—I wasn't doing much better myself. So we sat there in an awkward silence for some minutes while I pondered different choices. I finally decided on the old therapeutic standby: If all else fails, ask someone how he or she is feeling. I made this suggestion to Peter. He complied and asked her.

Wiping her tears, Angie answered, "Oh, I don't know. Sad, I guess. Unwanted. Confused."

Peter drew from the sheet before him. "Is this symbolic for you in any way?"

Angie paused and stared off. "Well, actually, yes. You leaving me symbolizes that I've failed as a wife. But also, it's almost as if it challenges everything I've ever believed in. It makes me wonder . . . wonder if everything I had believed in was just a fantasy. You know, if I'm the good, dutiful wife, the kind and attentive mother, I will have a happy, healthy family. Well, all that has been blown to smithereens now." As if to make her point, she blew her nose.

Peter asked, "So your world is sort of falling apart, too?"

"Yes, Peter, my world has crumbled. At first it was awful—I couldn't believe it and I blamed it all on you, of course. But these past couple of months— probably because of some of the books I've been reading or something—I've been wondering if this was inevitable. I don't mean you moving out but rather that my illusions had to come crashing down around me. I don't really know . . . just some random thoughts I've been having."

Peter seemed quite interested in what his wife was describing. "Okay," he said, "Let's try this one next." He glanced down and read from the sheet in his hand. "What are your life aspirations or dreams?"

Angie peered at him. "Do you really want to know or are you just fulfilling the exercise?" This bit of spunk on Angie's part took me by surprise. I filed the information away for later use.

"No, it's not just the exercise. I really am curious about your dreams."

"Well, okay. You know how much I loved doing art projects with my students?"

Peter nodded.

"Well, I've been looking into graphic design schools."

Peter's eyebrows went up. "You have?"

"Yes, in Seattle."

Angie tentatively described what she had researched. A couple of times I stepped in to assist Peter in differentiating between statements that were opinions and ones that were clarifying or supportive.

After the intervention was over, I checked in with the couple.

"So, how was that exercise?"

Peter nodded his head. "Pretty interesting. I had no idea how much I didn't know about Angie."

Angie concurred that the exercise had had some interesting and insightful components. Doors had opened, if only slightly, between them. They had had a taste of a different kind of interaction around this very difficult topic. It would be a process we returned to frequently throughout the course of treatment.

I often give couples in crisis homework assignments, sometimes because doing so can help me with my own anxiety about a difficult couple (at least I'm doing something!). But also, in a case like this, I want to give them some structure outside of the therapy sessions. To say Peter and Angie's old marital home had toppled to the ground was an understatement. These two were at a loss as to what to say or do when alone with one another, except when it came to handling "business." Assignments could give them a new foundation upon which to relate. To try these, they needed to separate talking about the "business" of their lives (something both were familiar and comfortable with and upon which they fell back when they were uneasy with each other) from more "personal" conversations. They needed to move from feeling wary of one another toward feeling more trusting and comfortable. A new avenue just might give them that possibility. Their first assignment was a combination of two exercises: the "stress-reducing conversation" and alternating leadership on dinners together.

I began with the stress-reducing conversation. "This is how it goes: One of you is the speaker. The speaker is to talk about what's on your mind and what's in your heart—both, the stress in your life and also the excitement, opportunities, and joys. The one topic I want you to avoid at this time is your marriage. Talk about anything else: your work, the stock market, the kids, something that happened to you that day that was meaningful in some way. Meanwhile, the listener's job is to listen, ask clarifying questions, and offer support. Don't try to offer solutions unless the speaker wants you to—just try to be a good ally. Each person gets between 10 and 20 minutes to be the speaker."

Ideally, a couple does this frequently over a week. With an emotionally distant couple, it's wise to start them out more slowly. In this case, I recommended twice a week. It's important to give a couple assignments in which they can experience some success. Peter and Angie's rituals of connection at that time were a few weekly phone calls and dinner approximately once a week. Because Peter was no longer in the home, there was a fair amount of business that had to be attended to. I asked if they could take care of business in their phone calls or e-mails and be willing to meet twice a week for dinner. Yes, they thought they could. I then asked that they alternate leadership on the evenings out. This means the person in leadership thinks about where he or she wants to go or do; if one would like to take in a movie, perhaps, or a walk, one proposes the idea to the other. With this intervention I was trying to move them away from the common married-couple mentality of "we're just having dinner out" and toward one person taking charge, giving the evening some thought, and offering leadership, which is more reminiscent of dating. During the evening out they were also to have their stress-reducing conversation.

I explained, "This exercise can feel a bit mechanical or awkward at first. We are self-conscious and awkward the first time we do most things—driving a car, writing a report, or kissing someone. So let's have a practice run here. Again, remember that this is not the place to discuss your feelings of discontent in your marriage, only the stresses outside of it. So who would like to be the speaker?"

Peter and Angie looked at one another. Peter shrugged and said, "I guess I could start."

"Great. I will slip in and assist you if needed."

Peter sat for a few moments looking down while Angie gazed at him with anticipation. Peter then took a deep breath and began. "Well, I guess I could talk to you about some of the changes going on at work. You remember that new foreman I hired about 6 months ago?" He went on to describe some of his current work challenges. Angie listened attentively and asked appropriate questions. When they were done, I congratulated them, noted how well they had done, and then asked Angie to take on the role as speaker. She squirmed in her chair.

"Well...I don't really have much to say." Peter looked at her intently as she stumbled around for words. "I...well, I had thought that by now I would be doing *something*. Substituting or volunteering myself as a tutor somewhere or something. But the truth is I haven't had any desire or energy for much of anything." Angie laughed nervously. "If I can't talk about our marriage, I can't think of what else to talk about. I know you're not interested in hearing about the housework I do or the bills I pay for us. Or my gardening. I can't talk about my conversations with our kids, because...."

We had hit a land mine. Angie's primary stress—what she thought about day and night—was their fractured marriage. She ruminated daily on why Peter had moved out and what she could do differently to change things. She found she had nothing to say that was outside the marriage. Knowing their strength in the SRH was at the seventh level—common goals, roles, philosophies, and dreams—I cast the net a bit broader and encouraged Angie to instead talk about her dreams.

Angie paused. "I don't know what to say. I flip-flop between the dreams that include Pete and the ones..." Her implication hung in the air.

I stepped in. "Sometimes the topic in the stress-reducing conversation can be quite intense. But much of the time it's lighter. You know, about something that grabbed your attention that day, or that week... something you saw or something you've read recently."

Angie tried again and this time shared a recent insight gained in the individual therapy that she had recently begun.

Once they understood the concept of the stress-reducing exercise, I went to the next item on my agenda. Peter needed to assume more responsibility for his depression and his unhappiness rather than projecting it onto Angie and their perpetual problems. To this end, he needed to identify what triggered or amplified his low moods and, simultaneously, explore what excited him and engaged him. (Peter had refused psychotropic medication when his individual therapist recommended it. I also believed it would be advantageous for him, but I didn't feel I yet had the clout to encourage him in that direction.)

So I asked Peter where in his current life he felt alive, where he felt joy. How did he connect to himself and to others in his life? After a few minutes, he began to describe times when he was able to hang out on the site with his workers, when there was a time crunch and he'd pick up a hammer and together they'd meet their deadline, bantering, cursing, joking, and supporting one another all the way. As he spoke of these times, he became animate and had a gleam in his eye. He mentioned he was most comfortable with these guys, as they were blunt and straightforward. Remembering his strong desire for clarity in his marriage, I took this as permission to be quite direct with him. However, I also recognized that he might not desire the same style from a female professional. Peter was goal-oriented and liked and took pride in getting his tasks done. Homework would give him a way to break down the changes asked of him into small, digestible bits, as well as give him a clear focus. He needed a tool put into his hand.

We came up with the idea of a daily chart, using his own words, such as *charged, alive, juiced, dead, depressed,* and *uninterested* (I vetoed *bored*). Peter was proud of his expertise with computers, so we drew a sketch in my office of a chart that he could then put on his computer. The adjectives were placed vertically on the left-hand side of the page, and a timeline in 3-hour increments was placed horizontally. Each column was for a particular 3-hour block of time. Peter then proceeded to chart his "aliveness," noting in the spaces what he was doing/thinking that contributed to feeling "dead" or "alive." The goals here were twofold: to assist Peter in taking responsibility for his inner states by recognizing the multitude of factors coming to play, and to give him a concrete way of understanding his own patterns and needs.

He eagerly tackled the assignment, proudly bringing in his charts each week and describing what he saw in them. In the second treatment session, as Peter was going over what he had learned that week from his charting, Angie noted, "I haven't seen you this animated in a long time!"

Peter paused and practically glared at her. "I'm like this every day at my job. You just never took any interest in what I do there!"

His hostility surprised Angie and me. *Defensiveness and criticism,* I silently noted. Which meant he had heard Angie's statement as an attack.

Into the tense silence I softly asked, "Peter, what did you hear Angie saying to you right then?" Angie was sitting tensely, biting her lip, fighting back tears, no doubt blaming herself for his outburst.

"Well, she said that I've been a jerk! That...that...I was some deadbeat at home."

I looked at Peter's red face and Angie's scared look. I thought: Do I educate them about flooding and self-soothing? Or do I do a "Dan Wile"? The tension in the room seemed to hold a lot of hidden meaning, which I wanted to mine and not sidestep.

"Is this a familiar place for the two of you?" I asked quietly.

"You've got that one right," Peter said with a snort. Angie nodded and blew her nose. In Dan Wile style, I said, "What I want to do now is to further this conversation for the two of you. I believe there is more here than meets the eye. I know there's a lot I'm wanting to understand about the tension in the room. Toward that end I'm going to encourage you both to continue this discussion, but at times I will step in and speak for one of you. When I do, your job is to clarify if what I said is true for you or not. Okay?"

Peter did not look convinced but he nodded curtly. Angie indicated that she was game.

"Peter, I want to start with you, Okay? I'll speak to Angie as if I'm you. When I'm done, modify or correct what I've said." Peter raised the left corner of his mouth wearily and lightly rolled his eyes, shrugging an "all right." I noted the hopelessness emerging as derision and contempt. For the moment, I stayed on task with wanting to understand each of their stories more fully. The contempt I would tackle later.

"Okay, then." I looked at Angie and saw that her gaze was on me. I sat forward in my seat, clasped my hands in front of me, and looked down, trying to gather words for how I was perceiving Peter's position based on his defensive response. A few moments passed and I began.

"I don't think you really meant to criticize me by what you said just now, Angie, but the fact is I felt criticized. For most of my life I've had someone breathing down my neck about what I'm doing right or not right." I suddenly remembered Peter's stories about his mother's very high expectations of him and of her style of teaching through criticism. "Yeah, yeah, my mom adored me, but you know how sharp her tongue could be." Angie nodded. "Well, if it wasn't you telling me everything I've done wrong, how I've spoiled everything, then I've been telling myself."

I glanced over at Peter. His eyes were glued to me, so I kept going.

"I guess what I need to tell you is, I just can't take that anymore. I don't want to make you wrong—I know you have your own feelings and needs—but I just can't take feeling criticized by you or anyone else anymore."

To Peter I said, "Okay. What fit and what didn't there?"

He rubbed his chin and then said, "I don't think it was as bad as you make it sound, how my mom treated me, but besides that, you've got it pretty well."

"Okay." I turned to Angie. "So now, Angie, please respond to Peter as if he had just said what I said."

"I . . . I had no idea, Peter. Well, I guess I did. I know I can be controlling at times. The house has always been my domain and you know I like things a certain way. But I never meant to be critical of you. Never! And I've *never* thought of you as a deadbeat!" There was a pleading and a whining tone to Angie's response. Angie had come to believe that Peter had moved out because she wasn't witty enough, fun enough, or spontaneous enough. Peter was "bored" with her. She easily recalled statements he had made prior to moving out that supported her interpretation. As a result, Angie came to the therapy with an agenda to understand what she could do differently to make Peter happy. Her one-down position wasn't going to help the situation. Neither was Peter's penchant to hear criticism in neutral statements.

Peter paused, looked at me, then at Angie.

"Well, you're damn right the house is your domain. You chose the furniture, you chose the wall colors, you chose the china. I don't see why you want me there at all—you have the damned house!"

Angie's voice was desperate. "Damn it, Peter! I don't want our little perfect house! I want you. I never asked your opinion because you were so busy. I thought it would burden you to drag you into all of those decisions. I never thought you were interested! Let's sell the silly place and start all over."

Peter paused and pondered his hands in his lap. I waited.

"Don't do that, Angie. Let's just wait and see. Let's just wait."

Peter was pulling back, whereas Angie wanted more engagement. One of my goals with this couple was to assist them in clearly speaking their needs and wants to one another and sidestepping their attack-defend pattern. I turned to Angie.

"Angie, I want you to tell Peter what it is you are needing and wanting from him at this point in time."

This was harder for Angie. Her frame of reference was to find out what she needed to change to keep Peter around, not ask directly for what she needed.

"Well, I don't know. . . ." She pondered my question for a while. "I guess what I would like is for Peter to want to spend time with me . . . but how can I ask that of someone? Either he does or he doesn't!" Angie was close to tears.

"You're right. We can't ask someone to *want* to be with us. But we can voice what we like and don't like, and to give our needs and wants a voice. Say, if we would like to go out to a particular place or hear some music. Or to ask our partner to speak respectfully to us." Angie nodded as I continued. "In a marriage each person is both a teacher and a student to the other. For example, no two people feel or express caring in the same way, so we need to let our partner know what does or doesn't work. You could ask Peter for some action that shows you that he cares about you. In this way you are being a teacher to him."

Angie thought about this for a while and then spoke up. "I would really appreciate it if you would tell your mother about the separation. I don't answer the phone for fear it's her. I just can't keep lying to her for you." Peter had been adamant that his parents not know that he no longer lived with Angie. Since he had moved out close to 6 months earlier, she had been keeping up a facade with them.

Peter stared down at his hands. "You're right. That hasn't been fair to you. I'll think about that one."

There was a short silence. Then I spoke up.

"Do you both feel a difference in how you are talking now compared to when you started this discussion?" I reminded them that the discussion had begun with Peter describing what he had learned about himself using his daily mood chart, and how an innocent statement by Angie had set them off. They agreed they felt less tense and defensive.

From this point we turned to discussing the four horsemen. I asked which ones they recognized in their marriage. They conceded that they saw all four. I clarified to them that I would now begin to stop them and identify the horsemen as they spoke.

Closely related to the horsemen is flooding. With most emotionally disengaged couples, I try to work in a discussion about flooding within the first three sessions. As flooding is the first step of the distance and isolation cascade, it is critical to teach a couple how to recognize it and how to respond to it. The best time to teach self-soothing is when someone is actually flooded in the therapy session.

I didn't have to wait long for the opportunity to arise with Angie and Peter. In a terse interchange, I asked them both to stop and take their pulses. Peter's was 111 and Angie's was 124. After describing DPA, I had them come up with a time-out signal. They chose the signal of putting one's hand over one's eyes. Then I gave them the instructions for a time-out: "Either one of you can use the signal at any time. Whoever gives the signal is the one in leadership. What this means is you are then responsible for making sure a break is taken, anywhere from 30 minutes to a few hours. You are the one who will be responsible for setting a time, no sooner than 30 minutes and no longer than a week after the time-out signal was given, when the two of you will sit down and discuss the issue that catapulted you into the flooding or the four horsemen. That person, the one in charge, is responsible for remembering the topic, for making sure the follow-up meeting happens, and for setting the tone of that meeting."

Typically there is one person in a marriage who will not—or feel like he or she cannot—stop an interaction when it is going nowhere but downhill. The reasoning typically is: "We never finish our discussions. If I let him/her walk away, we'll never finish this one." Many times these individuals are also trying to manage their anxiety by keeping the dialogue going. I try to convey that when someone is flooded, nothing gets resolved. Indeed, to follow one's partner and keep the fight going only makes things worse. The person who is leaving needs to calm down. The person who "stays" needs the reassurance that the topic will be discussed. Having the conversation later generally increases the possibility of discussing it calmly, giving the couple a much better chance of having a productive dialogue.

In the following weeks and months, I assisted Angie and Peter in recognizing when one or both of them were flooded. On numerous occasions I had them practice the visual clue, as well as the steps following it.

With these tools in place—dreams-within-conflict, stress-reducing conversation, weekly rituals for connections, a time-out signal and steps for follow-through as a response to flooding, and Peter's monitoring his moods—we were in the swing of therapy. Each week Peter would bring in his chart and talk about what it revealed to him. He noted he woke up feeling optimistic, but the minute his thoughts went to Angie, he felt guilty, which led him to feeling blue. Successfully meeting challenges at work raised his spirits. But even with that, he found he suffered from low mood, low energy, hopeless thinking every afternoon around 3 or 4 P.M. and in the later evening. He also found that drinking alcohol worsened his evening blues. Peter's new therapist wouldn't let him linger too long on blaming his depressed state on his marriage. Clearly the broken state of his marriage and the resulting loneliness and disengagement contributed to Peter's depression—but it wasn't its sole source.

During this time, Peter's father suffered a stroke. Peter's own expectation of himself, and those expressed by his parents to him, highlighted his role in his family as the son who could make everything right. Through all of this Peter began to examine his parents' expectations for him and what Angie did that triggered his anger and rebellion at those expectations, along with his guilt when he didn't meet them. This work also served to help clarify his priorities. It became clearer to him just how important the values of family, commitment, and perseverance were to him. While he was in Montana assisting his parents with his father's illness, he ran into an old best friend—who was taking Prozac. His friend openly discussed his own need for medication and how it had helped him. Peter returned more open to the idea of medication for himself.

Over time, Peter began to see how his depression permeated every aspect of his life and how it had contributed to the breakdown of his marriage. He also began to identify what he needed to feel more alive—both in his life and in his marriage. Our work in my office assisted him in asking for what he needed without falling back on criticism or defensiveness. For instance, he needed Angie to let him join her more in the kitchen, cutting the vegetables any way he wanted. Living alone he had found he enjoyed cooking and he wanted to see if he could enjoy it with her.

Angie's work, the brunt of which she did with her individual therapist, was to not fall into thinking "I'll do whatever he wants just to keep him" but rather to identify her own needs, sexual and otherwise, and to begin to voice them. In my office, Angie's work was to look at her part in the crumbling of the marriage without taking all of it on: to look at her passive-aggressive behaviors and how she had gotten what she wanted in the past from Peter by using innuendo and guilt. It took much longer for Angie to get clear on her needs and to feel comfortable asserting them. She eagerly took my instructions on what was and wasn't criticism, defensiveness, and contempt.

By the third-month check-in, the couple's rituals of connection were more frequent and more satisfying for both of them. They reported finding themselves falling naturally into the stress-reducing conversations and were having them three to five times a week. It took several weeks for them to get the hang of using their time-out signal outside of the office. When they did start using it, it typically was Peter who initiated it; Angie rarely wanted to disengage. They reported that when they did return after the time-out to discuss whatever the topic had been, they were able to talk about it more calmly. Peter surprised Angie at the three-month check-in with a weekend away for the two of them—their first time away alone in years.

As their fondness for one another returned, they resumed a sexual connection. Peter requested that Angie explore some sexual fantasies of his. He also wanted Angie to join him in a class on God and physics. Peter wanted to reexamine some of the spiritual beliefs he had learned as a boy and he wanted someone to talk to about these explorations. Angie jumped at these opportunities, although each area took a fair amount of negotiating, dialogue, and compromising.

With the time-out process mitigating the arguments that had previously eroded goodwill between them, and their rituals of connection beginning to restore a sense of closeness and friendship, we began the next tier of therapy: continuing with building the friendship while developing more skills for handling conflict. We began by exploring the difference between solvable and perpetual problems, as well as the different means for approaching them.

Understanding perpetual problems helped Peter put some of their earlier conflicts into perspective: It wasn't the issues that were the problem, but how he and Angie had gridlocked over them rather than using dialogue, compromise, and acceptance. He began to successfully apply the concept of perpetual problems to his work life, where some employees were in gridlock with other employees.

Gottman's concept of enduring vulnerabilities also can be helpful with couples like this. I find it reduces defensiveness and encourages softened start-up for people. This is how I introduce it: "There is something called enduring vulnerabilities. We all have them. They are our individual vulnerabilities that endure over time. Experiencing pain or rejection is a part of everyone's life, but when some pain has been especially deep or repeated, it may develop into an enduring vulnerability. One example is a young girl whose father leaves the family when she is 12. She becomes pregnant at 17 and her boyfriend abandons her. Eventually she marries a man and together they have a good marriage for 6 or 7 years. At that time she learns that a year earlier, while he was inebriated, he had slept with a woman who was their neighbor and whom his wife had considered a friend. The husband feels horrible about his betrayal, takes full responsibility, and truly wants to mend the damage he has caused. Is she going to stay? Probably not. This isn't her first major betrayal by an important man in her life, but her third. So she leaves her husband and continues on as a single mom. Some years later she and another man fall in love. She sees him on the dance floor at a party and falls in love with his gracefulness and warmth. They become committed to one another. But this man loves to dance, and this woman is far too shy to dance with him in public. When they go to parties, he wants to dance. *She* wants him to dance. She trusts him. But as she watches him with other women something tightens up inside. This is her enduring vulnerability. It isn't his fault. It isn't *her* fault. It simply is what she brings to this relationship. If his response to her anxiety is defensiveness and criticism—What's wrong with you? I'm not flirting; I'm not going home with anyone but you. I'd dance with you if you'd only get over your shyness!—you can imagine how that would affect her. She would probably close up to him over time. But if he is able to see it isn't his fault that his sweetheart has this vulnerability, and if he is able to respond with understanding, then he and his girlfriend will move closer together. For instance, if he could say, 'Hon, I know it sometimes bothers you when I dance with other women but at other times you're fine with it. The problem is, I can't tell the difference. Could we come up with a private signal that you give me? When I see it, I'll stop the dance as gracefully as I can, and come and sit by you. Would that help? Or do you have other ideas?' "

I used this concept of enduring vulnerability with Peter and his experience of taking neutral statements as criticism. We were able to capture his sensitivity to neutral statements on videotape. We would then play them back and let Peter describe what he "heard" as opposed to quibbling over what Angie had said. As we continued to work with this issue, both of them came to see that Peter was highly sensitive to feeling criticized, even when Angie's statements were benign. Angie then began to see it wasn't something she was doing, and this helped her to not respond defensively. Once Peter was able to own that he did indeed have this enduring vulnerability, he took his defensiveness as an indicator that he had felt attacked—and understood that it was his job to check out with Angie if what he *believed* she had said was what she had wanted to say.

By our fifth month of working, Angie and Peter were negotiating to have him move back into the family home. They were meeting on their own several times a week and going away for weekends once or twice a month. They rediscovered their love of hiking and bird-watching. They learned to hold the difficult conversations for a time when both felt rested and were ready to discuss the topic at hand. We practiced dream-within-conflict and aftermath of a marital argument often in my office, so they could access those processes at home. Peter still questioned if he wouldn't have been happier if he had met a woman with whom he felt a "spark," but he came to accept his decision to stay in this marriage and to see the gifts it had to offer him. From her individual therapy, Angie developed stronger assertiveness skills and a clearer picture of what she wanted in her life, with or without Peter. By their eighth month of therapy, she still bent to his will more often than not, but on the topics that mattered most to her, she held her ground in ways she hadn't before.

CONCLUSION

The emotionally distant couple can be a challenge. Obviously, the case offered here is of a successful therapy. It certainly looks easier on paper than it feels in the office. Generally speaking, the first step is to assess if there is enough left in the marriage to build upon. Does each member of the couple have the motivation to do the work to rebuild the basic structures of friendship in their marriage? Without these elements on your side, therapy would be an uphill battle. With them, there is hope. There certainly are times when the answers to these two questions aren't completely clear, which is what I tried to illustrate with this case.

Using dream-within-conflict early on in treatment, and often thereafter, can do a lot to loosen the affectless mire an emotionally distant couples lives within and to begin the process of creating bridges of connection. Next, assist the couple in building a structure into their weekly lives of rewarding rituals of connection (common activities, the stress-reducing conversation, and so on). Meanwhile, there needs to be some stopgap measure for the interactions that disintegrate into the attack-defend pattern (the time-out agreement). Finally, new processes for handling conflict are taught: how to process fights, learning to dialogue through perpetual problems, and learning the skills of compromise. Certainly the ultimate goal is to assist the emotionally disengaged couple in becoming emotionally reengaged with each other and with their own lives.

REFERENCES

Boegner, I., & Zielenbach-Coenen, H. (1984). On maintaining change in behavioral marital therapy. In K. Hahlweg & N. S. Jacobsen (Eds.), *Marital interaction: analysis and modification* (pp. 27–35). New York: Guilford Press.

Chapter 9 ✻

Stepfamily Issues and the Sound Relationship House

Trudi Sackey

My first encounter with John Gottman's principles of the SRH was in 1996. Having worked with couples for many years, I was looking to refresh my skills and was intrigued by Gottman's research-based model. The idea of developing interventions from empirical evidence of how couples actually interact, rather than from a therapist's idealized notion, struck me as both compassionate and compelling. The SRH theory gave me a framework to hold much of what I already had observed and believed to be true in working with couples.

My former beliefs were confirmed. It is easier to address difficult issues with a partner that you believe likes you (emotional bank account). A positive perspective also helps relationships go smoothly. Likewise, conflict can be more easily resolved if couples treat each other as well as they would a houseguest. Gottman had elegantly observed and stated the obvious.

As that first 2-day training continued, I thought about these ideas and how they played out in the lives of the couples in my practice and in my own life. At that time, I was newly engaged to a man who had never been married and had no children. My daughter from my previous long-term marriage was a young adult. I wondered how the SRH principles would play out in the stepfamily couple I was about to form. I wondered, too, how they would apply to the issues and concerns of the stepfamily couples with whom I worked.

I had for some time been a professional affiliate of the Stepfamily Association of America (SAA), pioneered by researchers Drs. Emily and John Visher. This organization is dedicated to all aspects of support for stepfamilies, including the education of the public and clinicians about stepfamily life. SAA also advocates for stepfamilies through its support of interface among researchers, clinicians, and public policy makers.

The United States Census Bureau statistics and research suggest that one out of three Americans is now a stepparent, stepchild, stepsibling, or some other member of a stepfamily (Larson, 1992). More than half of Americans today have been, are now, or will eventually be in one or more step situations. The most common stepfamilies where children reside are stepfather families or combined stepfather-stepmother families. In the latter case, the stepfather's children from the prior marriage typically do not reside in the stepfamily.

According to research there are few differences in happiness or satisfaction reported between first-married and remarried couples (Vemer, Coleman, Gagnon, & Cooper, 1989). Bringing children into marriage doesn't lower the odds of marital success (Martin & Bumpass, 1989). Likewise, there was found to be no difference in the frequency of marital conflict in first-married and remarried couples, particularly if both adults are remarried (MacDonald & DeMaris, 1995).

Among the factors affecting marital quality and stability for stepfamily couples are the quality of stepparent-stepchild relationships, with stepfather-stepchild quality key to wives' satisfaction. Ambiguity of role expectations for stepmothers and their relationships with children was cause for instability in marital relationship (Bray, Berger, & Boethel, 1994). Further research concluded that higher attachment to the former spouse decreases intimacy in remarriage (Gold, Bubenzer, & West, 1993). And when role expectations are realistic and boundaries with former spouses are clearly defined, marital satisfaction is higher (Weston & Macklin, 1990). Research also found that a key to stepfamily stability is a mutually satisfying couple relationship (Bray et al., 1994; Brown, Green, & Druckman, 1990).

I wondered how the Gottman SRH theory could be useful in working with the growing numbers of stepfamily couples in my practice. What are the commonalties in first-married couples and remarried couples with children, and what are the differences? I was interested to know what aspects of the SRH theory could be particularly useful with stepfamily couples. Good marital adjustment was a thread common to all marital satisfaction. By putting together what I had learned about the normal stages of development in remarried families and applying the principles of the SRH theory to the couple interaction, I hoped to have a useful working model for working with stepfamily couples.

A stepfamily, like all relationship systems, is in a state of becoming. The normal stages of stepfamily development as described by Papernow (1992) include a seven-part cycle. They range from the burden of fantasy, based on misconception and unrealistic expectations of the early stages of development, to the mature stages in which authenticity and resolution of stepfamily relationships can occur.

I view partners coming together in remarriage with children as travelers from two different established cultures and histories, where grief through death or divorce is part of the cultural landscape. The longing of the human heart to reconnect in love, despite its having been broken, is a glorious phenomenon. In remarriage each partner has taken the opportunity to become once again hopeful and willing to risk that marriage can be a safe place for making dreams for one's self, love, and family come true.

I conjectured that the SRH methods and the understanding of stepfamily developmental stages could be woven together as I worked to help couples navigate the complicated stepfamily landscape. The following assessment and treatment of a stepfamily couple is a clinical example of this synthesis.

LISA AND DAVE

Lisa, 40, and Dave, 43, came to the clinic, self-referred. This marriage was the second for both of them. Lisa had been widowed 2 years before she met Dave. Her daughter from that marriage, Pam, who was now 17, lived with her and Dave. Dave had divorced his previous wife in his late twenties. He had two children from that marriage: Zach, who was now 19 and away at college, and Sarah, who was 16. Both had lived with Dave, and with Lisa and Dave after they married, since the divorce.

History

Lisa and Dave had recently separated after 8 years of marriage. Both were distraught and confused. They considered each other their "best friend," but for the past several months anything they attempted to talk about became an angry shouting match. They became so alarmed about the fighting that they were afraid to engage in even small talk together. Their sexual relationship, which had been a source of comfort and pleasure for both of them, had all but stopped. The fights had become so frequent lately that Lisa became worried about anxiety in Pam, who was involved in a highly competitive academic program. Lisa was concerned about the effect of the "blowups" on Pam's chances of success. Dave agreed that the fighting was bad for Pam and had reluctantly moved out of the family home to a rented condo in their neighborhood. He continued to share parenting duties for Pam's after-school activities. Dave missed being with Lisa and Pam, especially because Zach, had gone off to college the previous year. "Stanford University," Lisa proudly interjected. Dave said that his daughter Sarah had gone to spend a year with her mother in California. Dave explained that, although Sarah had visited with her mother in recent years, she had not lived with her since he had gained sole custody of his children at the time of his divorce.

Dave's ex-spouse, Vicky, had become addicted to cocaine and gambling after Sarah's birth. Vicky's behaviors had been emotionally and financially costly to Dave. He had loved her and did everything he could to help her, but when she began to neglect and endanger the children, Dave had to take action. At age 29 he found himself a single father. He became a real hands-on dad. With the support of his parents and siblings, Dave was able to care for his children. Now that he was no longer worried about their safety, Dave was able to rebuild his accounting practice.

"It hasn't been easy for Vicky," Dave explained. "Over the years she's gotten help for her problems and has become a chemical dependency counselor herself. She's really pulled herself out of a bad place." He went on: "About 6 years ago Vicky married a good guy named Ron. Zach has visited his mother in the past 5 years but never seems to really connect deeply. He's always wanted to come home early to be with his pals. Sarah, on the other hand, really enjoys the time with Vicky and Ron, especially when Ron's little boy is with them. He's 8 and Sarah just loves him. She practically begged us to spend this year with Vicky."

Lisa and Dave didn't like the idea of Sarah's being away for so long, but agreed, as long as Sarah kept her grades up and returned home for her senior year. "Besides," said Dave, "She wanted it so much and I have to say that Vicky has worked so hard to be a better mother, I felt guilty saying no."

The room became silent. I noticed a red flush beginning to creep up Dave's neck and redden his cheeks. His breathing became shallow as he noticed Lisa looking distractedly at her fingernails, her mouth pursed. Lisa shot Dave a daggered look and turned to me. "I am so sick of Dave telling everyone what a transformed angel Vicky has turned out to be! My God, the woman has put us all through hell! Granted, she has made changes—and good ones—for the kids, but the way Dave tells it, we should all be grateful she's in our lives!"

I noted Lisa's affect and strong reaction to Dave's story. "It sounds like you've been through a lot together," I said. After a short time, Lisa nodded. I saw that Dave's face was becoming more flushed as he noticed Lisa sighing and rolling her eyes.

Dave broke the prolonged silence, speaking with considerable annoyance. "Look, Lisa, of all the people in the world, I'd expect you to be the one to understand. You are a mother! I really don't get why Sarah's and Vicky's need to be together is so upsetting to you!"

Lisa sat very still, stone-faced as if she had left the room.

I took note of the contempt I saw in Lisa's eye rolling, and the flush of Dave's neck and face, which could indicate flooding. I also noted Dave's cautious, prolonged silence before he voiced his frustration, as well as his criticism and contempt of his wife for not understanding Sarah's need. Finally, I took note of Lisa's stonewalling. The four horsemen were definitely present here. This was a conflict-avoidant and characteristically soft-spoken couple. Each partner was highly sensitized to anger and conflict in their families of origin. The effects of criticism, defensiveness, contempt, and stonewalling, which lead to flooding and emotional disengagement, would need to be brought to their awareness. I had noted in the Gottman assessment packet that each had rated high on flooding and four horsemen. Their attempts at repairing conflict were also rated as needing improvement. I had not seen physical or emotional abuse noted in their written assessments. This exchange between Lisa and Dave, which for a less avoidant couple could seem mild, was for them very painful.

I waited a few minutes for their flooding to deescalate and asked if this was the kind of "blowup" they had talked about earlier in the interview. They both nodded sadly.

"We'll be looking at the ways that you've learned to express differences in feelings between you in your marriage," I said.

"Or haven't!" quipped Dave, catching Lisa's eye. They exchanged a brief smile.

Repair attempt received, I thought.

"Well, I'm ready to learn a new way," said Lisa.

Dave followed with, "Me too."

Willing to accept influence, I thought. "Setting a positive intention is a good start," I said. I was feeling hope for Lisa and Dave and wanted to offer it to them.

Returning to the oral history interview, I asked the couple, "How did you meet?"

Lisa was first to reply. "Our kids introduced us," she said.

Dave went on to say, "It's been a running joke, our kids gave us away at the wedding."

Lisa continued, "Our wedding invitation said "the children of Lisa and Dave request your presence at the marriage of their parents. Everyone thought it was so cute! The children were friends at the extended day care. That was 10 years ago now. We'd go for pizza with the kids sometimes. The girls especially have always been great friends. They'd have sleepovers and we'd share birthdays. Before we knew it, we became like a family."

"Lisa was such a big help to me," said Dave. "I didn't know half as much as she did about what Sarah might need. Lisa treated Sarah like her own. If she were shopping for Pam she'd include Sarah, too. You know, hair barrettes, stickers, and little stuff. It really meant a lot to me to have Sarah's life somewhat normal."

"It was good for me to keep busy then," said Lisa. My husband, Carl, had died of a sudden heart attack 2 years before. He was just 38 years old! I was just beginning to come around from the shock when I met Dave. Carl was a wonderful man, and we had a good marriage. His mother and I are still friends. Carl left us with enough financial support, I'm grateful to say, but finding a life purpose again was hard. If it weren't for the kids, I don't know what I would have done."

Lisa continued: "Dave and I had a lot in common, both raising children alone. Dave is the most dedicated father I've ever seen. We understood one another. Zach and Sarah, for all they'd been through with Vicky, were really sweet kids. That was Dave's doing. I never heard him say a bad word to either of them about their mom. As angry as I feel right now about Vicky, I still admire Dave for that. Anyway, one thing led to another . . . our families just seemed to fit."

"So, 2 years later," Dave interjected, "we were married with three children between us."

Wanting to understand more about their fondness and admiration system, I shifted the interview to ask about how the couple spent time together and alone, without the children. Dave and Lisa looked at each other and laughed. Lisa started by saying, "I can hardly remember."

"There hasn't been much time," Dave went on. "We did have a honeymoon week, of course—that was a while ago."

"What do you remember about that time?" I asked.

"It was wonderful!" said Lisa. "Really the longest time Dave and I had to be alone since we had met. We rented a cabin in the mountains. We hiked, cooked, and canoed. Remember the bear, Dave?" The couple laughed as their faces softened.

"It seems like a thousand years ago. Yeah, I remember all the flowers you pointed out to me. I'd never known anyone who knew more about the woods." Dave smiled at Lisa. "We used to leave the kids with their grandparents once in a while and go on mushroom hunts. Then as my folks got older it was more difficult for them to take the kids. Anyway, the kids have been so busy with sports and activities. It all takes time." The couple remained silent for a time.

I wanted to understand how Dave and Lisa were turning toward versus turning away from each other in their current life. "It sounds like you both enjoy the outdoors," I said. "How does it figure into your lives these days?"

"We are so involved with other things," explained Lisa, "I can't find the time to take myself for a walk, never mind a date with Dave. We finally got Zach settled in college, and Pam is a senior this year, which means another round of college applications! She is playing select soccer and piano. The schedule is murder! Now I have to worry about Sarah being with Vicky, and how that's going to affect her grades." Lisa began to cry as she lamented, "Everything is falling apart and I'm afraid I'm going to lose Dave."

"I'm scared, too." replied Dave. "I don't want to lose you or our family. I just don't know how to keep everyone happy. Why can't we all just get along?"

"It sounds like you both have a lot at stake," I said. Dave and Lisa looked at each other and nodded. "Can each of you talk about what you would like to see come about in this work in therapy?"

Lisa began. "I want Dave to come home, but the blowups have to stop. I'm so confused about what's going on. Sometimes I even know I'm over the top about Vicky and Sarah. I just don't know why. I have so much I have to do with Pam. Every time Dave and I try to talk it out, there is no time and we get nowhere."

"I'm relieved to hear you say that you want me to come home," said Dave, tearing up. "So much has changed. Lately, I don't know what's happening! Zach is away at school, Sarah's in California most of the time, Pam is so busy. It seems the only time we have together anymore is on the way to or from an event. What happened to us? What a mess! I guess one good thing about this separation is that I've had some time to think when I'm alone. I miss Lisa. It's been a very long time since we've really talked about us. When I try to say what's on my mind it comes out wrong. I want to change the way we talk. I hate the blowups too."

Listening to Lisa and Dave's story, I was struck by the complexity of their family system. Using a family genogram, I noted Lisa, Dave, and their three children, and the strong alliances that remained with their ex-spouses and ex-spouses' families. Lisa's disapproving facial expressions and Dave's physiological responses at the mention of Sarah's going to live with her biological mother were an indication of a gridlocked issue.

All stepfamilies have a history of loss through death or divorce. I wondered what dreams were locked up in these prior relationships. I wondered what meanings could be shared and understood by this couple. Grieving their former marriage issues could facilitate their ability to deepen their present relationship.

In individual interviews with each partner I began to better understand the particular culture of this marriage. I was interested in understanding their meta-emotional structure. Dave and Lisa were both very soft-spoken people. They described themselves as conflict avoiders. Lisa had grown up in a household organized around her rageful father's moods. He would scream and badger Lisa and her brother. Her mother was "helpless" in standing up for herself or her children. Lisa learned to protect herself and her family by becoming the family organizer. She made sure that others took care of their chores, helped her brother with his homework, and picked up the house before Dad got home. She was a straight-A student and had married well.

Dave's family had been conflict avoiders of a different style. Both his parents were social activists and pacifists. His grandparents on his father's side had been missionaries in Africa. He held strong convictions that conflicts could and should be worked out without anger for the greater good. He had childhood experiences of his parents' fostering kids in troubled family situations.

Assessment

I assessed Lisa and Dave's situation from the Gottman SRH theory and from the perspective of stepfamily developmental dynamics, with particular emphasis on the adjustment of the couple. From the perspective of stepfamily couple adjustment (Bray & Kelly, 1998), I was interested in discovering how each spouse had integrated their stepchild's biological parent into his or her way of conceptualizing the family. Lisa was willing to acknowledge the positive changes that Vicky had made in her relationship with Sarah. I wondered what distressed her enough that she continued to so strongly resent Vicky. From the perspective of stepfamily dynamics, I was interested in exploring how this couple was able to manage change in their lives. Lisa and Dave's relationship had been born out of traumatic, unexpected changes in both of their lives. Lisa's loss of Carl through sudden death and Dave's loss of Vicky through addiction and divorce had set them each on a roller-coaster of dramatic changes. They had joined forces against these outside storms and shared pride for their successes with regard to their children. I saw strength in their ability to rally together for the common good of the family. In Gottman language, it was easy to see couple efficacy and to help this couple glorify their struggles. I also wanted to help Lisa and Dave draw on their strengths as a couple.

Dave and Lisa had sustained losses that were important to understand as elements in the relationship. Hope for a happy couple relationship was also an important overriding element. I wanted to support and strengthen Lisa and Dave's hope for a more joyful future together as a couple, while supporting them in honoring each of their past histories.

This couple was efficient at handling chaos and change for others. I wondered, as their children launched into the world, how Dave and Lisa would handle the change of just being a couple for the first time in their 10-year relationship.

In further assessing the needs of this couple, I wanted to understand how successful Lisa and Dave had been at separating from their former marriages. How did they create and understand appropriate boundaries between residential and ex-spouses?

As is common with many stepfamily couples, Dave and Lisa had focused on the well-being of their children to the detriment of their couple relationship. They had organized their family life around creating a "perfect" place for their children. I wondered how their children would describe their family life. How could I help this couple redefine their stepfamily culture? They needed a culture that could honor their past marriages, as well as the relationships between their children and their children's biological parents. They also needed to affirm the struggles and triumphs of their current relationship in order to define themselves as a "we" and strengthen their couple bond.

Dave and Lisa had defined their relationship as parenting partners. I wanted to help them strengthen their friendship and understand the meanings of their resentments regarding Sarah's time with her mother. I believed this could lead to unlocking the gridlocked conflict that had lead to their unwanted separation. Understanding their own meanings and those of their partner could lead to shared meaning for the couple.

I also wanted to consider a family meeting with as many members as possible to get a better idea of the current culture of the stepfamily. I realized this would be difficult. Pam was the only child currently living with Dave and Lisa.

I was concerned with the seemingly unrealistic expectations of perfection that Dave and particularly Lisa were holding of stepfamily. Through psychoeducation in current stepfamily developmental models, I hoped to normalize their struggles and offer them more workable realistic expectations, so that they could move toward satisfying long-term goals for the family. I would also give the couple information about community support groups and reading materials created for stepfamilies.

Incorporating SRH theory, I would facilitate the couple's understanding of their dreams and aspirations, for themselves individually and as a couple. As their children were entering the launching stage of family development, I wanted to help Dave and Lisa make explicit their current shared meaning system. Gottman describes this as a deep interest and knowledge of each other, knowing each other's injuries and healing, knowing each other's strivings and triumphs, and knowing each other's life dreams. I believed that from a perspective of shared meaning, I could help Dave and Lisa understand each other's current frustrations, expectations, and fears, as well as learn the tools for effective conflict discussion and resolution.

In our short time together I had seen the DPA that occurred in each of them when conversation became charged with negative emotion. When DPA occurred, their conversation went off track, the four horsemen came galloping in, and the communication shut down. However, I had also seen the couple offer and accept influence and repair. Even in this time of crisis, there was fondness and admiration and loving memory for the past. They were proud of their accomplishments with their children and of each other. I was hopeful that Dave and Lisa could build on their strengths by learning how to physiologically soothe themselves and each other, soften the start-up of conflict conversation, and become more comfortable in allowing differences in their feelings and needs. The idea here was not to have the couple not engage in conflict, but to help them see that avoiding conflict or differences was actually preventing them from remaining in contact with one another, to the point that they had headed down the distance and isolation cascade.

One of my tasks would be to help them become more comfortable with conflict so they could move the gridlocked issue into a dialogue between them.

Like all of us, Dave and Lisa carried their own personal points of view and philosophies. Growing up in the families they did, they had formed ways of being in the world that included wonderful adaptive strengths and challenging vulnerabilities. Lisa learned to become very competent. The downside of this adaptation was that her own dreams and needs did not occur to her easily, and when they did, she couldn't allow herself to ask for what she wanted. Lisa, in her need to avoid chaos, had become a perfectionist. She held unrealistic expectations of herself and others.

Dave held an adaptive strength of social consciousness and responsibility that he learned in his family of origin. This had helped him move ahead and be accepted in many social settings. The vulnerability for Dave was his difficulty in setting boundaries with others and his guilt for longing to have his own desires and needs met. Dave's anger, which was not allowed to be expressed in his original family, came out in self-righteousness. Understanding, without blame or judgement, each other's positions on the issue of Sarah's year with her mother and the meanings that each position held would begin to provide the safety for Dave and Lisa to explore their needs and goals. This would allow them to move toward workable compromise and problem solving.

Neither of their adaptations to the world left them room for joyful play in their lives. The stories they told about their short honeymoon together pointed out a longing for more. The Gottman assessment paperwork indicated a strong fondness and admiration system, confirming what I heard in the initial interviews. However, the love maps and turning toward assessments indicated a need for improvement. Their emotional bank account was low. I would begin my intervention with them by strengthening the positive perspective in the relationship to create a foundation of safety so they could move toward the reconciliation that they had both voiced they wanted.

Their stepfamily had been evolving since before the beginning of their marriage and would continue to evolve from this time on. I didn't see Sarah's being with her mother for a school year or Lisa's response to her own or Dave's feelings as a crisis event. I characterized each of their responses to Sarah's time away, to Zach's being off at college, and to one another as normal. I pointed out that the ability to handle change is one of the hallmarks of stepfamily adjustment. Big transitional changes such as these often bring out unresolved issues.

To further my understanding of the culture of the stepfamily and of Dave and Lisa's assessment process, I suggested a meeting be set with as many of their children as were available. A time was set for Lisa and Dave to come in with Pam the following week. I wondered about the impact of all of the family changes on Pam. She was the only child to witness her parents' separation firsthand. We talked about the possibility of meeting with all of the stepfamily at a later date.

As this session continued, Dave said, "You know, Lisa, I'm beginning to feel a little calmer about what's going on. I'm still confused, but I think it will turn out all right. We've been through a lot together."

I wondered if Dave was turning toward Lisa or asking for reassurance from her.

Lisa replied, "Yes, we've gotten through a lot together. I want to get through this, too. But I need time to understand what this is about."

I thought Lisa did a good job of validating Dave's statement without discounting her own need for time. She continued, "We've got the rent paid on the condo for the next 30 days. Let's use the time to really work on this."

Dave said, "I agree." Then he laughed and said, "I guess this is what Gottman would call a big time-out!" Lisa gave him a quick grin.

Repair attempt delivered and accepted again, I thought. "I'm glad to hear you're both seeing this time-out as an opportunity to observe and reflect upon the interactions between you," I said, framing their choice as positively as I could.

I asked the couple to discuss needs regarding logistics—bill paying, visits to each other's residence, phone calls and so on—as well as sexual boundaries and expectations between them during the separation time. Dave and Lisa were comfortable with a daily evening phone check-ins. They agreed to have dinner or lunch together on therapy days and joked about its having taken a separation for them to make a date night. The question of sex left them in an awkward silence.

"This is a painful one for me," said Lisa in a small voice. "I love you, Dave, but I just can't do it right now."

"I know, but I just don't understand. Sex used to make us closer," replied Dave sadly.

I let the silence support their grief in this issue for a time. "Sexual closeness has been a painful loss for both of you," I said. "We'll be working on the bottom levels of the SRH, rebuilding your emotional bank account together and getting you reconnected with your love maps and fondness and admiration system. That's where the roots of a good sexual relationship begin. I suggest a moratorium on sexual intercourse until you're both ready to move forward in your sexual relationship."

"That would take the pressure off of not knowing what's expected," Lisa said.

Dave added, "Honestly, for me too." The couple agreed that touching, hand holding, kissing, and even cuddling could be okay, if they both agreed. Once the parameters were set, they both looked brighter and more relaxed.

"I think we've been avoiding each other because we didn't know what we were expected to do," Lisa commented to me. I asked her to turn her chair toward Dave and speak directly to him. I wanted to begin to turn the couple toward each other in their communication, moving the conversation from the traditional triadic marital therapy model into a more dyadic Gottman method form. My goal was, as Dan Wile (1993) said, "to help this couple have the conversations that they needed to have."

As the extended feedback session was coming to an end, I asked the couple to continue reading John Gottman's *Seven Principles for Making Marriage Work*, paying particular attention to the discussion of DPA and flooding, and to begin to notice their own physiological responses to stress and be aware of their own breathing, especially in times of stressful conversation between them. I asked them also to become mindful of the ways in which their partner was turning toward them and their own turning toward their spouse in behaviors and thoughts. I suggested that they do this with as little negative judgement—and as much compassion for themselves and their process—as possible. If they found themselves getting stuck in negativity, I suggested to just notice it and try to let it go. They had given themselves 30 days to focus on understanding issues between them that had taken years to grow. They didn't have to solve them the first day or week of therapy. And it would be okay to have some fun along the way. I would see the couple for an extended 75-minute session once a week, as well as the appointed stepfamily session with Pam and any other family configuration that seemed appropriate.

The couple left discussing where to eat dinner. Their mood was much lighter than when they had arrived.

STEPFAMILY SESSION AND ASSESSMENT

When I entered my office waiting room to greet Dave, Lisa, and Pam, I noticed Lisa sitting on a bench quietly next to her daughter. Dave was sitting across from Pam and Lisa, leafing through a magazine. Lisa introduced Pam, who smiled and said hello as she reached out to shake my hand. As we walked to my office I noticed Pam was neatly dressed and presented in a friendly, adult way. The family arranged themselves with Lisa and Pam claiming the sofa and Dave sitting in a single chair. I began by thanking the family for arranging their schedules to be here together.

Pam replied, "Yes, I'm missing a study group to be here."

Looking a little annoyed Lisa said, "You said it was all right! How are you going to make it up?" Pam looked quickly at Dave, rolling her eyes.

"It will be okay, Lisa, I'm sure she knows what she's doing," Dave said in a placating tone.

Lisa mumbled, "Oh, never mind," and looked at her hands. "We're here now."

I continued, "I'm interested to know, Pam, what do you understand about being here with your parents today?"

"Well, I know they're trying to work out their problems. Dave moved out."

"How is that for you?" I asked. Pam sat in silence for about a minute. She looked at her mom, whose eyes were tearing up. "I hate it," Pam said emphatically. "Now Mom's a mess and I have to take care of everything!"

"That sounds pretty hard."

"Yes, especially with my brother and sister gone, too. I'm stuck with everybody's chores. I'm going to college in the fall. If Mom and Dave don't get back together, what am I supposed to do? "And where is Sarah going to be? She's supposed to be coming back home in the summer."

"There have been a lot of changes to deal with, Pam, and it sounds like you're angry and you're worried about the future," I said.

"Pam, I didn't know you were thinking about all this. You didn't say!" cried Dave.

"How could I?" said Pam angrily to Dave. "Everyone's gone!"

"But, you're doing so well," exclaimed Lisa, tearing up again, "I thought . . . "

"How would you know?" Pam shot toward her mother. "All you think about is Sarah and Vicky."

Lisa's arms crossed her chest as she turned slightly away from Pam on the sofa. Her face tightened and a red flush was creeping up toward her cheeks. Dave was looking down at the floor, suddenly seeming more interested in the carpet pattern than what was being said in the room.

As I observed this exchange, I was struck by the forthright way in which Pam was able to express her feelings. The fact that Lisa and Dave appeared surprised by her anger and worry was consistent with the avoidant emotional style they had presented earlier. Pam had been harboring her feelings for some time and was going to seize this opportunity to tell Dave and Lisa while she had them in the room together. Pam had identified Dave and Lisa's gridlocked issue, which was also gridlocked for the family. The issue could not be talked about without one of the four horsemen showing up.

Acknowledging to the family that it was normal for stepfamily relationships to feel confusing at times, I asked Pam to tell me who was in her family. I began a genogram on the large pad of paper kept on an easel in my office. This would serve to further my assessment and allow Pam to inform Lisa and Dave about how she was viewing the family.

Pam identified Lisa as her mother and Dave as her dad, with Sarah and Zach as her sister and brother. She explained that she had another father, Carl, who had died when she was 5. I included Carl on the genogram as I asked Pam what she remembered about him.

"Not much," she said. Pam gave a sideways glance to her mother and paused.

I made a mental note of Lisa's stonewalled expression and wondered what was behind it.

"So," I said, "Dave is your stepfather and Sarah and Zach your stepsister and stepbrother." I made these adjustments to the genogram as we went along.

"Technically, you could say so," answered Pam. "Dave is my only real father, as far as I see it, though, and Sarah and Zach have been in my life almost as long as I remember."

"Pam, you do have a real father and that's Carl," said Lisa in a tense voice. "He loved you very much."

Pam crossed her arms. "I don't remember that. All I remember about him is the two of you fighting at night and me crying in my bed."

The room was quiet for a while. I noticed Dave's shocked expression as he sank further into his chair. I made another mental note to explore this later, remembering that in the couples session, Lisa had characterized Carl as a "wonderful man."

Pam continued, "You never want to hear the truth! Like with Sarah, she has a real mother and that's Vicky! You expect me to love someone I can't even remember, except to be afraid of, and Sarah isn't supposed to want to be with her own mother who she loves! I don't even tell you when I get e-mail from Sarah because you'll be mad at me for talking to my own sister. Sarah wants me to visit her at Vicky and Ron's house. Sarah has a little brother that I've never even seen!" Pam took a deep breath and softly began to cry. Dave and Lisa looked at Pam and toward each other sadly.

I added Vicky, Ron, and Zach and Sarah's stepbrother, Michael, to the family genogram. This assessment/intervention of the genogram illuminated the complexity of the unexpressed differences in the family. Pam had her unique perceptions regarding the family, as well as whom she felt was important to include as family. This certainly differed from Lisa's perspective.

Lisa's defense of her former husband, Carl, against Pam's memory of Carl's anger was an important note that I would explore in a later meeting. Dave's apparent surprise about that issue and his withdrawal from the conflict discussion left me wondering what he was thinking. These threads would be picked up as the couples sessions progressed.

INTERVENTION

The changes in the development of the stepfamily could not be accommodated until these gridlocked issues were unpacked and understood. I would attempt to help the couple and thereby the family engage in communication with one another that was honest, respectful, and appropriate to their stepfamily development and to the development of each individual. For the time being, I would work toward improving the understanding that Lisa, Dave, and Pam held of one another's unique perceptions and needs, while keeping in mind the inclusion of others in the family sessions in the future.

I considered the merits of continuing this couple's work to include further family sessions. One of the great strengths of this couple was the value they shared as parents, which was a source of pride in the marriage. The session with Pam, although uncomfortable for the family, had opened up issues that had been avoided in the system. I felt there was enough emotional safety for Pam, Lisa, and Dave in the system to warrant going forward with the family work. During the course of treatment I saw Pam, Dave, and Lisa together a total of three times. Lisa and Pam were seen together twice. I saw the stepfamily (Lisa, Dave, Pam, Zach, and Sarah) for one 2-hour session. Although I will refer to those sessions in this chapter, the emphasis will remain on the couples sessions.

As noted earlier, I considered the family from the perspectives of the stages of stepfamily development (Papernow, 1992), the adjustment of the stepfamily couple (Bray & Kelly, 1998), and the Gottman SRH theory. I wanted to see how interfacing these ways of looking at the stepfamily and couple adjustment could be useful in helping Dave and Lisa reach their goals of understanding and reconciliation.

I included psychoeducation in the sessions with Lisa and Dave throughout the course of their work. I explained that the tasks that couples need to accomplish for successful stepfamily adjustment are: (1) for each partner to integrate their stepchild's biological parent into his or her way of thinking about the family; (2) to develop the ability to manage change in their lives; (3) to successfully separate from the former marriage; and (4) to create and understand appropriate boundaries for former and residential spouses.

In considering Dave's and Lisa's adjustment to these tasks, I was impressed with their abilities to adjust to change in the past, when their children were very young. Now that changes were happening according to the needs of their soon-to-be-launched adolescent daughters and young adult son, their current inability to adjust to change came to light. These difficulties highlighted the remaining, and as yet unmet, tasks to be focused upon.

Lisa had not developed a way of thinking about Vicky that was integrated into the couple or stepfamily. This was alienating her from her husband, her stepdaughter, and her biological daughter, as was evidenced in the family session. Lisa's deceased husband had become a kind of nonentity to the couple. However, I remembered the surprise on Dave's face when Pam had talked about her negative feelings regarding her father in the family session. I suspected Carl had not been integrated into the couple's knowledge of each other's internal worlds. Also, I assessed that Dave and perhaps Lisa had not separated successfully from their former spouses. Dave's guilt about Sarah's begging to be with her mother was a place to explore. The boundaries for former and residential spouses, in this case, Vicky and Lisa, were brittle. Although she agreed to Sarah's spending the school year with Vicky, Lisa was left feeling powerless and abandoned by the decision. This needed exploration and understanding.

I then discussed the stages of stepfamily development with Dave and Lisa. In the early stages couples struggle with getting stuck in the fantasy of what each may have hoped or expected the family and their own roles would be. As awareness grows the family moves into the middle stages, where differences in perspectives and needs can be aired and new action taken. The family is able to mobilize and reorganize. In the later, more mature stages of development, authenticity within and between family members grows. Finally, the stepfamily is able to accomplish true intimacy and resolution of issues. The navigation through these stages for stepfamilies is a long process. I reminded myself and shared with the family that the normal range of time to move from fantasy stage through to resolution stage is 4 to 12 years.

As I looked at the structure and development of Lisa and Dave's stepfamily in relationship to the development of their SRH, I saw areas of strength and areas of weakness. Lisa and Dave had great inner strength and resolve when it came to meeting the challenges they had faced as young parents. Lisa had dedicated herself to raising her daughter after her first husband's untimely death. Dave had dedicated himself to parenting following his divorce from Vicky. Their intention in joining forces to form a family was only meant for good—the "greater good," as Dave had talked about in an early session. They jumped into what they had assumed was a marriage of shared meaning. The fact that they had done so without understanding the dreams, personal meanings, and aspirations they held about their marriage was an error that was now being uncovered. Both partners' ex-spouses were essentially out of the picture when Dave and Lisa met. They attempted to blend their families together rather than encourage a natural shift in relationships. This had greatly effected the loyalties in biological parent-child relationships.

For many years Sarah and Zach did not see their biological mother. Early in the relationship, Lisa took on the role of "savior" with the family, which at the time endeared her to Dave. Although there had been excellent improvement in Vicky's mothering of her children, the subject of Vicky had become taboo in the stepfamily household. Loyalty binds developed for all of the family members.

Pam, too, was encouraged to blend with her stepfamily without grieving her losses or sorting through her transitions at the time of her father's death. As Pam was facing the grief and fear of the possible loss of her current family, the feelings that had gone underground earlier in her life were beginning to surface.

Dave and Pam, although well-intentioned in their wishes to avoid negative feeling and conflict, had created an unrealistic expectation of family
homogeneity (blending) that did not allow for differences in perspectives and
needs. I wanted to help the couple and the family move into the middle stage of
stepfamily development of airing differences, which Pam had started to risk in the
family session.

In SRH terms the positve perspective in Dave and Lisa's relationship needed to
be strengthened if they were going to feel safe enough and have the courage to risk
sharing their inner worlds. In further sessions Lisa and Dave explored each other's
inner worlds through exercises using love maps. The couple drew on the strength
of their fondness and admiration system by using the appreciations checklist
exercise. Dave and Lisa worked on rebuilding their emotional bank account
through increasing their awareness of bids for connection. These interventions
helped to increase each partner's positive perspective of the relationship. In time,
the work they did to strengthen the lower levels of the SRH provided enough
safety between them to explore feelings and needs and differences.

As noted earlier, I taught Dave and Lisa about DPA and its effect on one's ability to process information effectively during stressful conflict situations. I taught
them to take their heart rates and recognize the stress sensations in their own body.
They learned to become aware of their own emotional flooding and be sensitive to
their partner's flooding. Learning about DPA was both enlightening and relieving
for Dave and Lisa. Each had been interpreting their partner's withdrawal as lack
of caring. Gaining the understanding of the four horsemen and their relationship
to the physiological response to stress helped them be more compassionate. I instructed Dave and Lisa to take a time-out of at least 20 minutes when DPA was
present. They agreed to honor the time-out and not leave the situation before they
had agreed upon a time to rejoin each other. I also taught physiological soothing
and self-soothing through relaxation, breathing techniques, and refraining from
stress-maintaining thoughts while they were taking a time-out. The couple felt empowered and encouraged by the way they were able to brainstorm their time-out
rituals. They even found some humor—Dave suggested they keep a George Carlin
comedy video in the VCR when he was visiting Lisa, just in case. Lisa was able
to recognize this joking as Dave turning toward her and an attempt to repair. As
therapist, my goal was to stay out of their dialogue but still encourage awareness
and shape their being in contact with each other.

In the following session Lisa and Dave were excited to report that their use of
the time-out ritual had been successful during the week. Lisa had become upset
about a phone call from Vicky, and she was able to ask for a time-out when she
noticed her complaint turning to criticism. Dave did not withdraw and honored the
reunion time they had agreed upon. The couple was beginning to see the problem
of their issues as a process between them rather than a fault of their partner's
character.

At this point in the couples work, I had seen Lisa and Pam together for two
sessions. The issues of Pam's conflicted loyalties between Sarah and Lisa were
brought to light. Pam shared that she felt disloyal to her mother if she talked
about communications with her sister, especially if anything positive was said

about Vicky. She also felt angry that she wasn't free to openly support her sister. As the tension had grown in the household and Dave had moved out, Pam found herself withdrawing from contact with Sarah. For that, she felt guilty and very sad.

Lisa was able to hear her daughter's complaints in sessions without becoming defensive. She listened and validated Pam's right to her feelings. Her daughter's pain was very difficult for Lisa to hear. After a silence, Lisa explained to Pam that it was never her intention to cause a distance to develop between Pam and Sarah. She said tearfully that one of her greatest joys was to see the love that her children had for one another.

Lisa and Pam arrived at our second meeting looking more open and comfortable with each other. I was interested in exploring the issue of Pam's biological father. Referring to the family genogram that we had begun earlier, I acknowledged that of all the relationships in the family, the one between Lisa and Pam held the longest history for them.

"I guess I forget how special that is sometimes," Lisa said to Pam.

I asked Lisa to talk about her life with Carl—how they had met, what she liked about him, and what her life was like at the time. Pam listened quietly with interest. I asked if she'd heard the stories before.

"No, I didn't think Mom wanted to talk about it," she said, glancing at Lisa.

"I hadn't wanted to talk about Carl's death," Lisa said to me. I encouraged her to address Pam. "You're right, Pam, I thought I was protecting you, but now I think we should talk about it."

The sessions with Lisa and Pam began to shed light on unspoken feelings and secrets that were impeding the development of the stepfamily and couple. Airing differences was essential to creating the foundation for authenticity and intimacy in the stepfamily relationships, as well as for the couple.

Two months had passed since Lisa and Dave had begun therapy. In that time they had gained awareness of the meta-emotional system of their couple relationship and how it grew out of the families in which they were raised. In turn they were now aware of the impact their avoidance of differences and feelings was having on their relationship and the relationships in their stepfamily. Their fondness and admiration system had been strengthened and their intention to reconcile was clearly stated by each of them. It took a relatively short time for this couple to rebuild their emotional bank account. Having learned about DPA, flooding, and physiological soothing and self-soothing, the couple felt much more comfortable with the idea of differences and even conflict. They were coming to realize that although they had intended to create harmony in the family through avoidance of conflict, they had created distance.

They also were relieved to know that they didn't have to resolve their differences right away. They were able to offer and accept repair when conflict and flooding occurred between them. I encouraged them to keep their Gottman repair checklists in a handy place in their homes. They had become more conscious of turning toward each other and accepting their partner's bids for connection. Lisa and Dave reported more affection between them. They had instituted the appreciations checklist into a daily ritual, sharing at least one appreciation each day. I intervened to continue strengthening the lower levels of the SRH, before going to problem solving of the couple's issues.

I gave Dave and Lisa a pack of Gottman love map cards to take on a dinner date. The instruction was to not talk about any of their children during dinner, and to spend at least a half hour answering the cards for one another. They reported that the exercise was a lot of fun.

"I really had to think about some of those questions," Lisa said. "I'm not sure what my favorite color is anymore, let alone my favorite poet!"

"I'm wondering about our dreams and aspirations," Dave said to Lisa. "Since doing the love map work, I've been thinking that the aspirations I have are for the kids, and for me, too, but I wonder about yours and mine."

By the end of that session, the couple decided that Dave would move back home. Dave was concerned about how Pam felt about his coming back home. I suggested a family session before the move was to occur.

In the family session, Pam was relieved that her parents were reconciling. When I asked Pam to tell her parents how the separation had been for her, she expressed that she was sad and also angry with both of them for Dave's leaving. Dave was able to hear and acknowledge Pam's anger without becoming defensive or stonewalling. Pam again spoke about wanting to feel more freedom in her communication with her Sarah, without its causing a problem between her parents.

Lisa, at first, was understanding. However, later in the session Lisa tried to diffuse the tension in the room with humor, saying, with a laugh, that Pam was so busy she didn't have time to miss Dave and Sarah. This only served to minimize Pam's feelings. I pointed out this process to the family, talking about the meta-emotion system in the family. Lisa could hear me talking about the process without becoming defensive and began to cry softly. After a time, I asked her to talk about the feelings that her tears were expressing. She told her family of her sadness and anger about the changes that had occurred in the family. Dave listened and didn't stonewall. He offered his hand to Lisa and she held it.

Expression of intense feeling was beginning to be less threatening to the system. The brief separation that had served as a time-out was no longer necessary. Dave and Lisa had a safety valve in the time-out and an ability to allow their feelings. As their sessions continued, I sought to normalize the process of problems in marriage for the couple. They were surprised and relieved to learn that Gottman's research showed 69% of problems to be unsolvable. Differences in personality, values, and worldview between partners were to be expected. I explained that understanding the meanings of the positions that Lisa and Dave took with regard to their gridlocked problem of Sarah's year with Vicky would do more to help them come to compromise on this issue than would rushing toward problem solving. The couple was also relieved to begin to understand the complexity of the stepfamily system and how the stresses they experienced regarding the changes that were occurring in the family were normal.

I recommended reading for Dave and Lisa that would give them a more realistic expectation of themselves and stepfamily life. As a way of further normalizing and informing the process of stepfamily, I recommended the couple contact the

SAA to receive their magazine and gain access to other stepfamilies and support resources.

Dream-Within-Conflict Intervention

This intervention is a very powerful tool and can be quite dramatic. It may, at times, look like a "magic bullet" in terms of evoking deep feelings from clients. In order for the couple to gain benefit in strengthening their understanding and empathy of each other, the conversation should go on between them in session and not through the therapist. In this way the voice of the spouse who asks a question like "help me understand" becomes the voice of comfort and empathy. Of course, the therapist must guide and model. But the goal is to remove him- or herself from the conversation as much as possible and shape the intervention toward a dyad. If the dream-within-conflict intervention is attempted and not successful, it is a good indicator that the lower levels of the SRH need more strengthening.

In this session, I explained to Dave and Lisa that they would be exploring the conflict between them regarding Sarah's spending a year away with Vicky. Each of them would take turns as a speaker and listener for 15 minutes. I had asked the couple to review the chapter in *Seven Principles for Making Marriage Work* on overcoming gridlock, so this format and the ideas of dreams would be familiar to them. In addition, I gave the couple a list of sample dreams, such as justice, honor, a spiritual journey, adventure, having a sense of order, unity from the past, and so on.

I explained the job of the listener as one of creating safety. "It is the job of the listener to listen well enough for the speaker to tell you the dream behind his or her position in the issue of Sarah's going to live with Vicky." I gave Dave and Lisa a list of sample questions to ask to help with clarification of dreams and meaning—questions like "What are your feelings about this? Will you help me understand that? What do you wish for here?" The idea was to be interested and suspend judgment, I told them. Under no circumstances was the couple to begin problem solving. The purpose of this exercise was to create understanding.

Lisa and Dave were sitting in swivel chairs across from me. I asked them to turn toward each other.

"I'm pretty nervous," Dave said. Lisa said that she was as well.

"This is a very important issue for each of you," I said. "Remember, you don't have to resolve it today. This exercise is about understanding better. Let's start with some deep breathing." I led the couple through a brief relaxation exercise to deescalate their anxiety.

Dave began as the speaker. With the help of Lisa's nonjudgmental listening and acceptance of his experience, he was able to begin to better understand his own dreams and meanings as well as share them with Lisa. When there was a long lull in Dave's story, I encouraged Lisa to prompt him and to show her interest with a question. This helped Dave clarify his ideas.

Dave's dream in having Sarah spend the year with Vicky had to do with his core values of forgiveness and his sense of responsibility to humankind. His dream had to do with healing his whole family and the world. He felt that if he didn't encourage the reconciliation of Vicky and her children, that he was contributing to discord in the world. Lisa asked if this had anything to do with his parents' teachings of activism and pacifism. He said, "I never thought of Vicky in those terms, but it certainly fits with how I see myself." He admitted that in the past he had felt guilty about having taken the children from Vicky. More recently, though, he was feeling remorse and grief about what had happened to his young family long ago. He became quiet and tearful. "I guess supporting the relationship between Sarah and Vicky is a way of forgiving myself for the pain I caused both of them long ago, and supporting healing for Zach as well," he finally said. "It's my responsibility to put my own feelings aside. The kids are safe with Vicky now. But I have another dream, too. It's that that you and I, Lisa, could be a team in this, just like we have been in the past. I know this situation hurts you, but I thought you were on my side. Maybe that's selfish of me. My dream is for us to be a team."

"What do you know about that dream?" Lisa asked.

Dave thought for a few seconds. "When I was a kid, my parents were busy with all kinds of groups—the church, civil rights, antiwar groups, you name it! Our house always had people in it and something going on. I'm almost embarrassed to say this, but my parents were there for everyone else. I was lonely—nobody was there for me. When you came along and wanted to help me with Sarah and Zach, I thought, 'Wow, someone's here for me!' My dream is that we can be a team in our relationship."

At the end of 15 minutes I asked the couple to switch roles. "I've been thinking a lot about this," Lisa began. "This is really hard for me to talk about, Dave. I'm afraid you're going to be mad at me." She began to cry. I expected that she was going to come forward with information about Carl and her former marriage.

Lisa took a deep breath and began again. "My dream seems so complicated. You know I've had a couple of sessions with Pam. She has been remembering some things about her early life with Carl and me. I can't lie to her anymore, or to you. The fact is that Carl wasn't the wonderful guy I always make him out be. It's true he was a great provider, but he never wanted children. When I got pregnant he was very upset. He wanted me to terminate the pregnancy! You know I couldn't do that. After Pam was born he all but disappeared from our marriage. He worked all the time. We argued all the time he was home. He seldom spent time with Pam. I was lonely with no one I could talk to. I had even thought of leaving my marriage but my parents thought Carl was a prince. They were finally proud of me. And Carl's mom was very sweet. I think she knew things weren't right, but she adored her son. Her own marriage to Carl's father was difficult. He was angry and put her down in front of people. I felt sorry for her, and she loved Pam."

She continued, "When Carl suddenly died one day everything changed! Everyone felt sorry for me and Pam. They were all talking about Carl and what a great man he was. Everyone wanted to help us. I just went along with the story of what a great person Carl was. I didn't mean to lie, I was just protecting everyone—Pam, my mother-in-law, my parents, and maybe me."

"Help me understand that part, " Dave said.

"How could I complain then? Carl had just died."

Dave leaned toward Lisa. "I'm so sorry. I had no idea that you had all that trouble with Carl."

Lisa sat silently for several seconds, looking down at her hands, which were resting in her lap. She answered Dave in a shaky voice. "It seems so foolish now, but I couldn't tell you back then with all the trouble you were having with Vicky and trying to take care of Zach and Sarah. I should have let you know about me, but I thought you needed me to be strong. I'm glad that Pam is making me look at this now. She has a right to have her past validated and maybe I do, too."

Dave and Lisa remained silent for a time. Rather than return to the dream-within-conflict intervention right away, I decided to first give the couple a chance to process this disclosure.

"It took some courage, Lisa, for you to come forward with this," I said.

Lisa nodded, remaining silent. Dave continued to turn toward her.

"I'm wondering how you are feeling now?" I said.

Lisa answered in a small voice. "I feel a little foolish, like I said before. I also feel angry that Dave didn't know about this. I know that doesn't make sense. How could he?" She paused a few seconds. "I guess I'm worried that Dave is mad at me."

I noticed that Dave was continuing to look at Lisa with compassion.

"Can you check this out?" I asked Lisa. "Will you look at Dave and ask him what he's feeling?"

She nodded and looked at Dave. I asked Lisa what she saw.

"I see love," she said and paused again, looking away. She took a deep breath and turned again to Dave. "What are you feeling about what I told you?"

Dave replied, "I can't say I understand it all, but I know I'm not mad at you. I knew it was horrible for you when Carl died. I had no idea it was horrible for you in the marriage, too. I'm sorry you were so alone in it. Maybe I was too focused with my own problems to give you a chance to tell me about yours."

Lisa leaned toward Dave. "It's not your fault and maybe not mine either. I'm just glad to be telling you now."

As I directed the couple back to the dream-within-conflict intervention, I wondered what part this disclosure played in Lisa's dream. I said, "You're right. Blame isn't useful here. Remember that understanding the meanings behind the positions you hold needs to precede any problem solving."

Dave asked, "Lisa, tell me more about what Sarah's going to live with Vicky means to you."

Lisa began, "When Carl died, my life had been lonely for a long time. The relationship with him had really shaken my confidence. I'd thought I'd known him but found out I didn't. Then I met you. As we started to interact around the children I could see your dedication to them, and to being a good father. You were kind and funny, even though you had trouble with Vicky. You needed and admired me. This was all I'd ever wanted in my marriage with Carl. I thought my dreams of family were finally coming true! They did come true until Vicky started coming into the picture more and more."

Lisa stopped. I noticed that her breathing became shallow as her face flushed. I waited a few seconds and commented, "It's easy to become flooded as these dreams are explored. Lisa, take a few deep breaths and start when you feel more calm." After a few moments her smile indicated that she was ready to begin once more.

"I guess I'm feeling like I'm losing my dream again," Lisa said.

"Like you lost the dream with Carl?" asked Dave.

Lisa nodded and continued. "I'm afraid that Sarah isn't going to love me anymore. I know it sounds crazy, but I feel like you aren't going to need or love me anymore, Dave."

The room became silent. Dave searched the sample listener questions I had given him. After several seconds he asked, "Will you help me understand more about that?"

"I know you needed me when Zach and Sarah were younger. You were on your own and Vicky wasn't in the picture. We've worked hard to get the children through school and into college. Now I'm afraid that my job is over."

"But that's not true!" Dave interrupted. Lisa stopped.

I intervened, saying, "Remember, Dave, the idea here is not to argue with Lisa's feelings. Just try to understand them."

Dave tried again, searching the sample questions. "Does this relate to some belief or value you hold? What about your family history?"

She thought a moment and answered, "You know that I was the organizer in the family where I grew up. My mother relied on me to keep things under control so my father wouldn't go into a rage. She was so helpless! I used to feel sorry for her. Now the thought of it makes me mad. I used to do my brother's homework so my dad wouldn't pick on him. I got A grades so my father wouldn't hit me, too! I was loved by my brother and mother, and at least not punished by my father. I guess I learned to believe the way to get love and avoid hurt was to take care of people's problems. I learned to value perfection as the goal."

"Help me understand how this relates to Sarah being with Vicky," Dave continued.

Lisa thought a moment and began, "As Vicky becomes more reliable and a good mom, I feel that Sarah doesn't need me as much. It's not you and me dealing with the problem of Vicky anymore. I feel like you don't need me in that arena. Zach is on his own and doing well. How do I matter if there's nothing to fix?" Lisa began to cry softly.

"So you feel that Sarah won't love you and I won't need or love you if she gets closer to Vicky?" Dave asked.

"That's it," Lisa answered, looking at Dave. She hesitated a moment as her face brightened. "I just realized, that the real dream I have, under the fear, is that I could be free of organizing and taking care of everyone. That I could just be loved for being me. Maybe I could truly learn to relax!"

The key to unlocking the gridlocked conflict issues between Dave and Lisa lay in understanding their dreams-within-conflict. As their work in therapy progressed, Lisa and Dave were able to find ways of honoring Dave's dreams of contributing to the healing of the planet by promoting healing in the stepfamily. The couple found ways of honoring Dave's dream of becoming a team with Lisa. Lisa learned that she could be loved without having to put her own dreams aside or be constantly doing for others. Lisa learned to state her needs. She also began to risk saying "no" to the requests of Dave and others.

As their friendship continued to deepen and their marital perspective became more positive, Lisa and Dave's ability to tolerate differences in the other's personality, worldview, and needs increased. Issues that had been intolerably painful to discuss became more tolerable, even welcome.

The vulnerabilities and differences in Dave's and Lisa's personalities didn't go away. Sarah's living with Vicky continued to be a tender issue with potential for conflict. In later sessions, Dave and Lisa learned which areas of this issue were central to their core beliefs and values. These were the areas in which they could not yield to one another. They also learned about their areas of flexibility and how to accept influence and compromise. Their perpetual issues had moved from gridlock to dialogue, where differences could be talked about without the four horsemen getting in the way.

One such issue arose when Lisa and Dave came into conflict about visiting California to attend Sarah's school play. Lisa, Dave, and Pam were excited to see Sarah in her first starring role. However, Lisa was not comfortable attending a party at Vicky and Ron's home later that weekend. Dave and Lisa were able to come to a compromise on the issue, with each one feeling honored in terms of their core needs. Lisa offered that she would be willing to invite Vicky, Ron, and Ron's son to dessert after the play, as Sarah would be staying with Dave, Lisa, and Pam at their hotel that night. Dave was very happy with Lisa's offer and agreed that he would not bring up the party to Lisa again. As Lisa became more comfortable with the idea, she was able to honor Pam's request to be with Sarah at the party that weekend. Dave responded by saying that would give him a chance to take Lisa to dinner while they were away. That response pleased Lisa. She felt that her need to create a boundary for herself was honored. She felt loved, even though her needs were different than Dave's and Pam's. Lisa was also glad to be able to turn toward Vicky and her family in a way that felt congruent to her. Dave felt his need to support Sarah's turning toward Vicky was honored by Lisa. He felt that he and Lisa were a team, even though their needs were different. Pam was relieved to be able to be with her stepsister without feeling guilty about being disloyal to her mother.

In summary, I treated the couple through their separation and into their reconciliation. As Dave and Lisa reported more regularly that they were having conflict discussions outside of our sessions in which the four horsemen didn't take over and flooding wasn't halting communication, we began to meet less frequently. I have continued to meet with this couple and family from time to time. These sessions have tended to be around transition times, such as planning house rules when Zach returned home from college and when Sarah returned to live with Dave and Lisa.

The couple and family continued to work on rituals of connection. Each person had individual needs and motivations that were different from the others. Vicky had sent a note to Lisa thanking her for the invitation to dessert after Sarah's play. Lisa in turn began to include Vicky and Ron on her holiday card list. These small ways of turning toward one another continued to set a positive tone for the whole stepfamily. Sarah continued to connect with her stepbrother, Michael. Zach, too, began to take an interest in Michael and eventually Michael became part of everyone's family map. This brought the two households together in an organic way. Dave and Lisa continued to enhance their own love maps. They created a new set of goals and rituals as they moved toward becoming a couple alone for the first time in their marriage.

CONCLUSION

Dave and Lisa had been too involved in making a project of their shared family. Their lack of true intimacy had stunted the stepfamily development. As I had conjectured, weaving together SRH theory and understanding of the stages of stepfamily development had worked well to provide assessment and treatment for the couple and family.

The SRH methodology helped Lisa and Dave to shift their perspective on their marriage from negative to positive. This allowed the couple to hear one another as friends rather than adversaries. Their understanding of the meanings of their conflicted positions helped Dave and Lisa move toward shared goals in their relationship and toward the mature stages of stepfamily development.

As contact, intimacy, and authenticity grew between Dave and Lisa, the tone in all of the stepfamily relationships moved toward more authenticity. Differences could be aired, and effective problem solving and compromise became possible for everyone.

REFERENCES

Bray, J. H., Berger, S. H., & Boethel, C. L. (1994). Role integration and marital adjustment in stepfather families. In K. Pasley & M. Ihinger-Tallman (Eds.), *Remarriage and stepparenting: Current research and theory* (pp. 69–86). New York: Guilford Press.

Bray, J. H., & Kelly, J. (1998). *Stepfamilies.* New York: Broadway Books.

Brown, A. C., Green, R. J., & Druckman, J. (1990). A comparison of stepfamilies with and without child-focused problems. *American Journal of Orthopsychiatry, 60,* 556–566.

Gold, J. M., Bubenzer, D. L., & West, J. D. (1993). Differentiation from ex-spouses and stepfamily marital intimacy. *Journal of Divorce & Remarriage, 19*(3–4), 83–95.

Larson, J. (1992). Understanding stepfamilies. *American Demographics, 14*(7), 36–40.

MacDonald, W. L., & DeMaris, A. (1995). Remarriage, stepchildren and marital conflict: Challenges to incomplete institutionalization hypothesis. *Journal of Marriage and the Family, 57,* 387–398.

Martin, T. C., & Bumpass, L. L. (1989). Recent trends in marital disruption. *Demography, 26,* 37–51.

Papernow, P. L. (1992). *Becoming a step family: Patterns of development in remarried families.* New York: Gardner.

Vemer, E., Coleman, M., Gagnon, L. H, & Cooper, H. (1989). Marital satisfaction in remarriage: A meta-analysis. *Journal of Marriage and the Family, 51,* 713–725.

Weston, C. A., & Macklin, E. D. (1990). The relationship between former-spousal contact and remarital satisfaction in stepfather families. *Journal of Divorce & Remarriage, 14*(2), 25–47.

Wile, D. B. (1993). *After the fight.* New York: Guilford Press.

Chapter 10 ❀

The Use of Metaphor

Sarah L. Rattray

Understanding and acceptance can be especially challenging when clients feel flooded or defensive in therapy sessions, let alone in their marriage. A couple walking in the door of the therapist's office has a lot at stake. They are focused on their pain and their desire for change. Sometimes listening to theoretical ideas, approaches, or suggestions is difficult. For some couples, the concepts may be new and they may have difficulty understanding them. Others may understand the concepts on an intellectual level but have difficulty applying the new concepts to themselves or their relationship. Metaphor can often help ease the clients' anxiety about new concepts. A metaphor provides a gentle, indirect, but often clear and powerful illustration of a concept. Because the illustration is not the issue the clients are grappling with, it can be easier to hear and understand.

I often use metaphors to explain GMCT concepts and to illustrate helpful points. Clients also like metaphors that they can easily relate to. With a traffic engineer I might talk about timing of lights and flow; with an accountant or a mathematician, balancing equations; with a physician, healing; and with an artist, light and form or even purchasing canvas stretchers.

I am not concerned with how close I come to the client's real profession. If my understanding of what a traffic engineer does leads me to the wrong metaphor—if she doesn't work with lights and flow but instead with another aspect of traffic—she will fill in the blanks in her own mind with a metaphor that works for her.

With all due humility, I will sometimes say, "Of course I don't know what is really involved in the coordination of traffic lights" as I offer the metaphor. Fortunately, clients do not get hung up on the particulars of a metaphor, as they so often get hung up on the particulars of the real issues they are trying to talk about. Also, if clients' feelings of professional expertise are enhanced, it invites clients to accept the therapist's expertise about relationships and suggestions for change. By using metaphors that relate to clients' lives, the therapist can demonstrate respect for them, their knowledge, and their professions, which in turn invites their respect for concepts the therapist will discuss with them. Thus, the mood in the room can change with the use of metaphor. When arms are crossed defensively and heads are shaken in disagreement, most couples will nod and open up to a brief story being told to them. There is often little to disagree with in the metaphor being told; it helps when the metaphor is distant enough from their issues that clients have no stake in taking a contrary position.

I offer the following illustrations to show how I have used metaphors to explain Gottman concepts or otherwise reach clients who were having difficulty accepting the influence of therapy.

TWO SUBJECTIVE REALITIES: THE BLIND PEOPLE AND THE ELEPHANT

Really understanding and incorporating the concept of "two subjective realities" is essential for clients who are working on building a Sound Relationship House together. The concept allows them to move away from an "I'm right, you're wrong" stance and toward one of mutual understanding. Although this is an essential idea, it can be a difficult concept for many. People naturally assume that there is really only one objective truth (hopefully, theirs). They believe that if they can just explain their perception emphatically enough, one of the outcomes of therapy will be that the therapist will divine the objective truth and issue a pronouncement about how to proceed now that the truth has been discovered.

In the initial session of a 3-day therapy "marathon" I conducted with clients who had come to my office from another state, they told their account of the incidents that brought them to therapy. When the first client finished, the partner jumped in, agitated, emphatic, and contemptuous, exclaiming, "How can you possibly do therapy with us after such a skewed account? What my partner told you is so far from the truth that you can't possibly be effective. If I try to tell you what really happened there will be no way for you to know what was the truth. Why are we wasting our time if my partner can't even tell you what really happened?"

I introduced the concept of two subjective realities and said, "I am comfortable hearing two different realities, or two different versions of what has happened. I would like to hear your version in just a moment. But first I want to tell a little story to explain what I mean by 'two subjective realities.' Perhaps you remember the fable of the five blind people who have their first encounter with an elephant? They all approach the elephant and feel the part of the elephant they contact. Afterwards they tell each other what an elephant is. The first blind person says,

'An elephant is a rope with a tassel at the end.' The second blind person says, 'An elephant is a wall.' The third one says, 'An elephant is a tree trunk.' The fourth says, 'An elephant is a flapping tapestry hanging down.' And the fifth says, 'An elephant is a thick, flexible hose.' What you encounter is real; what your partner encounters is also real. Neither of you sees the whole elephant, and it is your experience that shapes your perception and perspective."

At this point the clients nodded their heads in understanding—the metaphor penetrated the brick wall each had built around their own perception, and allowed them to feel the possibility of two subjective realities. They understood the concept at an initial level and were willing to set aside their doubts long enough to proceed. They had literally been ready to walk out the door on the therapy, and perhaps the relationship; they now sat back, willing to continue working at least a little longer.

I more commonly introduce two subjective realities to clients when they are talking to each other about a shared experience, usually a conflict. Sometimes, filled with the desire to "win" the conflict, clients will hear the concept as a new opportunity to convince their partner that their own perception of reality was really the objective truth. These clients may understand the concept on a superficial level, but because of their overwhelming need to defend their perception, be unable to really incorporate the concept enough to see reality from their partner's viewpoint.

A client in one couple, after hearing the subjective reality of the partner, said, "You said that I was furious and out of control yesterday. That isn't what happened. I was just telling you what I thought. You think I'm some kind of lunatic. That's not how it was at all. I was just trying to make my point, and I was not out of control—in fact, I wasn't even furious." Clearly these clients had different perceptions and couldn't see each other's perspective. I went further with the metaphor to better explain two subjective realities. "Let's take two of these blind people and their realities. For one blind person the elephant really is a rope with a tassel, and for another it really is a wall. We know that one blind person came in contact with the tail and the other with the side of the elephant. When you talk with each other in the future, I will be teaching you to say, essentially, 'I can see that given that you came in contact with a different part of the elephant, that given your perspective, that given your own personal experience with this issue, that you would come to the conclusion you did. It makes sense to me that you see it the way you do, however, I still have my own experience. It is okay and understandable that we had two different experiences.' The person who got hold of the tail will never look back and feel it as a wall, and the person who felt the side of the elephant will never remember it to be like a rope. But they will come to accept that the other person truly did have a different experience, and each experience can lead both to a better understanding of the elephant."

I return to this metaphor in future sessions when couples are having difficulty hearing each other, reminding them that one is describing a rope and the other a wall. Recalling this metaphor helps quickly bring back the concept of two subjective realities, and along with it a greater ability to listen to the partner's reality.

Letting go of the belief that there is one objective truth can be hard for some people. It can be equally hard to understand that exploring their partner's subjective reality is valuable in relationship building, no matter how far the partner's reality might seem from their own. One client said, "I could accept it if my partner said an elephant is a rope, since an elephant really does have a ropelike tail. But what if my partner said that an elephant is blue and fuzzy? An elephant isn't blue and fuzzy, so how can I accept this? Don't I need to convince my partner that an elephant isn't blue and fuzzy?" We went on to discuss his belief that there is one objective truth, and that one of them will be able to know it. When we are discussing an elephant we, as sighted people with experiences of elephants, know what an elephant "really" is. Within a relationship, though, we are like the blind people. We don't have the benefit of seeing the whole elephant, and our goal is to connect with our partner, to gain new understanding and acceptance of our partner's point of view, of our partner's inner world. We can then begin to experience how that inner world connects with our own, and how it informs our relationship. I stated, "If my partner said an elephant is blue and fuzzy, I would want to be curious about that. I would ask my partner to explain more to me about their experience, to help me to understand it from their perspective. I might tell them that from my perspective the elephant seemed gray and that I am confused about their color perception—could they tell me more about that? In this process I would hope to learn more about my partner, their perceptions, and what is important to them."

This metaphor, with its gentle story and clear illustration of the folly of believing that a single point of view constitutes the whole of reality, can open a dialogue leading to the incorporation of two subjective realities. Other metaphors can help the dialogue progress.

TALK CLEARLY ABOUT WHAT YOU NEED: LEMON YOGURT

In teaching the concept of softened start-up we recommend that people talk clearly about what they need. Rather than venting frustration by saying, "Why don't you ever take a turn with the cooking?" we encourage them to start softly and positively with "I appreciated it when you took a turn with the dishes last week. I'm burned out on cooking right now. Could you please take a turn planning the meal and cooking tomorrow? I'd be willing to do the shopping." This approach addresses the speaker's needs in a positive, nonthreatening way, allowing the listener to take action without taking offense.

But some clients have a hard time asking clearly for what they need. It may be that they expect their partners to know what they need with a minimum of information or without being told anything at all. "If you really loved me, you would know by now what pleases me!" When that expectation is not met, their frustration prevents them from saying clearly what they need. I have heard many interchanges such as the following:

Partner 1:   Why don't you ever give me a hand?
Partner 2:   I didn't know you needed one.
Partner 1:   How could you not know? Didn't you see what I was doing?

Partner 1: Why isn't there anything to eat in this house?
Partner 2: It's full of groceries.
Partner 1: Well, there's nothing that I want to eat.
Partner 2: What do you want to eat?
Partner 1: You should know by now.

Partner 1: I need your caring and support.
Partner 2: Okay, in what way?
Partner 1: You know, caring and support.
Partner 2: What kind of caring and support?
Partner 1: Why can't you just give me caring and support? You know what
            I mean, you know what I need.

When clients are stuck in this dialogue loop of frustration and thwarted expectation, they flood easily and end up in attack-defend mode. Without first breaking the loop, attempting to work with these clients' actual needs can be too difficult. These clients are not ready to hear that their partners do not know what they need, because the approach is unclear. The clients are not yet ready to hear that they have to take the responsibility to state their needs in clear, unambiguous, and polite terms.

I used a "lemon yogurt" metaphor to break the dialogue loop with one couple I worked with. One partner did not feel noticed or cared for, but was not making his needs explicit. He was too frustrated to talk about this directly. I said, "Suppose you were really hungry right now, and what would really hit the spot would be your favorite lemon yogurt. You could tell your partner that you were *hungry*, but she may or may not know that what you really want is for her to go out and buy you some food.

"A better thing to tell your partner is that you would like her to *buy* you some food. But she might not know that you mean at that moment, and she might think you wanted her to take a turn going shopping at some point.

"A better thing to tell your partner is that you want her to go to the store *right now* and buy you some food. But when she comes home with the wrong thing you might feel hurt that she didn't get what you wanted.

"A better thing still to tell your partner is that you would like her to buy you some *yogurt* right now. But if she came home with a flavor you were not in the mood for you might feel misunderstood.

"An even better thing to tell your partner is that you would like *lemon* yogurt. But she might then return with the wrong style of yogurt, and you could feel ignored, because she never noticed the style that you always buy yourself.

"The best thing to say would be '*I am very hungry. I would really appreciate it if you would buy me a lowfat French-style lemon yogurt right now. Would you please buy me four of them, because I know I'll want two now, and I would like to save two for tomorrow. If they don't have lemon you could get blueberry for me.*'

I find that using an explicit, detailed, extreme, or picky example of stating a need couched in a safe metaphor allows clients to see all the various ways their own real need, explicitly stated, can help their partner better take care of them. It's easier to learn that specificity helps when a metaphor is used as explanation, because using an example from their real lives might invite a response along the lines of "But they should *know*, after all these years!"

ACCEPTING RESPONSIBILITY: THE CAR ON THE TENNIS COURT

In the GMCT model, as in other couples therapy, it is important to be balanced. We want each partner to feel we are being fair, focusing our comments and cautions on each of them in turn. However, I have worked with couples where one partner has an issue that interferes with the relationship or the therapy to such an extent that it needs to be focused on first so that therapy can then proceed in a more balanced way.

I worked with a couple with one partner who continuously interrupted her partner or me. I initially attempted to ask her to wait a moment, then I tried to hold up my hand to get her to stop. I then paused to explore what the interrupting was about for her—what it meant to her. I thought I was being kind and careful, but she felt otherwise: "Why are we sitting here talking about the meaning of interruptions? Why are you sticking your hand up at me, and wasting our time talking to me? I'm interrupting because you need to be focusing on my partner more, not just me."

I worked with another couple with one partner who became flooded so quickly and so easily that I needed to talk to him for a while about self-soothing. My goal was to help him stay calm long enough that we could return to talking about the issue between the two of them. Although I tried to be careful and well-intentioned, the client said, "Why are you talking only to me? Why are you making this only my problem? What about all the things that my partner does wrong? This is not all my fault. It's not me who is so harsh and blaming. Why aren't you calling my partner on that?"

I would like these types of client to be able to accept responsibility in a gentle, nonblaming way. A metaphor I first found helpful with a couple who played tennis together is the "tennis court and the car." (This metaphor can easily be adapted to fit different couples—it could be changed to a ping-pong table with model plane on it, or card table with sewing machine on it.) I introduced it like this: "Suppose you want to play tennis with your partner on your tennis court. Tennis is a nice back-and-forth game that the two of you can share equally in. The two of you can put up the net together, get out the balls together, and take turns hitting back and forth to each other. You can take turns retrieving the balls that go out of the court. However, suppose you personally parked your very own antique convertible on the court while you were rebuilding the car. It now becomes your sole responsibility to clear that car off the court before you and your partner can play tennis together. This does not mean that your partner doesn't want to play tennis or that you are bad or wrong for having the car on the court. It simply means that you were the one who put the car there in the first place, and you may need to be the one to accept the responsibility to move it off the court now, before the two of you can begin to mutually play tennis together."

This metaphor is easy to accept and agree with. It helps to make a transition to the client's acceptance of and agreement with the possibility that he or she may have a little more work to do first. With one couple I used a version of this metaphor and then explained, "I know how important it is to you to work out your different approaches to money management. Before I can talk to the two of you about that, before we can get back to playing cards, we need to get that sewing machine off the table. We need to take a little bit more time exploring what's going on when you interrupt, because it's blocking the card table—it's blocking our ability to have a productive discussion about money management." With this couple, the client's reaction was a grudging "Well, okay, but we'd better get back to the real stuff soon." That response is sometimes as good as it gets, but it's enough for a start.

SELF-SOOTHING: EMPHASIZING IMPORTANCE

Some tools we teach in GMCT are accepted as important and powerful by clients, and they go home ready to incorporate them into their relationship. "Stop criticism and replace it with complaints without blame" is a clear and strong message, and the knowledge of the pain criticism causes can motivate couples to listen and try to change. Other tools sometimes seem too simple, trivial, passive, or subtle to some clients, and they don't take the suggestions seriously or give them enough time or attention. Teaching clients to take a break when they're getting flooded, to calm themselves down before returning to a discussion, and to soothe themselves in general when they are anxious are important examples. It is harder for them to see how taking time out to relax will help lessen the pain they are experiencing in their relationship. Advice or directives in this area are often ignored.

I worked with a couple in which one partner was a physician. He had quite a bit of stress in his life, was on edge at work, and whenever his partner spoke to him about any kind of an issue other than polite chatter he quickly flooded. This overwhelming anxiety became so aversive that he wanted his partner to appear happy all the time. I tried to discuss and suggest self-soothing, relaxation, and various stress-management techniques. I asked him what he could do for relaxation to help his body return to a resting state, so he could cope more effectively. He said: "I find skiing very relaxing. I would like to get away by myself for a few days. I used to get a massage—that was great. Of course, I know about deep breathing and progressive muscle relaxation. I know all that stuff. I just don't have the time for any of that. Please just tell my partner to stop bringing up unpleasant things."

As he was a physician, I chose the following metaphor: "Suppose you were recovering from a car accident in which you fractured your hip. In order for you to regain your freedom of movement and to fully heal, your physician told you that you needed to go to physical therapy twice a week. This would not be as dramatic or immediate as getting pins put in your bones, or a cast on your leg, but it would be just as important in healing all the way. Even if you felt you didn't have time to go to physical therapy, that you were too busy, your physician would probably explain that you have a choice. If you want to walk well again, and even be able to run again, you need to take the time to go to physical therapy. Otherwise you may not heal correctly or completely, may have chronic pain, or may never be able to run again."

I then went on to say: "What I am telling you now is that if you do not take the time to relax, soothe yourself, heal your stress with relaxation and self-care, your marriage is not going to improve the way you want it to; it will become chronically painful or won't work at all. I understand that you are busy and feel you don't have the time, but this is the kind of choice with the kind of consequences we are talking about."

He responded, "Okay. I get it. Point made. Maybe I can make an appointment with that massage therapist again." As a doctor who had given similar advise to his patients, and believed it, he could hear this metaphor and come to grips with his own choice in accepting healing treatment. Very often metaphors ease the way in allowing clients to abandon their resistance to change and move on to connect with their partners.

WORKING TOWARD COMPROMISE: REAL ESTATE NEGOTIATION

In beginning to work toward compromise, couples are encouraged to identify and discuss their core areas of inflexibility and then areas where they can be flexible. When some clients first hear their partner's core areas of inflexibility they are ready to give up. "That's it. She is too extreme. There is no way we're going to get anywhere on this." One partner in a couple I worked with was a real estate salesperson and the other was an attorney. They both seemed competent and capable in their professions, and yet with each other they were not willing to continue talking after their partner uttered a first sentence. This metaphor came to me: "When you are representing a couple who wants to buy a house, you will initially present an offer that is lower than the selling price, won't you?" Both clients nodded in agreement. "Usually the sellers will come back with a price that is slightly lower than their initial price, but higher than your offer, right? But they don't simply say no to your offer, do they?" Both clients shook their heads. I raised my hands in the air, one higher than the other. "The seller starts out at $300,000 and you offer $250,000. They come back with 295, and you respond with 260. They move to 290, you move to 270. You keep making moves, some smaller, some larger, step by step, one at a time, working closer together. Perhaps you ask for a roof repair. Perhaps they ask for a longer closing date. The dance is not over when the initial difference is first detected."

The clients nodded and smiled. They took a deep breath and were ready, tentatively, to work toward each other. They felt braver about not giving up at the first sign of difference. As the metaphor of negotiation related to an area where they both felt skilled, they were ready to try with each other.

REACHING COMPROMISE: METAPHORS THAT CONNECT

In reaching compromise couples are encouraged to look for ways they can creatively be flexible once their core areas of inflexibility have been defined. Some clients believe there is only one right way to do a thing. This can be a barrier when a couple is attempting to reach compromise. "The only way we're going to get a handle on our budget is to enter our checks into our ledger each night, and check with the on-line bank every day. You need to tell me what you have spent every day."

I try to come up with metaphors that will make the most sense to clients, that will speak their language. It is important to join with the client and acknowledge that some things do indeed need to be done right. Two plus two does equal four; a building does need to be built correctly or it could collapse. I look for a way to illustrate that there can be many different right ways to do something, perhaps drawing from the client's profession.

The just-mentioned couple with the money management issues were an artist who was willing to think of many ways to make changes and an engineer who could only see one way. I wasn't sure what kind of engineering she did, but I used the following metaphor: "When building a bridge it is certainly important to do it well. But there are many kinds of bridges—suspension bridges, floating bridges, covered bridges, and those bridges with arches. The designer of the bridge has some freedom in choosing the kind of bridge they would most like to use for their site. It will be important to be sure that once the kind of bridge is chosen, it is built safely and correctly, but the design can be flexible and unique."

I waited to see if the clients were nodding their heads in agreement, seeming to soften, and understanding the point. If they hadn't been, I would have continued with the metaphor a little longer until there was some momentum of understanding and agreement.

"The two of you agree that you want to work on your finances." They nodded. "You both certainly want to be sure that the math is done correctly—mistakes in addition and subtraction won't help." They nodded again. "There are probably several different ways you can meet both those requirements. How about discussing between the two of you a bunch of different ideas at first—be a little creative—and then narrow down to one or two you could both agree on."

They were able to proceed with an attitude of greater flexibility, coupled with the comfort that in the details that really mattered, the budget would be "done right."

CONCLUSION

As therapists, part of our job is to circumvent the defenses our clients present without directly assaulting them. Metaphors come at those defenses in a nonthreatening, easy-to-understand, impersonal way that allows people to lower their guard and grasp new concepts. Using the momentum of agreement with the metaphor can speed clients' acceptance of new ideas, other points of view, or new strategies. Using key words in the metaphor that relate to the concept being worked on, such as "healing" a fractured hip when working on "healing" stress, helps transition from the metaphor to the action you invite them to take. Using a metaphor that clients can relate to makes it more powerful, but general metaphors are very useful as well. I encourage you to take the opportunity to use metaphor with your clients when they are having trouble understanding or accepting what you are trying to teach.

Chapter 11 ❧

Marathon Couples Therapy

Andy Greendorfer

Marathon therapy at the Gottman Institute Marriage Clinic is an innovative and exciting way to work with couples. A highly intensive but time-limited, brief-course of treatment, marathon therapy gives couples an opportunity to work through specific and general marital issues much more rapidly than in traditional therapy. It is vigorous, highly interactive, and concentrated. Unlike more conventional models, which are constrained by session lengths, clients in marathon sessions delve deeper into marital patterns for longer, uninterrupted periods. Couples have frequent opportunities to increase their understanding and practice of new interaction methods. They can deeply explore problems, survive failed attempts at marital communication, and succeed where they've failed, all in a day. With a week of such work, they can make dramatic and lasting changes in their relationships.

Much of the design of marathon therapy is similar to typical GMCT but is condensed. The primary distinction is the extended time and frequency of treatment sessions. In marathon therapy the work takes place over 3 to 4 days, with 4 to 6 hours per day. This intense clinical model provides time for client self-evaluation, deep understanding of marital problems, both perpetual and solvable, and increased awareness of the implications of the four horsemen. Though a bonus when it happens, this method is not intended to resolve marital problems. Rather, its purpose is to provide a comprehensive look at the life of the marriage from its inception to the present and to develop effective marital management strategies—in other words, to "change the trajectory" of the marital relationship so couples can find new vision and hope in their troubled marriages. The Gottman model of treatment is particularly suited to this modality as it is a highly organized system of understanding but is not too prescriptive. The supporting Gottman materials, including books, tapes, and weekend workshops, allow for additional understanding of marital concerns.

Some couples seeking marathon therapy have already been in treatment that, for any variety of reasons, has proven to be ineffective. Other couples have never been in treatment but have found their old ways of coping failing them now; they want some relief from their marital angst. Often in crisis, these couples are looking for some ballast for their sinking ship. The design of this modality provides an alternative to more lengthy conventional approaches but still honors sound clinical practice.

One of the banes of therapy with couples is the need to end a session just when it seems that "we are getting somewhere." This sentiment is often expressed by one member of the couple or the other. How often clinicians have heard their clients say, "I wish we didn't have to stop" or "Last week when we left, we left feeling unfinished"? At other times clients have said, "We opened up so much last week, and I felt so unsettled.... I had a hard time returning to the rest of my day." Although this can become a manageable part of treatment, marathon therapy affords the opportunity for continuity and focus without the "intrusions" of normal daily routine. Although the model is built on the notion that emotionally based marital therapy is a highly productive approach, the exploration and then shutting down of emotion-laden material each week can be a struggle for many couples. Marathon therapy anticipates that there will be frequent occurrences of emotional arousal and utilizes this state-dependent condition to enhance opportunities for awareness and change. For example, the marathon model offers ample opportunities to understand and practice the management of DPA, which can, in turn, enhance marital communication.

First, who can best do marathon therapy (as it is through the use of self that much of the work is done)? There are a number of significant factors to consider. Primary among these is the therapist's ability to sustain a direct and active presence with the clients for several hours at a time. Most clinicians schedule 50 to 80 minutes per session. In contrast, marathon sessions are generally 4 to 6 hours per day and in some cases, longer. Though there are scheduled breaks during those hours, there is less opportunity to manage one's own psychological needs. Thus, the therapist needs to be able to fully give him- or herself to the process over these extended time periods, while at the same time maintaining strong clinical boundaries. This model requires a high degree of clinical endurance. The name *marathon* fits.

The therapist also needs to be flexible. He or she must be able to balance regularly scheduled clients and marathon couples. This may be the result of building a practice in which several blocks of time are held open during the course of a "quarter" for marathon sessions. In addition this modality is enhanced by spending a concerted amount of telephone time with both members of the couple in advance of the session. Although time-consuming and generally not standard practice for non-marathon couples, these calls aid in honoring the couple's commitment of time, money, and intent. Often couples have many concerns and questions that need to be answered before they can commit to such an intensive course of treatment. As is often the case, each member has a current understanding of the relationship and a strong desire to share his or her view. Although one does not do the narrative piece of the assessment per se, listening and fielding the couple's concerns is critical to the establishment of a strong therapeutic alliance. These issues will form the beginning of the work and will be more fully discussed later during the initial assessment phase of treatment. As with all clinical relationships, the establishment of a therapeutic alliance is critical to the work, and it begins with these phone contacts.

It should be noted that within the course of these phone conversations, the therapist's clinical office policy is also described in order to begin to establish the clinical boundaries needed for effective work. The conversation should include clear agreements about time, payment (including for the aforementioned phone contacts), and session format. Regular and customary administrative parameters are discussed. Then a written contract is mailed to the clients, who need to sign it and fax it back to the clinician. Fees incurred while setting up the sessions can be included in the final invoicing. In addition, the regular assessment material (written questionnaires) is also mailed to the clients with a cover letter outlining the session days and times, office location, and so on.

Some clients can feel overwhelmed by the impending intensity of the sessions. It is helpful for clients to know that although the work is intensive, breaks will be taken throughout the sessions. For clients who have planned several days for the work, staying in a hotel away from home can provide a distraction-free experience, which also augments the potential outcome. Often couples plan to recreate during the course of the marathon work and this can become a rich opportunity for the treatment process.

Clients need the assessment materials sent to them enough in advance that they can complete them in a thoughtful manner. The materials include the Locke-Wallace marital adjustment test, the Weiss-Cerretto marital status inventory, the 17 areas questionnaire, the SCL-90, the conflict tactics scale, and the Waltz-Rushe-Gottman emotional abuse questionnaire (EAQ). Also included are inventories about love maps, fondness and admiration, start-up, accepting influence, turning toward, negative perspective, repair attempts, compromise, gridlock, flooding, emotional disengagement, and the honoring of dreams. It is also important for the clinician to receive the paper work early enough before the therapy begins that it can be reviewed. Three weeks in advance seems to be optimum. I have found that when some couples look at the material their anxiety increases, making them ambivalent about coming to the sessions. Often one or both members of the couple will call after they begin to work on the assessments, as the questions often point to the very issues that they are struggling with. Sometimes the anxiety is great enough that clients request a delay in the session schedule. Although this may occur within the normative model of treatment, it is exacerbated with marathon clients due to the expense and the obvious commitment of time and other resources. These concerns can be allayed by normalizing the clients' concerns and providing additional information about the session format, which continues to establish a strong treatment alliance and also provides an experience of the model (i.e., the therapist's turning toward the clients). In cases where normalizing does not put the client at greater ease, a delay in the treatment is supported and a future phone appointment can be made to again consider the work.

In this modality, more latitude is given to the therapist, and to the client, in the manner in which time is utilized. The ebb and flow of overt and covert communication can be more broadly experienced and understood. This flexibility can be particularly useful when clients are flooded or have thinking styles that require a more considered pace than their partners. Similarly, the use of videotape, which I consider to be essential in marathon therapy, benefits from flexibility of time, as the playback and review process can be a lengthy one.

Taking breaks is another important facet of marathon therapy. As noted, the advantage to this modality is that the sessions can be paced so the intensity is managed without the time constraints. Breaks provide opportunities to help clients learn how to self-regulate when they are flooded, to practice taking breaks, to think about their role in marital interactions, and to return to the session to try again. In marathon therapy, the therapist can also use breaks to contemplate what interventions may be useful. Well-utilized breaks can also help the therapist to moderate his or her own emotional responses to the work although this should be continually occurring during the session time.

As with all clinical treatment, marathon therapists need to be well-grounded in their craft. It is indeed requisite that they are able to give their clients ample opportunity to move easily through the various levels of the SRH and reach to the underpinnings of the issues that compel the marital interactions. As in all good clinical process, being a part of a consultation group with other clinicians helps to hone skills. It is of course most helpful when the practitioner can be a part of a group that understands this modality of treatment.

There are a number of characteristics that determine whether or not a couple is a good candidate for marathon therapy. Clients who are the most interested in this kind of work are generally the most distressed couples I have worked with. Often they are on the brink of divorce or have reached the dangerous marital precipice just prior to separation. This highly emotional state can be a plus for treatment, as it is in this state-dependent learning mode that much cognitive and experiential information can be assimilated.

To ensure a successful course of treatment, couples who engage in marathon therapy need to have an ability to look at their own motivations and share these thoughts and feelings with their partners, even if this is a new or difficult skill. The extended session length renders defenses less effective, as the Marathon work provides numerous opportunities for the exploration of relevant issues. Of course, marathon therapy is contraindicated for the couples that have significant degrees of domestic violence or drug/alcohol abuse. These couples need to be referred to specialists to complete a successful course of individual treatment before marital therapy can begin. In a few cases where drug/alcohol use is present, this modality can be an opportunity to discuss the impact of the behavior on the spouse, and treatment can potentially be helpful. In other words, what applies for more standard treatment applies here. For couples in which there is untreated but clinically significant depression, anxiety disorders, or thought disorders, marathon therapy may also be contraindicated.

USEFUL METAPHORS FOR MARATHON WORK

Metaphors can often be useful in clinical practice, as they can free thinking from established cognitive frameworks. There are several that have worked particularly well in this modality. For example, when clients have trouble letting go of past hurts and resentments in order to do the clinical work, I suggest that "spending too much time with the past is like driving down the road and looking too long in the rearview mirror. It can be dangerous because you can't see where you are going and probably will crash. Conversely, not looking in the mirror at all is not safe because you can't see where you have been or what might be gaining on you." I suggest that a balance between glancing in the rearview mirror and looking down the road is an optimal way of considering history.

Clients often like this idea but say that they don't know how to achieve such a balance, so we discuss how entering marital therapy requires a certain degree of letting go and imaging possibilities. It is like going to a science fiction movie where the viewer enters the theater with a "willing suspension of disbelief." This is not a total abandonment of good sense, but rather an opportunity for something new to develop. Of course, ailing marriages are not movies, they are real life, with real pain. But change can be enhanced if, for only a moment, clients can suspend what they have always known about their partners, themselves, and their marital interactions.

Also useful is the hackey sack/tennis metaphor. Often in marital communication, couples work very hard to convince the other person that they are right about a particular matter. Partners banter back and forth about serious matters, waiting for the moment when they can prove how right they are and win. This is like a game of tennis with a good rally. There is much cross-court momentum and a period of lying in wait, which sets up the opportunity to slam in the winning point. To the winner, it feels great. To the loser, it can feel terrible. Have that happen often enough and you have "point, game, set." In essence, there is a victor and a vanquished. The ideal marital communication is more like a game of hackey sack. This game is generally played in a circle, where all of the participants stand facing inward. The idea of the game is to keep the two-inch stuffed ball, or "sack," in play and from hitting the ground. Participants hit the sack with their various extremities (mostly arms, legs, and feet). There is no wining or losing—the only goal of the game is to keep the sack moving. Effective marital communication is more like hackey sack than tennis. This is antithetical to the way most of us think about being in relationship, where we try to gain the advantage in order to be heard. Listening to the other person is often the furthest thing from our minds. The integration of this paradigm shift is paramount for the emergence of mindful and lasting change.

TOM AND LINDSEY

Tom and Lindsey contacted me in considerable marital distress. Both had read parts of John Gottman's *The Seven Principals for Making Marriage Work,* which had intrigued them, and they wanted to work within the Gottman model. They were feeling a mounting urgency regarding their marriage and, despite financial and scheduling exigencies, were hopeful about the possibilities presented in the marathon approach. Tom was very dissatisfied in the marriage and was asking for a divorce. Partnered for 2 years and married for 5, they were 2 months pregnant. For some time they had found that they were unable to work through issues of individual or joint concern. As a result of significant arguing that escalated to insulting, demeaning language, they had agreed to separate several months before. At the time of the initial contact they were living in separate residences.

Assessment

In extensive phone conversations, I learned a lot about Tom and Lindsey. Tom reported that he had returned to school after an unsuccessful career as a clothing sales representative. Lindsey had worked for a real estate company but planned to leave her position after the birth of their baby. The pregnancy was not planned, although Tom had always envisioned that he would be a father. Lindsay, however, was more ambivalent about her desire to be a mother. The pregnancy had put a significant strain on their relationship and was challenging them in unanticipated ways. Although Tom wanted to be a good father, things had gotten so bad that he thought divorce would be a better alternative than dealing with their marital distress. Lindsey concurred but wanted to give the relationship one last try. Tom was aware that his absence would have a significant effect on the baby, but he could not come to peace with himself about fatherhood, marriage, and the maintenance of his individual needs. He was an avid basketball player and played piano in a jazz band. He often spent his free time with his individual pursuits while Lindsey engaged in her own activities. He did not want to give up what had become a very fulfilling independent life.

Although not looking for another partner to fulfill his needs, Tom had become attracted to another woman who often came to listen to his band practice. She had expressed an interest in him and on several occasions they spent some private but nonphysical time together. Though it had not developed into anything "serious," his attraction alarmed him. He told Lindsey and cut off the burgeoning relationship on his own volition. It was this awareness that his emotions had stepped over the line that both scared him and drove him to seek treatment. Hurt and angry, Lindsey, too, took it as a symptom of a troubled marriage. Difficult as it was, however, Lindsey "marginally" forgave him and they jointly decided to delve into the issues that had created the distance in their relationship.

When Tom and Lindsey had recognized that they needed professional support to improve the quality of their marriage they had tried some counseling in their hometown, but they were dissatisfied with the results. They felt that the pace had been too slow and that the therapist had not interacted with them enough. Most importantly, they hadn't worked on problem solving skills or the underlying issues.

The practical approach of *The Seven Principals for Making Marriage Work* had appealed to them.

In the pre-session phone interviews, both Tom and Lindsey expressed trepidation about coming. They were anxious about what they might discover if they began to dig into their relationship issues. Driven by the depth of the marital crisis and the possibility that they might separate, divorce, and then have to parent alone, they jointly decided to come for marathon work. Given the impending birth of their child, they agreed that the maximum amount of hours would probably provide the greatest benefit. We agreed to meet for a total of 20 hours over 4 days.

In advance of the marathon session I sent out and then evaluated their questionnaires. The 17 areas questionnaire (which identifies solvable and perpetual problems) revealed difficulties with problem solving skills, intimacy, life goals, teaming, and finances. The Weiss-Cerretto indicated that both had seriously considered divorce, but at the time of the sessions, neither had sought legal counsel. Other questionnaires noted declines in the fondness and admiration system, and a specific inability to utilize softened start-up or to accept influence. Both members reported difficulty turning toward and making repair attempts. There was an inability to compromise and, given the overall profile, there was a highly negative perspective. They described feeling gridlocked in a number of areas including issues around the pregnancy, finances, and use of leisure time. Indicators of all four horseman—criticism, defensiveness, contempt, and stonewalling—were present. Both members described often feeling flooded at various times in their marital interactions. According to the data there was a mixture of times of emotional disengagement and times of connectedness. The Conflict Tactics Scale indicated that there had been some physical aggression by both of them during conflicted discussions, but both had reported that there were no incidents for over 2 years. There were no significant elevations on the SCL-90 or the EAQ. They spent little time together.

Prior to their courtship, neither Tom nor Lindsey was particularly interested in dating. They each focused on their career options and only dated occasionally. Introduced by mutual friends, they started off very cautiously in the relationship. During their courtship they went to clubs, hiked, and spent long weekends together. They particularly enjoyed doing things related to the arts; dance, music, museums, and film all were mutually held interests. Lindsey was attracted to Tom's forthrightness, his ability to problem solve, his physical person, and his respect for her. He treated Lindsey "with such respect, like I mattered." He found that her "free spirit was exciting, and it brought adventure and surprise to this world." He was also attracted to her unfettered joy of life, her attentiveness to him, her earnestness, and her "great body." Both acknowledged that they loved each other from early on in the relationship. They both also were aware that they didn't feel as free in their sexual relationship as they would like. Both said that their partner was overly critical and unable to accept them for who they were. Despite this they had a deep fondness for each other and continued with the courtship and ultimately with the marriage.

Lindsey was the youngest of three siblings. Her family relationships created a mixture of feelings for her. Her parents' marriage was very strained and they had separated 10 years prior to our sessions. Lindsey's father was very exuberant.

He could show a range of emotion in his marriage and to the children. Lindsey's mother came from a dysfunctional family in which emotion was not expressed. Her mother was counter-dependent and had given messages to all three children that they really didn't need to be married to be happy. Lindsey's mother was depressed, highly critical, and very demanding. In contrast, Lindsey's older sister was able to provide a model of emotional connectedness and effective problem solving. Overall, family communication was often riddled with sardonic and sarcastic humor that, although lively, hurt. It was indirect and passive-aggressive. As the youngest of the three siblings, Lindsey invariably felt unheard and invisible. Now, however, she was extremely close to her siblings and had a good adult relationship with both of them. There were no problems in her family with substance abuse or domestic violence.

Though different in many respects, Tom's history was also fraught with loss and loneliness. His father died when he was 11 years old. The long illness that preceded his death was very difficult for Tom. He was lonely and had to care for himself. His mother provided much of his father's at-home care and was emotionally unavailable during his latency and adolescence. Tom did not have a model for the understanding of emotion or problem solving during that period or any period of his life. Tom clearly remembered his mother's distress as the dominant emotional state in the home. Defined by the illness, the relationship between his father and mother was distant and at times hostile. Neither parent was equipped to deal with the range of emotions generated in the house. Issues related to the illness were not discussed in order to protect Tom's father (and mother) from stress and the increasingly present demise. After his father's death his mother did not remarry but had a number of relationships with men who were inattentive to Tom and his two sisters. Despite some emotional connection to his two sisters, the relationships had never been close. For the most part, Tom felt he was all alone in the world. Always hesitant about commitment, Tom did not want to replicate the difficult family pattern that he grew up with. He was cautious in most of his friendships and rarely got close to others.

THE THERAPY

Our 4 days of therapy transpired as follows.

Day One

Tom and Lindsey arrived at the office a bit late but were very excited about getting started. They had arrived in Seattle the previous day, spent some of the interim time sightseeing, and had discovered an intimate restaurant the night before. They took the opportunity to talk about the upcoming sessions. To their mutual surprise, the travel day had not erupted into discord. They had done well. There was little of the trepidation noted in the phone interviews. In fact, there was much joking and respectful teasing. There was physical touching—his hand on her knee and several brief but notable gentle holdings of her shoulder. Although I initially thought this to be anxiety or perhaps a "show for the therapist," it soon became clear that there was mutual respect and fondness between them. There were smiles and points of appreciation for the planning and implementation of getting to Seattle. Each had kind words for the other. I was heartened to think that they had more going for them than they themselves had realized. My initial treatment intervention was to enhance the awareness of this clinical impression of their strengths. However, before starting I had to gather more information.

The 1st day, a total of 6 hours with an hour-long break for lunch was spent gathering a complete relationship history. The joint meta-emotion/oral history interview was indeed a wellspring of information. I began to understand both through data and observation how each of them understood and utilized emotion in their marriage. This part of the marathon session took approximately 3 hours, with both Tom and Lindsey present. As I always do, I told them that there would be some individual time with me during the early stages of the work and that a decision on the timing of that would be made as the day progressed. (I generally accomplish this by midday of the 2nd day, waiting until there has been enough time for the problem areas to be overtly identified.) In the course of the interview, I saw that there was a fairly high degree of understanding of each other's overt love maps but there was little understanding of the meanings behind their needs and activities. The interview corroborated much of what the presession material had presented. They were having difficulty in their marital communication due to the presence of the four horsemen, particularly criticism, and they weren't able to talk about and process micro- and macro-problems in their relationship. Though they made many bids for connection, and many were accepted, they had little capacity to repair communication when things went awry.

> Greendorfer: I am so pleased to finally get a chance to meet you both. (*anxious laughter from both of them*) By choosing to come in for Marathon Therapy, you have made quite a commitment to the relationship. (*They looked at each other and smiled.*) I know from the phone conversations with each of you that there are many worries about the marriage and its future. (*an eye roll from her*) We will be working on these over the next several days. (*mixed smiles at each other*) As I reviewed your paperwork (*a grimace from him*)—and I want to talk about all that later on—I saw many ways in which you both seem to see things in a similar light. (*more smiles directed at each other, a touch from him on her shoulder*) Now I want you each to talk more about what brings you here and what you want to work on. Because you have set aside so many hours over the next several days, we have plenty of time to think about the relationship, the issues that are present, and see what we can do to bring greater understanding to the marriage. Tell me how you see things and how you think you got here.

At this point both Tom and Lindsey took a deep breath. Acknowledging that time and intent were both present seemed to make a difference to both of them. The initial treatment contract was now being reaffirmed and established. I knew that there was much to accomplish, but, because it was Marathon work, I could relax a bit knowing that there was sufficient time to cover much of the presenting problems.

Lindsey: Why don't you start Tom? I made the appointments and I want to see what you think.

Tom: All right. Well, I don't really know where to start. At the beginning of the relationship she was the one who wanted more of the relationship. As of last year, I was the one who wanted more. *(a nod from her)* I realized that things had gotten kind of bad, we were arguing all the time about the little stuff, and I began to realize I wanted to have something different. I had been thinking up to that point that there must be some ways that I could do things differently to be a better spouse but did not know what I wanted in a relationship. I have been doing a lot of thinking about this and realize that I need something more than what Lindsey is giving me. She is a wonderful woman with so many good qualities *(she interrupted with laughter: "I hate it when you say that!")* but ... well, I don't want to be hurtful, I don't know how straightforward to be but I need some other things as well. And now we have a baby on the way.... I mean I really do love Lindsey, that is not a question for me, but I don't know if this is who I want to spend the rest of my life with. It's really scary for me. Maybe it is just the mix between us, I just don't know.

Tom was having a very hard time articulating his concerns without hurting Lindsey. He verbalized positive feelings with congruent affect. He looked pained as he told her how he was feeling and repeated numerous times how he needed to voice his thoughts if things were going to improve. His genuine concern corroborated the assessment material, and I could see that there were still aspects of the fondness and admiration system intact. As I thought about the marathon work that was beginning to unfold, I knew that we were going to have to spend considerable time on his dreams of relationship and his approaching fatherhood, especially in light of the loss of his own father. I was also aware that he was sensitive to Lindsey's emotions and, as a result, conflict avoidant.

Tom: When we met I had a degree from college and I wanted to just play music. I have always loved to play music. *(a look of longing)* Lindsey liked that about me. *(a half smile from Lindsey)* I don't know if I can still have that kind of life any more. *(Lindsey slightly turns her shoulders away.)* You know, playing music and snowboarding. Of course I also want to have a really great relationship. *(no visible change in Lindsey)* These things are so important to me. You know, when I was growing up I didn't have all that and I know I want it now. *(Lindsey turns slightly back)* I just don't know if I can have it with Lindsey. *(Her eyes turn downward.)* She really is great and all that.

Tom's ambivalence about the relationship and unfulfilled dreams began to emerge. During most of the dialogue Tom continually looked away from Lindsey, either into space or at me. Although thoughtful, Tom appeared disconnected, as if he was instead reaching deep into hinself. I wanted to explore his ambivalence further but also build on their strengths. I thought about looking further into their love maps, fondness and admiration, and emotional connection.

Greendorfer: Lindsey, can you talk about how you see things?

Lindsey: Well, Tom and I were raised very differently and I just don't know if things are going to work out. Neither of us knows if this relationship is right. I don't want to raise a baby in a home where there is trouble all the time. I don't want it to be like in our homes that we grew up in. We both had problems. Tom's father was very hard to get along with. He had some very strong Catholic ideas. (*Tom laughs, uncomfortably nods, and verbally agrees.*) Not so true in my family. In my family there was not so much attention on religion, but we were more spiritual. I think this is another way that we are different.

Tom: You know, it's true, things were very different in our families.

Greendorfer: There do seem to be some differences here, but I am noticing how well you understand each other's worlds, the other one's family history, and how your partner feels about it. You seem to be aware of each other's love maps. That's a very good sign.

Lindsey: *(to Tom)* Well, see, we aren't all bad. We really do know a lot about each other. I totally understand where he is coming from because I know him really well. I know he loves me but sometimes I just... well, we get into so many arguments. We just don't seem to know how to talk to each other. *(Tom nods.)* What I really want is to be closer to each other, for you, Tom, to want me.

Tom: It really isn't a question of our marriage being bad, we really aren't miserable like so many other people that come into this kind of thing. It is just that I want a fantastic marriage. I really want us to be amazing partners for each other. I know that reality is never what we dream but I want to head more in that direction. I want to have a great relationship.

In marathon work, it is important to find various strengths within the relationship without being patronizing or rescuing the couple from their emotions. Again, this is often true in couples work, though in the "sequestered" Marathon setting there is opportunity to have these strengths accentuated to a greater degree. It is essential that strengths be found early so that the couple begins to see hope, some possibility or reason for change. This strengthens the fondness and admiration system. Often couples report at the end of treatment that helping them see these points of connection was a valuable first step to understanding one another. I proceeded to introduce the love map cards. Tom and Lindsey enjoyed this exercise, as many couples do, and found a deepening sense of connection in the process.

The morning session continued with dialogue about their competing needs. They were an introspective couple and work on individual family histories revealed a wellspring of unresolved emotion that was being projected onto the other one. She was looking for a partner who could be as enthusiastic as her father, showering her with attention. She had wanted a relationship in which teasing would be minimized, as it had been so hurtful in her life. She wanted connection like she had with her older sister. Lindsey's desire was to be heard and appreciated.

Tom's history led him to a desire for independence. He was fearful that he was going to lose this in the marriage, especially when the child was born. His self-reliant life was a powerful personal value. He was reminded of his feelings of anger when he had to care for his mother after the death of his father. Also, he was afraid that if he let himself be too close to Lindsey or the baby, he might lose them and thus he needed to remain independent. He was uncertain how to take care of Lindsey without taking over.

They had interactive interchanges about these histories and the impact that they were having on them. They did, however, continue to talk over one another, not listening to the other one's story and instead "lying in wait" to tell their own tale. It was time for a "psychoeducational instructional moment."

I had observed that Tom and Lindsey needed a "primer" on the concepts of the SRH. Even though they both had a familiarity with the concepts, I wanted to deepen their understanding of the framework. Often this education or reeducation is beneficial to the work. I often do this late in the morning of the 1st day, or sometime after the lunch break. Some education provides good reference points for the interventions and a common language to understand areas of marital challenge. With Tom and Lindsey the "lecture" took about 45 minutes. In the course of it, one or both of them commented about the various levels that needed work. I then added my observations of what I had seen so far in the sessions and what I had learned from the assessment material, and together we created a more complete treatment contract.

In order to refine this further, I used an intervention that has become standard with Marathon Therapy. In between each session, whether at the lunch break or the end of the day, I have couples do a two-part exercise. First, they write down what they have learned about themselves and about their partner. Second, they write down what more they would like to get from the therapy. Using this exercise, the couple continues to hone in further on the gridlocked, perpetual, and solvable problems. I gave Tom and Lindsey this assignment at the lunch break. When they came back the session continued.

> Lindsey: First I want to say that coming into these sessions was not so scary. I
> am beginning to see that we can learn a lot. . . . So, what I learned about
> Tom. I learned that Tom has a greater need for a very close relationship
> than I had realized and that this comes from wanting what he didn't
> have growing up. I never really realized that before. I always thought
> that that was just some kind of crap from him. I was pretty judgmental
> about all that. Now I see it differently. This leads into the second thing
> that I learned. I was threatened by his need for this closeness and now I
> realize that it's really important to him. I don't feel so threatened
> anymore now that I realize that. I really want him to be happy. (*Tears
> well up in her eyes.*) I also realized more about how this whole bunch of
> stuff is happening to us, to you, Tom, and how overwhelmed you are. I
> just hadn't realized that. (*Tom nods his head actively.*)
> Tom: I didn't realize how much I don't accept Lindsey for who she is. I have
> not focused on the positive things as much as the negative. And that has
> a lot to do with what I learned about myself. I am way too critical, too
> judgmental. It is really a minor effort that I can make to be less

judgmental. I just hadn't realized that and the effect it has on our relationship. *(Lindsey reaches across the couch and gingerly touches his arm.)*

Moments like this, of course, happen in non-marathon settings, too. However, marathon therapy sessions provide a building up of these understandings over the course of hours and days, rather than weeks and months of "regular work." Through this condensed and intensified work, these understandings can more immediately be utilized.

Greendorfer: So what more do you want to get out of our time together?

Tom: I want to understand more about how I can have it all. My life of piano, my work, and a family. It seems so hard to do it all. I also learned that I need to be less critical and listen better to what Lindsey wants.

Lindsey: I want to learn more about why we can't talk about stuff that is important without it breaking down to arguing and fighting. I don't want to do things like my parents did. I want to talk about the important things in our lives. I want to do it differently.

The 1st day ended with an intervention to continue to help them make connection. I used the positive adjectives checklist to further underscore the connections that they had with each other. Each of them had very engaging anecdotes that illustrated their feelings. Both of them found the other to be very intelligent and humorous. She was awed by his perseverance and creativity. He valued her beauty and loyalty.

Days Two, Three, and Four

Arriving on time the 2nd day for what was to be $5\frac{1}{2}$ hours of work, Tom and Lindsey were both tired. They had been out the previous evening and had reportedly had a good time with each other at a local restaurant. They slept in the same bed for the first time in several months, but did so without sexual intimacy. We started off with the "what did you learn exercise" based on yesterday's intervention.

Tom: *(to Lindsey)* I learned two things. I have to be more mindful, sensitive, when we are talking, be more tuned in to what you are saying. Once we get into that dynamic it is kind of hard to get out of it. I also learned that I need to know what I want in myself and communicate that with you. I didn't really ever tell you why I was feeling so trapped before we separated. I realize that it could have been different. I need to do better with all that.

Lindsey: I didn't know how much I needed to be appreciated in this relationship. And how much I need to appreciate you and say so. I learned that I also need to slow down and listen to you. I have so much to say . . . .

Tom: It is really good that you can say that you need me to appreciate you. I didn't realize that it really makes a difference. I want to do more of that. And you're right, I want to hear it, too.

Midmorning on this second day I spent time with both Tom and Lindsey individually. Each described in more detail how precarious the relationship had been prior to coming to the marathon sessions. Both were uncertain if there was going to be any real change, and their "mismatched relationship" was a theme for each of them. There were no "surprises" in these 40-minute individual sessions. There also were no reports of physical or psychological abuse, drug- or alcohol-related problems, or affairs other than what had been openly discussed. It provided a time for further recalibration of the treatment goals and an opportunity to establish a more heartfelt therapeutic alliance with both of them.

As the day continued Tom and Lindsey explored a variety of areas that had been "off-limits." With their newfound appreciation for each other, they were able to take more risks and say what they had been thinking with less criticism and defensiveness. The contemptuous feelings were discussed and their genesis considered utilizing the dream-within-conflict intervention. They continued to ask questions about various SRH concepts in order to more completely understand their issues. Of note was the practice of antidotes to the four horsemen. Each of the topics that were of concern—the pregnancy, motherhood, fatherhood, the "attraction to another woman," financial security, the need for independence, interdependence, the aging process, physical health, physical intimacy, and the sexual relationship—was explored. It was exhausting for both of them, but particularly for Lindsey, who was, after all, pregnant. We took plenty of time to reduce DPA. Decisions were made, compromises reached, and understandings deepened.

In the sessions I was very active, using a variety of interventions to help them get to these issues. Unless the client objects, I continually run the video camera during marathon sessions, and did so with Tom and Lindsey. The continuity of the marathon sessions offered ample opportunity to review the tapes, integrate understandings, and reference them at later points. The video playback was of particular value when there was subtle but observable contempt, acts of turning away, or attack-defend processes. In the following dialogue, each was able to see themselves and the not-so-subtle impact that their actions were having on the other. They further understood the need for being direct without being hurtful to the other one. I consistently noted moments of turning toward and turning away. If a picture is worth a thousand words, a moving one with sound is worth ten thousand. It is invaluable in exploring the subtle and not-so-subtle relationship interactions.

Lindsey: I know that you feel like you are going to lose so much of your independence when the baby is born. You know, this isn't easy for me either. I want her, but I have to give up a lot, too. I don't like the way my body is looking to me now. (*Tom is looking off in another direction.*) I'm afraid that I won't ever get it back again, you know, to the way it was before the pregnancy. I am going to want to dance again. (*Lindsey wells up with tears, Tom still looks off; suddenly, with vehemence, harsh start-up, and contempt, she continues.*) Are you listening to me? You never listen enough when I tell you stuff. Don't you get it? (*Tom was now listening, though somewhat blankly, perhaps flooded.*)

Tom: (*flatly*) I am listening but you don't see what is going on for me. (*with increased affect*) I am the one who is going to give up so much. My whole life is going to change. I want this baby, too, but you are really the one who has wanted to be a parent. This is all new for me. I don't know what I want. I need my independence to do my things, my music, my basketball, and just going out with my friends.

Lindsey: (*crying*) Why is it always about you? Go ahead, do what you want.

Tom: It's not just about me, but about both of us and the baby. I just want us all to be happy.

Lindsey: (*flooded*) That's a bunch of crap. You don't even care. It's just about you.

Greendorfer: (*leaning forward*) I need to interrupt you both here. I wonder if you understand what just happened. (*Both look somewhat flooded and quizzical.*) I think this would be a good time to look at the tape if that's Okay with you.... (*Both nod in marginal agreement.*) I would like you to watch the tape and then we will talk about what you see. Watch and listen to yourself in light of what we were thinking about yesterday and the learnings that you discussed this morning as our session started again.

The video was rewound. The room was silent; neither one looked at the other. Ten minutes of tape was replayed, including the previous dialogue.

Greendorfer: So what did you see or hear?

Tom: She tells me I don't listen, I think I am, but wow, I get it. There I am looking off.

Lindsey: I tell you that all the time. Why do we have to come all this way for you to see it? I am so tired of you not listening. It's why we have so much trouble all the time.

Tom: (*exasperated*) Forget it! I am just trying to learn something here about myself and you are all over me. Now who's not listening?

Lindsey: Okay, maybe you're right. (*A forgive-me smile appears*)

Greendorfer: So, there's a repair....

Tom: I was saying, I was looking off, I was listening, too, but I can see how that would piss you off. You just can't see that I am listening, too.

Greendorfer: That sounds a bit defensive, Tom. Can you try again?

Lindsey: See, that's what I mean.

Tom: Do I have to say it just right?

Greendorfer: If you wouldn't mind, try again. Think hackey sack, you know, like we were talking about yesterday and the day before.

Tom: Oh, yeah. I was thinking about all of this stuff and only sorta listening. When I saw the replay I can really see why that would make you mad. I'll try not to do that.

Lindsey: Thanks. (*Lindsey reaches for his arm, which has fallen outstretched on the back of the couch. She gingerly touches it.*) I guess I can get on you when I get flooded. I really saw it there, I mean on the tape, I just get so mad when you don't listen to me. (*Tom removes his arm and tenses up.*) I need to pay attention to getting flooded like that. I've always done that. It goes back to the way it felt when I was a kid, when my mom couldn't listen to me because she was so depressed. It just comes on so fast and then I go after you.

Other aspects of the taped interaction were reviewed. During the nearly 22 hours with this couple, the tape was utilized four times.

In the course of the 4 days we had an opportunity to work on many of interventions, including the aftermath of a marital argument, the repair checklist, and dream-within-conflict. These interventions deepened the couple's understanding of the four horsemen and gave them an effective working knowledge of their antidotes. By the end of the 3rd day, Tom and Lindsey were making more repairs, giving and accepting bids for connection, and accepting those bids more readily. They often laughed together when they used their old manner of interaction. They took some joy in teasing each other with the old style and then using the new tools. Lindsey was able to more quickly identify moments of feeling flooded and they took the requisite breaks, returning to the material later. The couple was able to deepen their appreciation for each other and the enduring vulnerabilities that they lived with. They were able to practice and practice again the techniques they were learning.

By the end of the last day Lindsey and Tom had reached some important decisions. It had been agreed that there was enough emotional connection between them that they would move back in together. They began to agree on some possible names for the baby girl who was about to become part of their lives. They planned to spend more time with each other and, above all, listen to each other without being dismissive like they had been before. They agreed to talk things out rather than stonewalling. Both members of the couple considered their new understanding of themselves as individuals as also useful for their marital partnership. They both knew that it was a beginning. Individual therapy and some continued marital therapy was recommended and they planned to follow up when they got home.

CONCLUSION

Marathon therapy offers an opportunity for therapists to help clients look more quickly and deeply at the process and content of their marital communication. It requires a commitment of resources that can give intensity to marital treatment, intensity that is difficult to create in more standard models. Clients who have participated in this mode have valued the focused attention that they have given to their relationships and have often grown closer in the process. At times, marathon therapy may help to clarify that the relationship needs to end, though this has been rare. Sometimes couples are interested in returning for more work within the marathon therapy mode. Although not all cases treated in this modality succeed, it can provide many couples greater opportunity for marital success when doubt and failure existed before.

Chapter 12 ❧

Bridging Psychodynamic Couples Therapy and Gottman Method Couples Therapy

Maureen Sawyer

In this chapter I describe how I have come to understand and work with two very different models of couples therapy. As a psychodynamically trained therapist, I discuss my enthusiasm and difficulties with implementing the Gottman Method Couples Therapy (GMCT). I will look at the concepts of affect regulation and internal working models to provide the bridge between these two very different models. Finally, I present a clinical vignette illustrating some of the clinical thinking of both the Gottman and the psychodynamic approaches.

BACKGROUND

My introduction to GMCT came when I attended the Gottman 2-day training for clinicians. John Gottman presented a theory and a method for working with couples that was based on his research at the University of Washington "Love Lab." His theory and methodology made good clinical sense. It was highly focused, client-centered, and nonpathologizing. I left the workshop very energized and excited.

However, when I was back into the trenches of couples therapy, with verbal bullets flying around me, I was quite confused and overwhelmed about how to use the model that had made such good sense. My initial enthusiasm was tempered. It was not easy for me to "just do" the Gottman method. Why was I having such difficulty using what I had learned? The first and most obvious explanation for my muddle and difficulty in applying the GMCT was the inevitable stress of learning and working with a new model. I knew that being exposed to new concepts and techniques was a far cry from knowing how and when to use them clinically, particularly in the heat of a couple's battle.

Then I began to notice that I was struggling with something else. I was having trouble fitting together psychodynamic therapy and GMCT. I would sometimes revert to "business as usual," which meant doing psychodynamic couples therapy to avoid not only the discomfort of doing new things, but also the discomfort of feeling conflicted. This felt like resistance, and was a more stubborn problem. I was gridlocked.

Yet the GMCT continued to intrigue me. I decided to pursue additional training. In 1999 I enrolled in the Advanced Training Program. Upon completion I became a clinician in the Gottman Institute. However, I experienced gridlock when I tried to integrate GMCT and psychodynamic couple therapy. I had two warring factions in me: psychodynamic couples therapy versus GMCT. They seemed at odds with each other. And as happens with a gridlocked problem, neither faction would budge. I obstinately remained focused on their differences. In my mind each theory ignored, devalued, and even vilified the other. I had a hard time engaging myself in a constructive internal dialogue between the models. I had to ask myself what I was afraid of and why I was so locked in resistance.

Part of the answer was that I had recently completed a several year psychoanalytic psychotherapy training program taught from a British object relations perspective when I began the advanced Gottman training. I felt threatened. I feared challenging and losing what I had just spent so much time studying. The battle in my head was between the loyalty and respect I had developed for the psychoanalytically informed model and an excitement for the new concepts of the Gottman model.

The two models differ in both theoretical orientation and methodology in some very significant ways. Here are some of the major differences that I have chosen to highlight.

First, GMCT is primarily dyadic. The therapist functions as a coach while providing active and specific interventions. The goal of treatment is to empower the couple with information and tools. The focus is on strengthening their friendship and teaching constructive conflict management, thus exponentially creating a more satisfying relationship. The goal of GMCT is to provide tools for the couple to effectively process issues on their own.

In contrast, psychodynamic couples therapy is triadic. The therapist's focus is on the *being* with the couple rather than *doing*. Unlike the GMCT, the psychodynamic therapist's interventions are not direct or targeted, and the therapist does not provide specific interventions. Instead, the therapist fosters collaborative exploration and understanding, and listens carefully to both what is said and not said. He or she pays close attention to countertransferential feelings and fantasies, looking for the clues to understand and speak to the couples' shared internal worlds of self and other. The therapist works to contain and reflect upon the couple's feelings, thoughts, and behaviors. Interpretations are made in a tentative fashion. They are to be chewed on, thought about, discussed, rather than swallowed whole. Gradually, and in the context of the therapeutic relationship, the couple learns the containing and reflecting functions of the therapist through identification and internalization. The goal of psychodynamic treatment is to have the couple effectively process issues on their own (McCormack, 2000).

Second, GMCT is quite structured compared to psychodynamic couples therapy. For example, GMCT has a highly structured assessment protocol that includes an oral history and meta-emotions interviews, individual sessions, questionnaire packets, and a play-by-play videotape of the couple discussing an area of conflict. The assessment process culminates in a therapeutic contract.

In psychodynamic couples therapy the assessment process is much less structured. The therapist invites the couple to tell their story in their own way with little or no direction. Factual as well as emotional information unfolds in a more organic fashion and on the couple's timetable. The therapeutic contract between the therapist and the couple is defined by an adherence to the therapeutic frame and the creation of a psychologically safe working space.

Both approaches value the expression of strong affect and believe that learning and insight occur best when the couple is affectively engaged. John Gottman refers to these times as the magic moments of learning. The approaches differ, however, in the means by which these emotional states are attained. GMCT actively choreographs these affective learning moments through the use of structured interventions and exercises.

In contrast, the psychodynamically oriented couples therapist strives to create an atmosphere that supports the organic emergence of strong affective states. The therapist functions as a container for the couple's powerful feelings and collaborates with them to explore and understand the meaning of what is happening. The therapist offers tentative interpretations carefully timed for the couple's consideration regarding the meaning of their defenses, anxieties, fantasies, and conflicts, and how they contribute to their problematic patterns of relating.

Third, in GMCT the therapist does not do the soothing. The couple learns to sooth themselves and each other using planned affect regulating interventions and exercises. Monitoring devices are used at times to help the client become more aware of his or her stress level.

In psychodynamically oriented couple therapy, the therapist's provision of soothing is central to the therapeutic change process. This holding and containing function aids in the regulation of the couple's dysregulated and at times unbearable affect. The therapist returns the unbearable affect in a "metabolized" form to the client via interpretation. The theory is that over time, the couple comes to identify with and internalize the therapist's soothing and affect regulating capacities. (Scharff & Scharff, 1991)

In addition, each model has its own distinctive language. Psychodynamic language talks about defensive projective identification, separation/individuation, and countertransference. GMCT talks about love maps, bids for connection, and positive/negative sentiment override.

When I thought about the models together there was dissonance. The transition and translation back and forth was at times dizzying and daunting. I found myself being critical of one theoretical approach, then the other. I had no fluency as yet between the two languages. In Gottman language, I was *gridlocked;* in psychoanalytic language I was *conflicted*. Both lead to the same feeling state: anxiety. If theories function in part as roadmaps for clinicians, I had two quite different roadmaps. I was lost, unsure of which map to use.

I thought about John Gottman's dreams-within-conflict intervention, which is used when the couple's problem is gridlocked (1999, p. 235). According to Gottman, "couples experiencing gridlock on a problem over a period of years typically have passed through a number of conflictual stages, beginning with dreams in opposition, moving on to entrenchment of positions, fears of accepting influence, vilification, and finally, emotional disengagement" (p. 235). But Gottman also stated in the marital workshop manual: "in the worst marital problems, the gridlocked perpetual problems, lie the keys to the greatest potential growth" (2000–2001, p. 14). As a clinician I had also internally passed through a number of those conflictual stages and I had certainly experienced much growth and would certainly continue to do so.

Being a student of the GMCT in many ways parallels the experience of the couples that come to us to learn new ways of relating. Both the student/clinician and the couple have to deal with resistance to change and letting go. Both cognitive and emotional space must be made to take in something new. Digestion and indigestion follow. Over time the new material is assimilated, transmuted, and made into one's own. As a clinician, I have had to let go of some my ways of thinking and working, just as in the course of marital therapy the couple must let go of some of their ways of thinking and patterns of relating. This process ultimately requires that the student/couple accepts influence and creates an opening in her or his mind for something new to happen.

My internal dream was to be able work in both models and integrate both models. I knew intuitively that each contains very valuable perspectives and methodologies. I also knew I would be the richer if I could endure the discomfort of the gridlock. So I have persisted with finding a way to honor each model rather than rejecting one for the other. I realize now that they are too disparate to be fully integrated. However, being able to draw upon each model more confidently and smoothly is a tremendous resource and benefit to me as a clinician.

AFFECT REGULATION AND INTERNAL WORKING MODEL

Affect regulation and the concepts of internal representations (the internal working model) have been for me the bridge between GMCT and psychodynamically oriented couples therapy. These intertwining concepts allow me to appreciate the value of each model.

What is affect regulation and how is it acquired? Most simply stated, affect regulation is a person's ability to manage and recover from states of hypoarousal and hyperarousal. The capacity for affect regulation is shaped through the myriad of interactions between the infant/child and primary caretakers. The infant, although a participant in the regulatory processes, has much less ability to regulate his or her own feelings. These feelings can be very intense and become easily dysregulated. Moreover, the infant relies heavily on the good will of the primary caregivers. This process occurs through the medium of normal caretaking.

In this process of interactive affect regulation and communication, attachment bonds are formed between the infant/young child and his or her caretakers. The style and quality of a child's attachment are defined as secure or insecure. The insecure attachment leads to anxious-resistant, avoidant, or disorganized patterns of relating. The secure attachment leads to flexible, cooperative, and organized patterns of relating.

It must be borne in mind that within each individual there is a continuum between regulation and dysregulation dependent upon his or her internal working model and the context of the interaction.

Communication and affect regulation happen around the quality of touch, mutual gaze, facial expression, and tones of voice or prosody. Initially, this process is primarily nonverbal. The quality of what Winnicott (1965) described as the "holding and handling environment" sets up a template of expectations for future relationships. This forms the basis of the internal representational world.

What is the internal representational world? The internal representational world is a template of self and other based on relational expectations. These representations derive from the "holding and handling environment."

Beebe and Lachmann (2002) defined three organizing principles as they relate to representation and internalization in infancy: ongoing regulations, disruption and repair of ongoing regulations, and heightened affective moments. Arising from this is a set of relational expectations. The quality of the infant/child's primary relationship informs how he or she experiences him- or herself and the other or object. In very simplistic terms the infant can view him- or herself as either predominantly good or bad and the object or other as predominantly good or bad, hence the terms the good or bad object.

The second of Beebe and Lachmann's (2002) organizing principles is disruption and repair. This refers to a "violation" of the expected of regulation "ongoingness" and how this is dealt with by either or both parties.

This is in keeping with the infant research of Edward Tronick who studied mothers and their infants to see what constituted "good enough mothering." He originally thought that it had to do with the mother's capacity to be attuned to her infant. What he discovered, to his surprise, was that the majority of interactions (70%) between mothers and babies were misattuned. What made these mothers better at mothering was their ability to realize the misattunement and make repair attempts to reattune with their babies. He also discovered that infants make repair attempts as well. When the infant is successful at repair, this becomes part of his repertoire and contributes to his or her sense of agency in the world (Tronick, 1989).

Conversely, an infant or a child who has been chronically unsuccessful in his or her repair attempts with his primary caretaker is at risk for a diminished sense of agency (Tronick & Weinberg, 1997). In addition, when repair works, children stay connected to caretakers and attempt to work out conflicts or stresses; when repair fails, children withdraw and attempt to soothe themselves.

Research has also demonstrated when conflict occurs, as it inevitably will, couples with a solid friendship are more likely to reach out to make interactive repair. Interactive repair is vital to affect regulation. Both parties must be willing to give and receive repair gestures. This ability is linked to their respective internal representational world and their internal working models as well. One can easily imagine how an infant or child's unsuccessful attempts could have potentially powerful implications for his or her sense of efficacy in future relationships, particularly intimate ones. The client with a childhood history of unsuccessful repair attempts is apt to have an internal working model that says, "Why bother with repair attempts. They don't work." Very often the person is unaware of this working model but it shows up in the form of resistance to making repair attempts.

Repair is much more likely to occur in an overall emotional climate of friendliness, respect, and admiration. This is a major premise of GMTC. In order to increase the likelihood of successful repairs, the Sound Marital House theory (SMH) has been custom-built to assist couples in strengthening their friendship and regulating their conflict. In fact, Gottman conducted an interesting and revealing experiment with his couple workshops. He did a 1-day workshop that focused only on the couples' friendship. Next he did a 1-day workshop that focused only on the couples' conflict. Then he offered a 2-day workshop that focused the first day on strengthening the couples' friendship and the second day on the regulation of conflict. The 2-day workshop proved to be significantly more effective than either of the 1-day workshops; both friendship and conflict regulation are necessary for marital satisfaction.

What then is the internal working model? The internal working model is based on attachment expectations, including expectancies of containment or the lack of containment. The internal working model is largely formed by the meaning each individual assigns to his or her history of affect regulating experiences, his or her attachment styles, and internal representational world of self and other. All these factors greatly influence how a person approaches relationships and the type of attachment he or she is likely to form: secure, anxious-resistant, avoidant, or disorganized.

Thus a couple's ability to have a satisfying relationship is intricately and deeply affected by their history of affect regulation, their internal representational world, and their internal working model. As a clinician, working from either approach, I view the couple's problems through the lens of their current internal working models.

An important commonality of GMCT and psychodynamic couples therapy is that each begins by attending to issues in the here and now. Relational patterns of interaction in the here and now are a reflection and expression the internal working model.

In GMCT resistance to interventions is a signal that attention needs to be directed to the client's internal working model. A particular resistance is linked to a particular level of the SMH. According to John Gottman, "it tells you why processes at that level of the SMH are systematically distorted in this marriage and not working properly"(2000–2001, p. 301).

In GMCT the interventions themselves are apt to stir up the resistance. According to Gottman the key to unlocking resistance is "exploring the person's meaning system, honoring each person as the profound philosopher of his or her own life, and serving as ally to both clients in this very personal life journey"

(2000–2001, p. 266). Questions are crafted to explore the internal working model. Gottman has designed a Resistance Interview with questions formulated to explore a person's internal working model. The questions are tied to the different levels of the SMH. Examples of the love maps questions are "What does it mean to the client to know someone?" and "What does it mean for this client to be known by someone?" This exploration often leads to the history of the client's enduring vulnerabilities and failed relational expectations. Gottman has also created questionnaires specifically designed to determine the presence of a low self-esteem or an antisocial internal working model.

In the course of treatment working with the four horsemen and other interventions such as dreams-within-conflict, the anatomy of failed bids, the aftermath of a fight, past injuries and healings are likely to trigger resistance and signal the presence of the client's internal working model. The therapist then takes the opportunity to explore further the client's internal world and its impact on the couple's relationship.

Other important GMCT interventions created to assist couples with the regulation of affect and internal working models are the triumphs and strivings, legacy and mission interventions and the repair checklist. These function as very tangible containers for the couple when dealing with conflict. There are even prophylactic exercises designed to minimize relapse such as the magic five hours a week. The exercises are literally portable affect regulators and can be used at home or elsewhere. The Gottman method provides many cognitive life rafts the couple can hold on to until they can reach terra firma individually and then with each other.

In psychodynamic couple's therapy, resistance is viewed as a signal of the client's or the couple's joint self-protective effort to ward off unbearable feelings and thoughts. These are feelings and thoughts that are so painful that they are kept out of conscious.

The focus of psychodynamic therapy becomes the creation of a safe space where feeling, thinking, understanding, and reflection gradually replace some of these defense mechanisms. In contrast to GMCT, the therapist's first task is to immerse him- or herself in the internal world of the couple through the process of transference and countertransference. In this way the therapist comes to experience, and thus know and understand, the pain of the couple. It is the therapist's commitment to this level of knowing and understanding along with provision of holding, containing, and at times even just surviving, that creates the possibility of change. Through this therapeutic process the couple slowly becomes less defended, more flexible, and open to him- or herself and each other. I find this approach is particularly useful when working with highly destructive couples, as they frequently seem less capable of using many of GMCT tools initially. These couples, after a period of more intense holding, are often better able to make better use of GMCT approach.

In psychodynamic couples therapy, projective identification is a central concept. It refers to a form of unconscious communication that includes "the phantasy of entering the object with the whole or part of the self which may lead to an altered perception of the identity of the self and object in relation to each other" (Box, Copley, Magagna, & Moustaki, 1981, p. 164). Projective identification is used to manage unbearable feelings and unthinkable thoughts. More norma-tively it is used for communication and to elicit empathy. Defensively, projective identification is used to "get rid of unwanted aspects of the self" or to control the other. A therapeutic goal is for the therapist to assist the couple to more effectively manage their unwanted thoughts, feelings, and shared anxieties by making the processes of thought, reflection, and discussion more available to them. The therapist accomplishes this via holding, containment, observation, and interpretation.

In GMCT the first two of the four horsemen, criticism and defense and the attack–defend cycle that often ensues, remind me of projective identification. In GMCT, criticism is defined as "any statement that implies that there is something globally wrong with one's partner, something that is probably a lasting aspect of the partner's character"(Gottman, 1999, pp. 41–42). In the marital workshops John Gottman described how one partner launches an attack by "putting a soccer ball of criticism in the other's body" that implies "you are defective"; naturally "if someone puts a soccer ball of blame in your body you take it out and put it back in the other person's body." This is the beginning of the attack–defend cycle or an attack–counterattack cycle. The "you never" and the "you always" declarations may be indicative of the psychoanalytic concept of splitting. The "putting a soccer ball of blame into the other" seems analogous to the defensive use of projective identification whereby one person puts unwanted feelings into the other and the other responds with a defensive counterattack. The defensive counterattack could be seen as loosely similar to a "noncontaining" and "unmetabolized" response in psychodynamic terms.

In GMCT the therapist teaches the four horsemen and their antidotes to the couple. A Gottman method of containment is the therapeutic intervention of stop action. When any of the four horsemen appear in the couple's interactions the ther-apist stops the interaction, identifies, and then labels the behaviors, thus height-ening the couple's awareness of destructive behavior. Implied in this stop-action intervention is the therapist's goal of transforming the couple's internal repre-sentational world and internal working model by restructuring their patterns of interaction.

Stop action as a method of containment is very valuable. Research has shown that a person learns best while in a particular emotional state. The therapeutic task is to promote state-dependent learning by having the couple engage directly with each other. It is imperative that the therapist be able to tolerate the couple's strong affect without trying to suppress or quash it. The therapist intervenes with stop action when the four horsemen (criticism, defense, contempt, and stonewalling) appear in the couple's interaction and directs them to use of the appropriate antidote.

Although the four horsemen and defensive projective identification are not the same clinical phenomenon, couples that engage in either or both are often very stuck in destructive relational patterns. As a clinician I find it very useful to be aware of and work with both in accessing the internal working model.

I will now present a clinical vignette to illustrate some of thinking of both approaches.

PAT AND PAUL

Pat and Paul have been married for close to 30 years. Their gridlocked issue was that Pat was outgoing and Paul was a homebody who did not like to socialize. Paul perceived himself as shy and feared rejection in social situations. In fact, he basically refused to go out socially with his wife. Furthermore, he did not want her to entertain at home. Pat, on the other hand, perceived herself as gregarious and fun loving. Friends and socializing were important to her. Over the years, Pat's frustration had increased as their lives had become increasingly narrow and restricted. She had worked very hard to find the perfect social situation for her husband to feel at ease in. Nothing had worked, and she had to attend social events solo. However, she still longed to have her husband join her, and she had dreams of them entertaining together in their home. Now she feared that they would become increasingly estranged as she went out and did things on her own. They were in a distance and isolation cascade.

Initially Paul had difficulty describing his stance, except to say that it he was an introvert and that introverts don't like to socialize. He was unable to articulate the symbolic meaning that his stance had for him. From a Gottman perspective, Paul would be viewed as a person out of touch with his dream. Pat could much more easily describe the meaning of her stance symbolically. She had a dream of a marriage where she and her husband could go out into the world and have fun together with friends. There seemed to be an undercurrent of hostility and a power struggle between them. Pat appeared to have the lion's share of the discomfort, whereas Paul quietly, and quite resolutely, maintained his position regarding his inability to be social. He posed no dreams of his own except in a vague and negative way. His dream could have been best described as not wanting to be taken out of his comfort zone.

The couple had trouble with the dreams-within-conflict exercise. Paul and Pat could listen to each other, but Paul had no dream to offer. Instead he maintained his negative stance, opposed Pat's dream, and made no counteroffer of his own. The process had dead-ended. The couple was unable to take the next step of honoring each other's dreams. Paul was clearly fearful of Pat's dream.

THERAPY

Using the Gottman method I decided to have the couple discuss their gridlocked issue in terms of Paul's fears of accepting influence. This intervention fit because of Paul's vagueness about his dream and his resistance to various attempts that Pat had made to accommodate his discomfort while still trying to get him to meet her in her dream. I viewed this couple as being in an uninfluenced stable state rather than an influenced stable state (Gottman, 1999, p. 33). I did not sense volatility. On the contrary, they were polite, soft spoken, and had fairly flat affect. I had the impression that Pat viewed herself as a nag and that Paul felt nagged. This prompted me to wonder about a distancer–pursuer pattern in their relationship.

> Therapist: Paul, why don't you discuss with your wife the fears that you may be experiencing with her desire to socialize? Tell Pat anything that you

can think of that might be contributing to your fears. Maybe you worry about what might happen if you let yourself be influenced by Pat and her dream. Tell her about those, too. (*turning to Pat*) Pat, your job is to listen. Only ask Paul questions that will increase your understanding of what it is like to be in his shoes. Perhaps it would help you to think of yourself as an anthropologist with a mission to understand Paul's worldview on this issue. Please set aside your own thoughts and feelings for the time being. Only ask Paul questions that would lead to a better understanding of his fears of accepting your dream.

Pat: (*sounding polite and flat*) Paul, tell me about your fears.

Paul: (*sounding stilted*) Well, you know I'm an introvert, and introverts are uncomfortable with other people. I'm more of a homebody. I find it exhausting to make small talk with other people. What's the point?

Pat: (*sounding exasperated*) Well, you don't have to just make small talk, you're smart.

Therapist: (*stopping Pat, containing her irritation and sarcasm, and redirecting*) Pat, remember your job is to listen and ask questions that will help you better understand Paul's experience.

Pat: Right, let me try again. Paul, whenever we try to talk about this you always have the stock answer, "I'm an introvert." To me the conversation is over then. There is no place to go.

I noticed his wooden response and wondered if he was flooded.

Pat looked at me and I decided not to intervene. I wanted to see if she would be able to get back on track by herself. She was.

Pat: So it seems pointless to you to make small talk with people?

Paul: Yes, especially if I don't know them and will probably never see them again. And besides, if I were to see them again I'm not sure that would help. That might even be worse.

Pat: What do you mean? I don't understand.

Paul: Well there's not a lot to understand. I'm an introvert. We've been over this a million times. I don't want to go over this again.

Paul's response led me to wonder if Paul was really unable, developmentally, to expand on his thoughts or if he was stonewalling, or both. He certainly did not seem open to Pat's inquiries, let alone influence. Pat again looked at me for help. She seemed exasperated. I decided to coach her, because coaching would provide holding and would help Pat manage her affect.

Therapist: Pat, why don't you gently ask Paul to tell you his story about friends and fun?

Pat: (*turning again to me with a tone of resignation and irritation*) I know the answer. We've been over that ground before. It's about Paul's mother. She ruined his friendships when he was a kid.

Paul: Well, it's true, she did, and making friends has never been easy since. It's risky. You know about my history with friendships. It wasn't worth it, and if I did try to keep friends, there was always a high price to pay.

Pat: (*becoming more exasperated and accusatory*) I know you said that it was hard and that your Mom was disapproving. I know. She disapproved of me, too. Anyhow, you've managed to stay friends with one or two guys, Bill and George.

I noted Pat's criticalness. Pat did not appear open to learn new information about Paul. She seemed to be taking a stance of "already knowing." I once again provided her with containment with a stop-action intervention.

Therapist: Pat, you sound irritated and critical of Paul. Remember, your job right now is to be curious about Paul's experience and feelings.

Paul: (*sounding defensive and somewhat angry*) Well, only with George. And I didn't introduce you to my family for a long time. Besides, my mother was mellower by then. It was awful with my friends.

I noticed that Paul had more energy and affect in his voice.

Pat: (*softening*) Why? What did she do? You've always been so closed-mouthed about it.

I noted that Pat was now showing genuine interest rather than assuming that she knew all the answers. This may have been because Paul's voice had more feeling and Pat was responding to his real emotions. I found that she needed less containment and direction. The couple had begun dialoguing directly.

Paul: Well, you know how when you're a kid, you want to bring kids home after school and have something to eat and hack around? I tried, but she always acted like we were a big bother. She'd get mad if I wanted to get us something to eat. She made it plain she didn't like me bringing kids into the house. I felt really embarrassed by her. She had to have everything so neat, and she was always so afraid we'd mess things up or break something. I don't know. What's done is done. It doesn't do any good to talk about it. It just makes me feel worse.

Paul seemed to have opened up, sharing more of his internal representational world. However, he quickly shut back down, perhaps defending against painful feelings by stonewalling. Does his closing-up signal his internal working model regarding disruption and repair? He seems to despair being understood and helped.

Pat: (*softly*) I know it's hard but, please, tell me more.

Paul: What more is there to say? She didn't like my friends. She was very critical and if I brought them home after school, she'd be either cold or say something to embarrass me in front of them. And after they left, she would be even more critical of them. It just wasn't worth it. My friends thought she was mean.

Pat: Well, I thought one of the reasons you married me was because I had friends. I'm different from your mom. I've always supported your friendships. So I don't understand why you feel like it's not okay to have friends now. Please explain this to me.

[Pat's voice is getting a bit shrill and more pressured, revealing her inability to manage her anxiety.]

Paul: (*flatly*) That's true. I thought with you I'd kind of get another chance to have friends. But somehow I feel like you are critical of me, too. Somehow I feel like you. Oh, I don't know how to describe it.

[Paul's flat tone of voice seemed in direct proportion to Pat's shrillness.]

Pat: (*defensively*) I don't think I'm critical of you with other people.

Therapist: (*noting Pat's defensiveness*) Pat, remember, your job is to ask Paul a question that will help him to tell you more about his feelings.

Pat: (*nodding okay and turning back to Paul*) What do you mean? I don't understand.

Paul: (*seeming truly engaged in reflecting and thinking and speaking less self-protectively*) I'm not totally sure. Maybe it has something to do with what happens before we leave the house. I mean, you criticize my clothes, my shoes. I feel crummy before we even start.

In the countertransference I am aware that I am relieved that Paul is finally expressing his feelings of anger rather than stonewalling or acting them out.

Pat: (*looking surprised and hurt, yet managing to remain curious and empathic*) How come you've never said anything about that? I don't get it. I didn't know it bugged you. I was just trying to help. Sometimes you even ask me to help you.

Paul: Well, somehow I always feel less by the time we get out the door. Then I think to myself I'm never going to let this happen to me again.

I noticed the absolutes of "always"and "never"in Paul's statements. I decided not to disrupt him with a comment. His expression of anger could have been too easily derailed.

Pat: What do you mean, "I'm not going to let this happen to me again."(*in a reconciliatory tone*) I didn't realize this was so upsetting to you. Why haven't you told me?

[Pat said this with a bit of curiosity. She was now more open and making a real bid for connection.]

Paul: Yes, well, what's to talk about? It's not going to make me feel better. It'll only make me feel lousy. What's the point?

[Paul had retreated again in an effort to self-regulate and rejected her bid for connection and understanding. His resistance and his need to be self-protective were quite evident. Pat turned to me for help. She sounded helpless and hopeless and ready to retreat herself.]

Pat: I don't know what to do with this. Where do I go from here? It's a dead end.

I sensed that Pat and Paul had reached this point in their discussions many other times.

Therapist: Stick with this. It's important not to give up. Why don't you encourage Paul to talk more about feeling lousy?

Pat: (*softening again and with genuine concern*) Paul, I didn't realize that you felt so terrible.

Paul: (*looking visibly sad*) Well, you know how difficult it was.

I was aware that Paul had progressed from flat affect to anger, and was now presenting with sadness.

Pat: I know, but I had no idea how awful you felt. How awful you still feel. I just mostly chalked it up to you being an introvert.

Pat's observation "how awful you felt" and "how awful you still feel" is an example of how the past is still very present and reflected in Paul's current internal working model.

Paul: (*moist-eyed and uncomfortable*) Yeah, well, me too. I was so lonely and embarrassed. I really wanted friends, but I knew it could never work out.

I noted that as Paul became more in touch with his own feelings, he also became more aware of the loss of his dream. Psychic space had been opened up for him to think and feel. His expression of affect was regulating for both of them. It diminished Pat's need to pursue. They were much more connected at this moment.

Pat: (*joining and empathizing*) I just feel so sad and bad.

Therapist: So, Paul, your dream of having friends has been pretty buried? Is there a part of you that would like to have fun too? Perhaps you squelch any thoughts and feelings you have about that.

Paul: Yes, but I really don't let myself think too much about the fun I'm missing out on. (*pausing for a few moments and then turning to Pat with a faint hint of enthusiasm*) Maybe we could have the Smith's over.

Pat: (*hesitating*) Well, I'm not sure you'd really be comfortable. I'm a bit worried. Paul, are you sure? Maybe I need to think of some other people.

I noticed that Pat looked a bit alarmed, and her eyes were slightly wider. Paul looked away and slumped ever so slightly in his chair. My psychodynamic self was feeling confused and annoyed with Pat for squashing Paul's fragile attempt to step forward. What was going on? My GMCT self noticed that Paul had made a bid for connection and wanted recognition for his effort to give Pat what she had been saying she wanted. Pat had not taken him up on it. My confusion at this seemingly incongruous response was a tip off to the presence of her internal working model. I decided to coach Paul in asking Pat what her reservations might be about his suggestion.

Therapist: Paul, why don't you ask Pat if there is a reason why she doesn't take you up on your offer. Ask if she has some concerns about having the Smiths come over.

Paul: Well, why didn't you take me up on it? What's your concern? I don't get it.

Pat: (*flustered, as if caught with her hand in the cookie jar*) I don't know. I just thought that it might be too much of a stretch and you'd be uncomfortable.

At this point I found myself thinking about Pat's family history. She had to compete with her brother for attention in her family. According to Pat, her brother was the family star and her parents' favorite child. He was also a superb athlete and very popular at school. This was so painful to her that she gave up trying to compete with him altogether. It was only after she left home and was in college that she felt that she blossomed socially. She made a niche for herself with her friends. Then she met Paul, who was shy and socially ill at ease. She was drawn to him because they shared similar traits. But more importantly he adored her and made her feel special in the way that she had always longed to feel in her family. With this in mind, I decided to coach Paul.

Therapist: Paul, ask Pat if there's ever been a time in her life when she felt socially uncomfortable.

Paul: Pat, I know you had a lot of friends when we met. It's hard to imagine that you've ever felt uncomfortable. Except I know it was hard for you with you brother, Tom.

Pat: (*pensively*) Huh. I haven't thought about Tom for ages. We've gone our separate ways for so long. I always felt so overshadowed by him.

It occurred to me that perhaps Pat was afraid of the very thing she said that she wanted. Maybe Pat was afraid Paul was a threat or competition for her in her group of friends. As long as Paul remained an "introvert," he could not upstage her as her brother had always done.

Therapist: (*coaching Paul again*) Paul, ask Pat if she can help you understand why she did not pick up on your offer.

Paul: (*reluctantly but with some feeling*) Pat, how come? How come you weren't happy?

Pat: (*again looking at me with some confusion and apprehension in her voice*) I don't know. I just thought it would be too much.

My psychodynamic self stepped in and I decided to offer to share my thoughts with them. They could be accepted or rejected by either Pat or Paul or both.

Therapist: Well, let me share some of my thoughts with both of you. Pat, I was confused at first when you didn't jump at Paul's offer to have the Smiths over. Then I recalled what you said about always having to compete with your brother for attention. You said that he was your parents' favorite and that he was popular at school. Then the saying, "watch out what you wish for" came to my mind. I was wondering if in some way it might bother you to have Paul be more social. I know that's what you've longed for, but perhaps at the same time there is a part of you that is afraid to risk having any competition with him.

Pat: (*looked pensive and sounded a bit defensive, but she seemed willing to consider what I said*) I don't know. I'll have to think about it.

Paul and Pat both had dreams and nightmares locked up in their respective positions. In Gottman terms, they were clearly gridlocked. Their discussion was not harsh, yet the four horsemen were clearly a factor in the pain and resentment between them. They seemed to be living lives of quiet desperation and drifting toward isolation and loneliness.

Clinically, I noticed that they were both very vigilant in a quiet way, carefully monitoring each other. Their communication style was highly coordinated and predictable, making it more difficult for them to change. This level of coordination was dictated by the needs of their internal working models (Gottman, 1979).

The dialogue makes it evident that Paul was squashed in his family of origin. His dream of having friends and being social were never realized. He was in touch with his nightmare of rejection and disapproval. In an effort to not feel pain, he had buried his dream and desire for friends and fun. This was an affect regulating strategy for him. Pat, on the other hand, appeared much more aware of her feelings and perceptions. Paul was squashing her dream of being social. However, she was not so aware of the nightmare beneath her dream: an expectation that her partner would upstage her. She had subtly maintained her balance by "protecting" Paul from social situations, always trying to find the perfect one. Her affect-regulating strategy was less obvious than Paul's. She had only been aware of her lost dream and she blamed Paul for it. Paul had felt endlessly nagged by Pat. Pat in turn felt helpless in the face of his total refusal to go beyond the bounds of his social comfort zone.

From a psychodynamic point of view, both had used defensive projective identification to manage their respective dreams and nightmares. There was an unconscious dimension to their gridlocked problem. Both of them had colluded to "protect" each other. Paul had projected his envious desire into Pat, whereas Pat had projected her own fears about socializing into Paul. In this unconscious arrangement Paul had been spared from facing his desire and perhaps "unbearable excitement" about friendships, whereas Pat had been spared the terror of being upstaged by her partner. The gridlocked problem encapsulated both of their fears and their dreams simultaneously.

CONCLUSION

This chapter provides an overview of two seemingly divergent forms of couple therapy. Upon closer examination, however, it is apparent that the major goal of each approach is to promote growth and change as well as increase relationship satisfaction. The difference between the approaches can be succinctly stated as follows: GMCT works from the outside in and psychodynamic couples therapy works from the inside out. In GMCT emphasis is on empowering the couple through the structure of the SRH and a library of interventions. A major tenet of GMCT is that seemingly small changes can have a profound ripple effect on the couple's relationship.

In psychodynamic couples therapy emphasis is on empowering the couple through intrapsychic growth and development via the therapeutic relationship and the holding and handling environment. A major tenet of the psychodynamic approach is that change will be more lasting because of the identification and internalization processes and does not ultimately depend upon the therapist's literal presence to be sustained.

I have discovered that both theories of change are true. Each approach assists the couple more adaptively to regulate and contain affect, to establish a more positive internal representational world, and to promote flexibility and change within their internal working models.

REFERENCES

Beebe, B., & Lachmann, F. M. (2002). *Infant research and adult treatment: Coconstructing interactions*. Hillsdale, NJ: Analytic Press.

Box, S., Copley, B., Magagna, J., & Moustaki, E. (1981). *Psychotherapy with families: An analytic approach*. London: Routledge & Paul Kegan.

Gottman, J. M. (1979). *Marital interactions*. New York: Academic Press.

Gottman, J. M. (1999). *The marriage clinic: A scientifically based marital therapy*. New York: Norton.

Gottman, J. M. (2000–2001). *The art and science of love: A workshop for couples*. Seattle, WA: Gottman Institute.

McCormack, C. C. (2000). *Treating borderline states in marriage: Dealing with oppositionalism, ruthless aggression, and severe resistance*. Northvale, NJ: Jason Aronson. Inc.

Scharff, D. E., & Scharff, J. S. (1991). *Object relations couple therapy*. Northvale, NJ: Jason Aronson.

Tronick, E. Z. (1989). Emotions and emotional communications in infants. *American Psychologist, 44*, 112–119.

Tronick, E. Z., & Weinberg, M.K. (1997). Depressed mothers and infants: Failure to form dyadic states of consciousness. In L. Murray & P. J. Cooper (Eds.), *Postpartum depression and child development* (pp. 54–81). New York: Guilford Press.

Winnicott, D. W. (1965). The maturational processes and the facilitating environment: Studies in the theory of emotional development. London: Hogarth Press and The Institute of Psycho-Analysis.

Chapter 13

When Parenting is the Issue

Mirabai Wahbe

We know that a drop in marital satisfaction frequently occurs after the arrival of children to a marriage, particularly for couples who are already experiencing difficulty in their relationship. Tension erupts between the partners over differing parenting styles, loss of physical intimacy, changing dynamics in the family, and other issues. Exploring each parent's dream-within-conflict as well as their internal working model when necessary can often open doorways toward greater understanding and compromise within the dyad. This chapter addresses a particularly complicated and difficult marital situation involving the issue of parenting, and it illustrates how the GMCT can be effective. The therapy focused on the Gottman concepts of *flooding*, *dream-within-conflict*, and the *internal working model*, as well as on *rebuilding the friendship*.

JACK AND BARBARA

My first impression of Jack and Barbara was, "What a handsome couple." Both in their early thirties, he was tall, athletic, and self-confident yet soft-spoken; she was attractive, petite, blond, and also self-confident. They seemed very enthusiastic about what they had learned at the weekend Gottman workshop they had recently attended and were eager to get more help for their troubled marriage.

Assessment

I began the process of assessment by doing an oral history of their relationship. Barbara was teary as she recounted her experience of their relationship. There had been so much hope and goodwill in the beginning. She had been married before and it had ended badly. She and her first husband had drifted apart and there had been much bitterness and hurt. When she met Jack, who had never been married, she thought she had found someone with whom she could really have fun, someone with whom she could build a life. They both loved the outdoors. They enjoyed skiing and traveling and they had many happy times at the beginning of their relationship. The relationship had begun as a good friendship, Barbara explained, and then they discovered that sexuality enhanced their friendship more than they had thought possible.

Jack nodded his head in agreement. He added that he felt he had found in Barbara a supportive and empathetic friend, something he had longed for but didn't dare believe he could have. They married and were very happy.

Three years after Barbara and Jack were married, tragedy struck: an unexpected pregnancy. They had agreed they wouldn't have children. Barbara had been told she was incapable of getting pregnant, and Jack was adamant that he did not want children. When Barbara became pregnant, their friendship quickly deteriorated.

As Barbara listened to Jack recount their history, she looked at the floor. I noticed tears sliding down her cheeks. "I just couldn't believe what was happening," she began. "Jack just suddenly distanced from me. I felt confused and abandoned. I knew Jack didn't want children, but when I became pregnant, I was so excited. My first thought when I found out was, 'Now I can be a mother.'" Her voice quivered as she spoke.

"All these years I believed I was defective, incapable of producing a child. To learn otherwise opened my world more than I ever thought possible. Of course I was aware of Jack's feelings about children, but somehow. . . ." Barbara paused and stared out over my shoulder. "Well, if I'm perfectly honest," she continued, "I guess I would admit that a part of me believed he had decided not to have kids because he hadn't met the right person. Because he had never loved someone the way he loved me. That decision was made long before he knew me. It sounds silly now, as I say it out loud, but I guess I expected Jack to be excited too; if not at first, well then eventually. We were so close—how could he not?"

Barbara wrung her hands in her lap. "Instead what I got was an absent husband. He literally disappeared. I could not believe that someone could change so suddenly and so drastically. He became a different person. Suddenly I was pregnant and alone. We continued to live in the same house, but Jack was so mad he didn't talk to me except for 'pass the salt' for almost the whole pregnancy. It was so awful, so painful." The tears fell freely now.

Barbara went on to explain that she had rationalized that Jack was just in shock—he would get over this and get used to the idea of having a child—so she did her best to be patient and wait for him to come around.

While Barbara told her story, Jack sat upright, arms crossed tensely over his chest. He seemed oblivious to her tears and her sorrow. Instead of focusing on her, his stern gaze was on me, as if to say, "Can we trust you to handle this and not make it all my fault?" Later I learned this had been his experience with their past counselor.

When Jack did speak his tone was cool and aloof. "I still don't understand how you could have expected me to be happy about having a child, Barbara. You talk about feeling abandoned, but I can't even begin to tell you just how betrayed I felt." Jack shook his head impatiently and continued. "We had this agreement, Barbara, an understanding. Kids were not a part of our marriage! You don't change an agreement midstream with someone just because you want to! My feelings for an abortion were completely overridden without any discussion."

Barbara winced, then turned toward Jack and fired back quickly and defensively. "Of course I couldn't talk about abortion! Abortion?! My god, Jack. Do you have any idea?! There was no way you could have convinced me to have an abortion. In my heart, I felt this child was a blessing—a miracle—a dream come true for me."

Barbara turned toward me and described how as a young girl she had yearned to be a mother and how she had believed she'd make a good one. In her first marriage she and her husband had tried to get pregnant but could not, even after undergoing fertility treatments. Barbara looked sad and distant as she spoke. "That was a very, very hard time for me. I was young and had always assumed I would have children. I felt like such a failure as a woman when I learned I couldn't have any." Barbara believed that the infertility issue was the beginning of what drove her first marriage apart. She had grieved deeply as she gave up the dream of becoming a mother. By the time she met Jack, Barbara had so accepted her "fate" that she could easily assure him that she did not want children. "I thought I had completely put the idea of children behind me," she said. "I believed that I had made peace with myself and looked forward to having an independent, fulfilling life without children."

They continued to describe the events of the birth of their daughter, now 6 years old, with as much sadness and despair as if it had just happened yesterday. The birth was a difficult one, as had been the pregnancy. Jack had attended some birthing classes and was present for the birth. Barbara began to cry again. "For me it was the most important moment of my life. Okay, Jack was there, in the room, but he really wasn't there. He actually fell asleep. I'm still so mad about it." She glared at him.

Jack looked down at the floor and shuffled his feet. "Damn it, Barb. Stick it in, why don't you?! You know how much I adore that kid. I feel like a total jerk for not doing a better job of welcoming her into the world. But I just couldn't. I just couldn't. I wish you could understand that." There was a pleading tone in his voice and a single tear in his eyes as he spoke. That was the first glimpse of Jack's real pain, undisguised by his otherwise aloof and defensive posture. I observed that his tears went unnoticed or at least not responded to by Barbara. She continued to glare at him.

Jack quickly regained his composure, sighed deeply, and described how their daughter, Sofie, had been a high-need baby. She had cried a lot, had colic, and had never slept more than a few hours at a time even at the age of one. Then his face suddenly softened and he looked off to the side, as if to hide his vulnerability.

"I will never forget the first time I held her, that tiny, tiny thing. I couldn't even begin to describe the tidal wave of feelings. . . . All I knew for sure was I was glad she was here—really glad. And amazed." He seemed in his own world as he remembered those first hours and days with his newborn daughter. "Yet I didn't have a clue what to do with her. From the beginning, I was completely helpless." He shook his head. "I was a total failure when it came to trying to stop her from crying. Barbara had the touch with Sofie and I felt like some huge clumsy ogre who she hated. I know Barbara has a hard time believing me, but I really did try to take care of her when she was a baby. I really did! But, okay, most of the time I just left childcare up to Barbara. She was so much better at it than I was."

Barbara sat listening to Jack, shaking her head, as if to say, "That's not how it was."

Clearly Jack had bonded with his daughter and had warmed up to her more and more, little by little, as time passed. But the change was so slow and tentative that Barbara had never really noticed it. Instead, she had continued to feel abandoned and desperate, her anger growing. Yet she still felt committed to the marriage.

Tension within the parental unit festered, and as Sofie grew, she developed more and more behavior problems. She had trouble following directions; she was stubborn and often defiant. She was fussy about everything—what food she would eat, what clothes she would wear. Daycare providers would eventually say they couldn't care for her.

"It went beyond temper tantrums," Jack explained. "She could kick and scream forever. She could be going along fine, and then suddenly something would upset her, and she'd be having a fit. There was no way to calm her down."

Jack acknowledged that he had no idea how to parent. They sought counseling, and took parenting classes. Jack participated in both. The counselor was helpful. In fact, when she learned that Jack had been adopted at birth, she recommended that he read the book *The Primal Wound,* which facilitated a breakthrough for him. It allowed him to begin to understand the impact of being adopted. (Jack later asked me to read the book and I did. It was an important step in the building of his trust in me.) Just as Jack began to develop some trust in their counselor, she moved away. At the same time Jack tracked down his birth mother, only to be told by her that she wanted no contact with him whatsoever. These two simultaneous losses served only to reinforce Jack's belief that you couldn't count on anyone, particularly women. As a result, Jack distanced himself more and more from his wife and child, and he became increasingly more isolated. His daughter was 3 at the time.

Despite this setback, they eventually sought out another counselor and started the process over again. The couple reported that this counselor saw Jack's behavior as the only problem. This was confirmed in a phone conversation with the counselor. The counselor had believed Jack was inappropriate with Sofie; Jack's expectations and discipline were out of line. He was aggressive and overly punitive. I looked carefully at Jack and imagined what that counselor had seen. Tall, with dark hair and dark eyes, he was athletic and muscular. His speech was controlled, his words articulate and commanding. He gave the appearance of constantly assessing the situation, sitting back and observing. His affect was often flat, and he seldom expressed emotion. The whole "package" could easily be interpreted as intimidating. Barbara's appearance and demeanor was almost the exact opposite of Jack's. She was vivacious, trusting, very talkative, and engaging, with a ready smile. She expressed emotions and feelings easily. It would be easy, I told myself, to assume Jack was the only problem. But that would have missed the pattern of interaction between them that I saw as the problem. Jack felt attacked by this counselor and refused to continue with him. Barbara, not knowing what else to do, continued with this therapist on her own, with Jack's blessings but without his participation. Barbara brought Sofie to counseling as well. Sofie's behavior grew worse and worse, despite her liking the counselor. The counselor told Barbara that Jack's alternation between verbal aggression and cold isolation from her and Sofie was the problem and that she must protect herself and her daughter. He assessed Jack as a dangerous person: Jack had experienced and witnessed violence in his childhood; that unresolved abuse in his childhood could lead to violent or destructive behavior as an adult; he had a gun collection; he was large in stature; he tended to be forceful in his opinions and was defensive. The fighting between Jack and Barbara was often very loud and filled with contempt and blame. Barbara admitted to the therapist that occasionally she did feel frightened of Jack. After 6 months, the therapist recommended that Barbara leave the marriage. Barbara, however, felt only more conflicted because she did not want to leave the marriage. Instead she decided to stop seeing that therapist. At home, she expressed more and more criticism and contempt toward Jack. He became increasingly more defensive and distanced from her even further.

It was at this point that they decided to attend the Gottman Couples Workshop. For the first time in years, they felt a glimmer of hope that things could get better between them. They recognized that the four horsemen (criticism, defensiveness, contempt, and stonewalling) were trampling their relationship. They recognized that although they could debate with each other, they were not able to listen. The dream-within-conflict exercise presented at the workshop sounded great to them, as it allowed them to discuss a conflict issue with the goal of furthering mutual understanding rather than resolution, but they were unable to do it. They couldn't even do the relaxation exercise together, where one person reads a relaxation script to the other. In no way could they relax in each other's presence. Frustrated, they decided to seek further counseling and contacted me.

INDIVIDUAL SESSIONS

After the first assessment session, I met individually with Jack and Barbara. In my individual session with Jack I learned that his adoptive parents had been neglectful and abusive. His father was an alcoholic. He bullied and beat Jack. His mother responded by excusing the father's behavior and telling Jack that it was all his fault. As a result, Jack grew up feeling hurt, abandoned, confused, and unwanted. Life as a child was a constant struggle. Jack succeeded at school, receiving accolades from his teachers. Yet at home he was derided for his intelligence, his vocabulary, and his academic achievement.

"I felt all alone. There was no one I could talk to about anything important. If I had a problem with the kids at school, or with a teacher, I just had to figure it out by myself." He had no close friends until high school and then only one or two friends through sports.

Jack spoke haltingly. "I just knew I never wanted to have kids. Why would I? My life as a child was hell. Why would I want to repeat that?" He was certain he did not have what it took to be a father and didn't believe the world was a good enough place in which to bring a child. He also felt that now as an adult he had a chance to build a life that afforded him some ease and some pleasure. He did not want to share his wife or his life with an intruder. He clearly felt betrayed by the pregnancy and birth of their daughter.

In my individual session with Barbara, she described how her father had died of a heart attack when she was just a year old. There was no life insurance and her mother had few resources. Her mother tried her best, but life was extremely stressful. She and Barbara were close but there were huge financial burdens, and the mother worked long hours. She had little time to maintain connections with any kind of support system, and her sole support came from Barbara. Barbara developed a sense of competency and independence in her role as the other adult in her family, and she received genuine support and encouragement from her paternal grandparents, who lived nearby. This combination helped her to develop a sense of self-worth along with a belief that a person should stick it out through hard times.

Barbara swore she would never repeat the pattern of her mother's life as a single mother, so she waited for Jack to "come around" to being a father. While she waited, however, Barbara's disappointment turned to bitterness and contempt. What was wrong with Jack? Why couldn't he adjust and learn to love and be close to his daughter? She began to see only his faults. She became critical. She knew Jack felt inadequate as a parent, but she couldn't hold back her criticism and contempt.

During our individual session I asked Barbara more about the nature of their fights and whether there had ever been any physical violence. Neither she nor Jack had indicated any physical abuse on the emotional abuse questionnaire and conflict tactics inventory, but given what Barbara had said about sometimes feeling frightened of Jack, and the previous counselor's assessment of him, I wanted to give her every opportunity to talk to me about her concerns. She explained that Jack could be verbally aggressive, but that she could match him without any difficulty. She could yell just as loud and be just as argumentative as he could. She said he had never thrown anything and never broken anything when he was angry. She went on to say that Jack never spanked their daughter. He rarely hugged her either. It seemed he was afraid to touch her.

THE CONTRACTING SESSION

The agenda for the fourth session was for me to give the couple feedback about what I saw in their relationship, based on our interviews and on the written questionnaires they had completed. We would then come to an agreement about our treatment goals and begin the actual work of therapy.

Aware of the agenda for this fourth session, Jack and Barbara sat on the sofa across from me, unable to look at each other. Barbara looked apprehensive; Jack seemed stiff and frozen. I wondered what was happening for them and decided to ask each of them what they were experiencing at that moment. They finally looked at each other and then Barbara turned to me and blurted out, "I'm afraid you are going to tell us that it is hopeless. I know Dr. Gottman said he could tell which couples were going to make it and which ones were going to get a divorce, and we both think you can see it too."

Jack nodded his agreement. "I know we are in serious trouble, and I'm afraid you will tell us it's hopeless." He stared at the floor.

I took a deep breath to center myself, collected my thoughts, and then slowly responded. "Yes," I said, "it is true that you have many issues to work on. You have each been forthcoming in talking about those. But in our previous sessions, I have also noted the strengths that you have." I went on to describe the strengths and resources I had seen. They were both survivors. They had emerged from childhood struggles with a great deal of inner strength and self-confidence. They had each been able to set a positive course for their lives and were working toward many of their goals. They were each working and attending classes to further their careers. They had purchased a home and had a sizable savings account that was important to both of them. They discussed finances easily and were mostly in agreement. They both enjoyed their sexual relationship despite the difficulties between them. There was trust and no question of jealousy between them. They were usually able to talk with each other about outside stresses. Housework and sharing responsibility for the day-to-day chores and tasks of running a household were not a problem. They often worked very well as a team, except around parenting issues. And in the area of spirituality they were able to support each other fully.

"So I can honestly say that I do not believe it is hopeless between the two of you." Their faces had been relaxing as I had shared their strengths, but now there was an audible sigh of relief.

"You have each stated that you are 100% committed to working on the marriage. That is another strength that you bring to this process. And despite not finding enough help so far through counseling and classes, you have not given up. You are here and I think there is a lot we can accomplish together." I asked for their response to what I had just shared with them.

Barbara began. "Your words ring true to me. It was nice to hear that we do have those strengths, that you can see them too. I've been so consumed by what's wrong with us, that I'd lost sight of what's right."

Jack nodded. "Yeah, I agree. I've always known that we have something right about us, but I never could have stated it as well as you just did."

They looked at each other and Jack reached out for Barbara's hand. She reached back and they held hands as we continued.

Next I outlined the areas that needed work. Of course there was the issue of parenting. There were other areas of difficulty as well, including relationships with in-laws, differences in desires for outside friends and social interaction, and differences in needs for togetherness and autonomy. They each acknowledged that these were their main areas of contention. To minimize defensiveness, I normalized their attack-defend pattern. I explained that they each felt wounded, and out of that pain, they had developed an attack-defend style of interaction that had made it impossible to discuss any of their issues without its escalating into a fight. Their fights involved screaming and yelling, with lots of name calling, blaming, and contempt, followed by emotional withdrawal. They could go for days and sometimes weeks without talking to each other. The main issue they fought about was parenting and all the issues associated with it. They each realized that their fights were adversely affecting their daughter, but felt at a loss as to how to change their behavior. There was a give-and-take discussion as I outlined these issues. The interaction pattern between them, I explained, was what we would focus on improving.

To this end, we would focus on two areas: their friendship and the way they handled conflict. Because both areas were equally important, we would weave back and forth between them. We would focus on rebuilding the friendship that had once been so strong and positive. But in order to rebuild the friendship they would need to learn all the skills of problem solving and moving from gridlock to dialogue, including softened startup, repair and de-escalation, accepting influence, self-soothing, and learning to accept one another. The goal was to increase the depth of understanding between them, particularly around the issue of parenting. We would spend time deepening their love maps, increasing the expression of their fondness and appreciation of each other, and practicing the art of turning toward. That was the treatment plan.

Jack and Barbara drew closer to each other on the sofa. Jack spoke first, his voice noticeably softer. "It seems that finally we have a plan. I know that when I have a plan I can follow it."

Barbara added with a small smile, "I also feel hopeful. That is true. You do follow through when you make a plan of action. Even over the last few weeks during these sessions, I have begun to feel closer to you again." Barbara paused and looked out the window for a moment. "But I also need to say that I'm still afraid that it won't work."

I nodded. "I think that's understandable and completely normal at this stage of the process. What you know and have evidence of is how it has been since the birth of your daughter. You don't yet have enough experiences of new interaction patterns to give you the confidence that change can happen. This will be our work together."

THE COUPLES THERAPY

From the beginning, Jack, although willing to learn new skills, was very defensive. He felt a strong need to question any new information or suggestion I offered until it made some sense to him. This process was demanding of me as the therapist, but I wanted to build trust with Jack and decided spending the time addressing his questions was worthwhile. I knew his defensiveness came from his inability to trust. Being defensive probably helped him survive his abusive childhood with some sense of self-esteem intact. My goal for him was to see that his level of defensiveness, though useful growing up and useful still in certain situations, was not useful in his relationship with his wife. But I did not expect him to give up that survival skill right away.

Sometimes in working with couples, pointing out the behavior is all that is necessary. With Jack, I knew I needed to focus on building trust and wanted to weave new information carefully with lots of support. I was also hoping that this would be good role modeling for Barbara. I wanted her to learn to be curious about Jack's way of processing information, rather than just reacting to it. Of course, I had the same goal for Jack.

I knew intervening on their flooding and teaching self-soothing was vital in their situation. Without it, reaching the goals this couple wanted to reach would be much more challenging. Consequently, I wanted to address their flooding as early in the treatment as possible. Their fights either escalated quickly out of control, or one or the other would engage in stonewalling, so learning to self-soothe and eventually learning to soothe the other would be essential in order to change the pattern of interaction between them.

Jack listened as I spoke about flooding, diffuse physiological arousal, and the need to take breaks when either of them had a pulse rate of 95 or more. "But," Jack began, "that doesn't work. If I try to leave, she gets even more upset and comes after me."

As if on cue, Barbara interrupted. "I have to or nothing would ever get re-solved. If I don't insist on continuing the conversation, you'd just leave. And then I'm just stuck with all my feelings. It's so frustrating! You leave and don't talk to me for days and then just pretend the whole thing never happened."

"Let me give you some more information," I said. "John Gottman's research is very clear on this issue. When your heart rate gets above 95 or so, people move into the fight or flight or freeze mode. It is virtually impossible to carry on a rational, constructive conversation when this happens. In your case, it seems you first both go into fight mode, each of you wanting to win the argument, which causes the escalation of fighting that is so unpleasant for each of you."

Barbara and Jack nodded agreement.

"Then what I see happening is that at some point Jack moves to the flight mode and begins stonewalling, which tends to escalate the fight response in you, Barbara, at which point you feel even more flooded and continue pursuing Jack to come back into the fight. Does this seem to fit your experience?" I was looking to each of them with this question. Jack nodded in agreement.

"Absolutely," Barbara replied. "That is my experience and I hate it. You are just so hurtful, Jack."

I decided to see if she would be able to go beneath her defensive shield, to identify more vulnerable feelings.

"I'm wondering, Barbara, if you feel abandoned at that point?" I asked her.

"Abandoned? I don't think so. And my father dying has nothing to do with this! This pattern started with Jack! I don't feel abandoned, I feel furious."

Taken aback by the strength of her response, I pondered what to say or do next. Obviously it was too soon to approach her vulnerability when she did not yet feel safe with Jack or with me. So I backed up a step, leaned forward and spoke softly. "I can see how frustrating this pattern has been for you."

Barbara tentatively nodded.

I continued. "Do you notice that nothing ever gets resolved when this pattern is operating?" At that point Jack jumped in.

"No, nothing gets resolved. We just go around and around. I see that now. So what do we do instead?" Jack asked. "This is so ingrained in us. Can it really change?"

"Yes," I said, "with a lot of work. It becomes very important to learn to pay attention to your body's signals. Do you know when you feel flooded, Jack? What signal does your body give you?"

Jack replied, "Well, let's see. I feel a rush of energy in my upper body, and my jaw gets tight. My stomach tightens also. And if I'm really flooded I can feel my temples throb."

"I'm not sure when I'm flooded," Barbara responded.

"Well, let's start now by actually taking your heart rate." Jack's heart rate was 55, which is somewhat low for a resting heart rate, probably reflecting how athletic and conditioned his body was. Barbara was surprised to find that her heart rate was 110. She was already flooded. I asked her what was happening inside her that was causing her to become flooded now. She replied that she had been thinking about their last fight. She added that she hadn't realized how easily she could flood.

I suggested that Barbara take a few deep breaths to see if this would help her calm down. It did. Her heart rate dropped to 80. We then explored what each of them knew about themselves in terms of self-soothing. For Jack, his primary method was leaving, whether it was to walk or run or ride his bike. Jack quickly saw how getting out of the house when his parents were quarreling or drinking was a way to soothe his fears and his upset. He was continuing that same coping now.

Barbara suddenly piped up and said to Jack, "You know what? I think that's what Sofie is doing when she goes to her room and dances so furiously to loud music. I think she is trying to soothe herself."

They both chuckled. Jack added, "And here we thought she was a young Mick Jagger." It was nice to see them connect through humor.

For Barbara, her way to self-soothe was to clean. Jack smiled. "I always know when she is upset about something. The house is spic and span."

With further conversation we discovered, however, that Barbara kept the argument going in her head. I spoke about how that would keep her physiologically aroused and upset. Barbara eventually realized that the conversations in her head were entirely focused on what was wrong with Jack. And that she could keep this up for a long time. "No wonder I feel so irritated all the time! I'm already mad at Jack when he walks in the door, even if I haven't seen him for hours. I guess I just never let go of the fight. Boy, I never realized I did that."

Jack was about to say something and I had the feeling it was likely to be something critical, so I put up a hand to stop him. Barbara sat contemplating her new awareness. We were all quiet for a moment or two. I wanted Barbara to have time to let this awareness really sink in. She then looked at Jack and said, "I'm sorry, Jack. I am beginning to really see how I've contributed to our problems."

Jack looked directly at Barbara. "Thank you for saying that. I don't want to do the wrong thing here, but I think that's the first time you have ever apologized to me for anything since Sofie was born. It means a lot to me to hear you say that. I always have the feeling that everything is all my fault."

Jack and Barbara continued to look at each other. After a few moments of silence I said, "That was a good example of repair." They each nodded. I wanted to reinforce what just happened, so I went on to talk to each of them about repair and then checked in with each of them to ask how that had felt. First I turned to Barbara.

"I felt very sincere in what I said. It's true. And I felt close to Jack when I said that. I guess I'm beginning to see that I'm defensive too and the distance between us is not just about Jack. It makes me feel closer to him. I think I'm really learning something here."

Jack responded. "It feels so much better to not feel like the bad guy for a change. I also feel closer to you Barbara, not just because you've admitted something you do wrong. It's because I admire your courage to face your issues. It gives me hope that I can do that too and that we can change."

"Let's talk more about self-soothing," I said. "It can be quite helpful to realize that's what you're doing when you, Jack, do some physical exercise to calm down or you, Barbara, clean the house. It is also a good idea to have more than one skill in your repertoire. I have a self-soothing technique that I would like to teach you. I encourage you to try it this week at home so you can see if it works well for you."

I remembered what they had said about not being able to do the relaxation exercise at the workshop. They were obviously experiencing a softening with each other. I thought this would be a good time to give them a "corrective experience." I gave them each a copy of the exercise from the workshop and asked them to do a little bit of it with each other right then.

"I remember this from the workshop," Barbara said. "We couldn't do it then. But I'm willing to try."

I gave them about 7 minutes each to do this, and instructed them to do it again at home at least once during the week. I was hoping that they could each begin the process of learning to relax just at the sound of the other's voice. Learning to soothe one's partner is an additional component of healthy marital interaction, but it was too soon to introduce this at this time. Just learning the relaxation exercise was enough.

I further reminded them to pay attention to their heart rate during any conversation that felt like it was starting to escalate. "If your heart rate is 95–100, take a break, and remember to not rehearse the argument during that break. Try at least 30 minutes of relaxation or distraction. Then come back and try the conversation again. If either of you starts to flood, take another break. I know this slows down the process of discussing the issue, but you probably won't make progress anyway if you are flooded."

At each session after that I gave them a new self-soothing exercise. It was important for a volatile couple like Jack and Barbara to have as many choices in their repertoire as possible. They found the "present time" exercise particularly helpful. In this exercise the person looks around the room and describes five things that he or she sees, five sounds that he or she hears, and five body sensations that come to awareness. The person then describes four things he or she sees, four sounds he or she hears, and four body sensations; then three, two, and one. I also gave them several different breathing exercises and visualization techniques and encouraged them to use their previous self-soothing methods as well.

Barbara and Jack agreed to work on these skills at home. Over the course of therapy, we came back to these skills again and again. Both of them realized that they flooded easily and became quite reactive to one another. They needed lots of practice, encouragement, reminders, and patience to establish these new skills of monitoring their internal state, self-soothing in the moment, and taking a break if they were not able to calm down. They also needed to commit to trying the conversation again when they both were calm.

Early in the therapy, the most difficult sessions were when we attempted to create a productive dialogue around their perpetual problem of different parenting styles. Barbara felt strongly that she knew what worked best with Sofie; Jack argued that his way was better.

By this time, Sofie was a difficult and aggressive child. She would physically attack Jack, which Jack took very personally and felt he should punish severely. Barbara would rush in and become angry with Jack. The behavior and feelings that had led to Sofie's misbehavior were then lost in the fighting between Jack and Barbara. This pattern was entrenched and after several sessions together neither of the parents had been able to change their judgments or their behavior. They were so entrenched in their positions that neither could listen with understanding to the other. They were not able to move from gridlock to dialogue, and rarely got out of the attack-defend mode on this perpetual issue. Jack felt that Barbara "coddled" Sofie and believed it made her behavior worse. Barbara thought Jack was too harsh and expected too much of Sofie. She tried to convince Jack that his behavior was creating power struggles with Sofie that only made the whole situation escalate. Most of their fights were variations of these judgments. They could not agree on how to parent.

I attempted the dream-within-conflict conversation. "There will be a listener and a speaker. The speaker's job is to talk about the dream, the hope, the wish that they have regarding the issue of parenting. The idea is to go as deep inside yourself as possible to help the other person understand what this issue means to you. The job of the listener is to ask questions that help the speaker go deeper. The listener needs to suspend their own agenda for the moment—they will have their turn—and only ask questions that help the speaker. Please avoid asking questions that argue for your own point of view. And avoid being critical."

Barbara chose to start. "My dream is easy. I just want to have a happy family. I want my child to be loved and nurtured. I think the job of parents is to guide and teach, not to punish and isolate. I hate it when you punish our daughter for some minor thing she has done."

I interrupted. "Barbara, see if you can just talk about your hopes and dreams without talking about Jack or what he does."

Barbara pouted. "But what if a big part of my dream is to have Jack stop being so mean?"

"I know you think that's the solution. But we are not trying to come to a solution right now. We are trying to increase the understanding between you so that eventually you will be able to come to a compromise that honors each person's dream."

"I can't do this. Not right now. Let Jack start."

I looked to Jack. "Okay," he said. "My dream is easy too. I just want to feel like I'm a good dad. I want to know that my daughter knows the rules and can behave accordingly. If she misbehaves, it's because you coddle her too much and she doesn't think she has to follow any rules."

I interrupted Jack. "Jack, try to just state your dream, your hope, without blaming Barbara."

Jack took a deep breath. "I want my daughter to respect me. I think it is very important to have respect from your child. If Sofie would only follow instructions, then I wouldn't have to be so stern with her. What choice do I have? Kids need to listen to those in authority. If Barbara could only understand that, we could straighten Sofie out and we wouldn't have these problems."

And so it went. The couple could do well for a few sentences, but invariably whoever was the speaker would blame and attack the other, sometimes overtly, sometimes very subtly. The listener would then go immediately into defend-attack mode. I pointed out this pattern several times. I interrupted again and again, but it seemed we were getting nowhere. Both Barbara and Jack would flood and need to take a break. At least they were making progress in that area. At home their fights no longer escalated out of control—they stopped before things became really bad. But when it came to discussing how to parent, they were not able to listen without going into attack-defend. I attempted to help them better understand where their issues were coming from. I used Dan Wile's technique of rephrasing and speaking for each person. I tried to explore their family of origin and how that affected their positions. Nothing seemed to change the gridlock.

In the meantime, both of them became increasingly frustrated. Sofie's behavior was deteriorating further. I recognized that Barbara's parenting skills were, in fact, more effective than Jack's, but I wasn't sure how to present this without his feeling once again discounted and ganged up upon.

During a particularly difficult session, Jack looked directly at me and blurted out in total frustration, "I feel completely incompetent. I know in my head that there is a better way, but I just can't change my behavior. I am a disciplined person and I should be able to do this, but I can't. To be completely honest, this feels weird to say, like true confessions or something. The times when I isolate and remove myself from the family as much as possible, I have noticed Barbara interacting with Sofie in ways that don't seem to escalate." I took this as an opening.

"Jack," I said. "That is such a powerful statement you just made. I appreciate your courage in being willing and able to share that. As we have discussed many times, a major step in stopping the attack-defend mode that the two of you have been in for so long is to shift into the admitting mode. Congratulations on being able to take that difficult step. I'm wondering if you would be willing to build on this insight. Would you be willing to let Barbara handle all the discipline issues with Sofie and continue to observe, this time not from a place of isolation, but from a place of clear intention to observe what works best for Sofie?"

Jack sat quietly for a moment. "I think that would be a good idea. I do want what's best for Sofie. But what do I do when I get upset that she's coddling her?"

"That's a good question. What I am suggesting is going to be hard. I am asking you to suspend your judgments for a month to see what happens. I know that one of your strengths is keen observational skills. I would invite you to think of yourself as a detective, just gathering clues to a mystery. Use all your self-soothing skills, and if it gets too much, call me. You will reach my voicemail, but it is totally confidential so you can leave any message you would like, and just pour out your heart and all your feelings and know that I am hearing you."

Jack sat quietly. He then said, "I think this might actually help. I really just want to be a good dad. Actually, it might make it easier on me for a while to not be trying so hard to be that good dad."

Jack did pay close attention to all his reactions and feelings. We discussed and processed his feelings and reactions during therapy sessions. As Jack watched Barbara and Sofie interact, he began to have more and more evidence of what worked with their daughter and what didn't. This helped break the pattern and Jack was able to observe and experience a different way of parenting.

This act of observing Barbara and Sofie interacting brought Jack to a major realization. He tried hard to not be like his own father, but in fact he was having the same impact on Sofie as his father had had on him. He was blaming Sofie for the entire problem, making it all her fault, conveying that there was something wrong with her, as his father had done with him.

He felt so terrible about this realization that for many days he could not speak to Barbara. Once again, feeling like a failure as a father, Jack withdrew. Unfortunately, his first reaction was to go back to blaming Barbara for getting pregnant in the first place. His anger at his own failure and at being in this situation at all brought him to despair and feeling suicidal. That was when the three of us decided that individual counseling for Jack would be helpful. He was not willing to risk seeing another therapist. After some discussion with Barbara and Jack separately and together, we all agreed that because there was good rapport and trust in our work together, it would be appropriate for me to see Jack individually.

We had one 3-hour session in which Jack allowed himself to become vulnerable and sobbed for the first time since he was a little boy. He shared his pain at being abandoned by his mother. He realized he felt jealousy toward Sofie because of the bond between her and Barbara. Barbara was a good mother and he wished he had had a mother to stand up for him like Barbara was doing for Sofie. His feeling was that neither his birth mother nor his adoptive mother cared enough about him to protect him and take care of him. He realized that he grew up wanting to be loved by a mother and never felt that love. He didn't trust women until he met Barbara. That's why the pregnancy was so hard for him. He was relieved when he made this connection. His distancing wasn't really because he didn't want to have a child with Barbara, because despite everything he said and did, deep down in his heart he was happy when Sofie was born. He now realized that the shock of the news of the pregnancy caused him to automatically go back to his earlier belief that women were not to be trusted. He felt he could no longer trust his wife. Until this session, he had not even realized he had made this decision at that time. He went back to the same defensive position he had taken in his family: Don't trust anyone. No wonder Barbara felt abandoned. This insight of his internal mindset made him eager to share this new information with his wife. It felt like a huge revelation. He realized that Barbara's becoming pregnant did not make her untrustworthy. He suddenly was able to hear everything Barbara had been trying to tell him. He emerged from that session with a renewed sense of himself and a renewed commitment to working on understanding himself and his daughter.

Over the next many months, Jack spoke of his pain in his adoptive family. He had known he was adopted as soon as he could talk. Sometimes his family would threaten to send him back. Jack tried to emulate his father because he seemed so powerful and capable. He realized that he had both identified with his father and hated him for being so cruel.

He also was willing to examine the important decisions he had made about himself and his world when he was growing up. We worked together to discover more of his internal working model and to begin to change some of the thought patterns that were no longer useful.

In this process he read several books that were helpful to him: Gershen Kaufman's *Shame: The Power of Caring,* Jean Clark's *Growing Up Again,* and John Gottman's *The Heart of Parenting.* This trio of books aided Jack in understanding his own childhood, what really happened for him in terms of his image of himself, and his beliefs about how to be powerful in the world. He began to understand that the way he had been parented left him with many conflicting ideas. He had read books on parenting before and had taken classes, but it hadn't really connected for him until he had taken the time to examine his own inner world. He now had the context he needed in order to change his behavior and his attitude toward his daughter.

Sofie continued to be a spirited, challenging child, but her behavior improved somewhat as her parents became a team. She was no longer caught in the middle of their fights. She did not act out as much as she had before. She now had her father's positive attention. As Jack became more confident in himself as the good father he longed to be, it was easier for him to show pride in his daughter. She responded well to this. However, some of her behavior problems persisted, and at my recommendation, Sofie underwent a thorough evaluation. It was determined that she had a mild form of sensory integration disorder. Both parents became well educated on the disorder and continued to work as a team in helping Sofie.

With these shifts in place, couples therapy resumed on a new level. Both Jack and Barbara worked hard to change old habits and patterns. As Jack shared more and more of his inner world with Barbara, she was finally able to understand his behavior and his struggles. Barbara let go of her angry and defensive stance. She was more able to practice softened start-up and de-escalation skills even as she talked about the most painful issues. Jack made every effort to respond to Barbara, to listen with understanding, to stay present and not stonewall or withdraw. They saw, heard, and experienced the changes in each other. They were delighted but also somewhat skeptical. Would these changes last or were they just temporary? As time went on, and the changes continued to grow and deepen, so did their trust in the process and in each other.

It became apparent, however, that each needed the other to listen to what it had been like before. They were having trouble letting go of past resentments even though things were better now. This process at times became touchy, but they were able to walk through it and stay connected. Barbara wanted Jack to know what it had been like for her living with his stubbornness, rigidity, and aggression. Jack wanted Barbara to really hear how her criticism and contempt had affected him. It was particularly hard for Jack to have these conversations; he really just wanted to let the past go and start over. But his wife was not able to make this leap. Finally he was able to realize that in order to start over he would have to help build a bridge back to his wife that included listening, being empathetic, and making amends for the behavior that had distressed her and their daughter. Barbara also made her amends for judging Jack harshly and for not understanding that Jack's parenting behavior came from his desire to be a good parent. She realized and expressed how hurtful this was to Jack.

We worked hard on learning the skills to self-soothe and on using the repair checklist appropriately and at the right time. They were able to listen and be present for each other's pain in a way they had not been able to before. There were many tearful sessions as they really listened to each other, with empathy and understanding. Their relationship grew closer and closer and their friendship was rekindled. It was easy again to express their fondness and admiration for each other. After 16 months of very hard work, we terminated the treatment.

CONCLUSION

I was surprised to see Jack and Barbara at another Gottman couples workshop about 6 months after termination. The time for a follow-up session was approaching, but we had not yet arranged one. Jack and Barbara came to talk to me during the coffee break. They were walking hand in hand and beaming. Barbara confided to me that at the first workshop she and Jack attended she had been envious of the other couples who seemed to be so connected with each other. She and Jack had barely been able to speak to each other. At that first workshop she had allowed herself to dream of one day being one of those couples. I looked at Jack. He had tears in his eyes and had his arm around Barbara. He looked at me and said, "Thank you. Our marriage is everything I hoped it could be and more." Barbara smiled at him. She said to me, "We are one of those couples now. And we have moved from gridlock to dialogue on all the important issues. It is such a relief and a pleasure to be here."

REFERENCES

Clark, J., & Dawson, C. (1998). *Growing up again.* Center City, MN: Hazelden.
Gottman, J. (1997). *Raising an emotionally intelligent child.* New York: Simon & Schuster.
Kaufman, G. (1992). *Shame: The power of caring.* Rochester, VT: Schenkman.
Verrier, N. N. (1999). *The primal wound.* Baltimore, MD: Gateway.

Chapter 14 ❋

Termination and Two-Year Follow-Up to Prevent Relapse

Michael T. Clifford

The ability to do effective follow-up is intertwined with the termination process. At termination, the couple's progress is measured according to John Gottman's "10 criteria for a healthy marriage." These criteria provide a helpful guage about readiness for termination for both the couple and the therapist. They are also used as a foundation for each session of the follow-up process and outline the structure of these sessions. The 10 criteria are as follows:

- The fondness and admiration system has been activated or reactivated.

- Love maps have been created and are being used on a daily basis.

- Each person accepts influence from the partner, especially the husband from the wife.

- The couple has created positive sentiment override and is maintaining it through more frequent moments of turning toward.

- The couple can effectively repair negative interactions.

- The couple uses respectful influence and positive affect in the service of deescalation.

- Each person knows how to soothe both the self and partner physiologically.

- The couple has the tools, without the therapist, to make the next conversation better than the last.
- The threshold of the "marital poop detector" has been set significantly lower.
- The markers of divorce have been significantly reduced, particularly negative sentiment override and the four horsemen.

These criteria are markers of ongoing health in the relationship, and are reviewed during each follow-up session and measured for relapse, maintenance of gains, or progress.

To do this effectively, two things are essential. First, the couples need to have clear goals for the outcome of their therapy at the outset of treatment. They must, with the help of the therapist, be able to identify what the problems are and what they wish to change. This is not always an easy or clear task. Many people simply want the pain to stop or to see their partner do that one thing that would bring immediate relief (for example, the husband wants more sex or the wife wants some help with the children).

Second, the therapist must have some clear goals in mind for what treatment can or should accomplish. The therapist needs to be able to realistically define minimal process goals for the couples in general, as well as realistic process goals for specific couple. These need to be blended with the goals of the couples themselves.

RESEARCH

The problem of relapse and weak effect of therapy is probably the greatest problem facing marital therapists today. In fact, the effects of marital therapy are so weak that attending marital therapy is positively correlated with getting divorced. A longitudinal study done by Bob Levinson and John Gottman (1983) found just that. They discovered a 0.5 correlation between getting marital therapy and getting divorced. This might mean many things. Some proportion of these cases may be due to clients' "dropping off their spouse" to alleviate guilt feelings when they have already decided to divorce. But some also must be attributed simply to the weak effects of marital therapy and the inability of couples to maintain gains over time using current methodology.

Jacobson, Schmaling and Holtzworth-Munroe (1987) conducted a study to determine the degree to which relapse was a significant problem in marital therapy. That study revealed that 100% of couples who maintained their gains posttherapy and 79% of those who subsequently relapsed reported that therapy was beneficial to the marriage. It may be that the therapy *was* helpful, but some couples could not sustain its gains over time.

Research by Jacobson and Addis (1993) revealed that only 35% of couples studied reached the nondistressed range as measured by the Locke-Wallace marital satisfaction test by the end of therapy. They demonstrated that even for couples who improved, 30% to 50% of those couples had relapsed after one year. This leaves a 17% success rate for long-term change for couples in marital therapy. So, clearly, it is incumbent upon us as marital therapists to address the problem of relapse.

One goal of the SRH model is to anticipate relapse, teaching couples to recognize its stages early, and giving them tools to use when it arises. It also attempts to give them a longer experience of success so they become more reliant on the strength of their marriage to address marital issues and life stressors.

GMCT is grounded in four research studies conducted by John Gottman, in which videotapes were made of couple interactions. A code was created for specific behaviors so that these behaviors could be clustered in a cross sampling of couples. These clusters were then matched with interactions of couples who reported both high and low marital satisfaction. The matching of these behaviors with a self-report of high and low marital satisfaction has created criteria for what a healthy marriage looks like. The definition of who is a "happy couple" and who isn't is critical, because couples who are not able to at least approximate certain levels of behavior have been predicted to divorce with over 90% accuracy in four prospective studies conducted by Gottman. Couples must be able to maintain these levels of behavior in order to derive lasting benefit from the therapy. If they relapse in one or more of the defined areas, the 2-year follow-up process ideally should provide them with the assistance they need to maintain their gains. We hope that if they are able to maintain those gains for 2 years, they will be able to maintain them indefinitely or with minimal help.

The Gottman Institute Marriage Clinic had addressed the issue of relapse by adopting a "mass and fade approach" during the therapy. This way of working is based on studies reported in the research literature. A significant study in Munich (Boegner & Zielenbach-Cronin, 1984) discovered that massing treatment at the beginning by holding several sessions close together and then slowly fading, or making the therapist less active and the sessions less frequent, provided the most lasting results.

Drawn from this were three conclusions: First, it was essential to make the couple as self-sufficient during therapy as possible so that they could process their own conflicts without the therapist after termination. Second, the therapist needed to take a mass and fade approach not only during the therapy, but also after it, allowing the fading process to span a 2-year period posttermination. Third, the follow-up process should first encourage the couple to make use of their own new learnings and newly built friendship, if possible, before restarting therapy. The thinking was that if the couple was relatively self-reliant just months before, the problem lay in a lack of maintenance of the new skills and relationship, rather than being in a new situation for which they were totally unequipped.

FOLLOW-UP IN GMCT

The Gottman Marriage Clinic made a 2-year follow-up process with couples a standard protocol as an extension of the massing and fading process, based on this dimension of the Munich study. Thus, Gottman Institute clinicians ask at the beginning of therapy that each of their couples agree to meet with their therapist every 6 months for 2 years following termination of treatment.

The primary goal of the follow-up process is to evaluate how the couple is doing with maintaining the therapeutic gains they have made. This is also the relapse prevention goal. Every 6 months after termination of treatment, the couple and therapist meet and review together the couple's gains at termination. Then, together, they look for places where the couple may be relapsing, determine why that is happening, and either make course corrections during the session or develop a plan to strengthen that area. They also determine together whether more therapy is needed at that particular time. Although a therapist might hope that the therapy was so solid that the only thing that would ever be needed again is a small boost, that is usually not very realistic. Sometimes gains made at termination are lost under new and challenging circumstances. Sometimes the gains were not as solid as they looked. Sometimes the couple leaves therapy in order to avoid dealing with some particularly difficult topic or dynamic.

The second goal is to identify the areas where the couple has maintained their gains. The therapist and the couple look at which specific areas are still strong and at what the couple is doing in order to maintain those gains. Knowing what they are doing well and doing more of it is a key element of this process. Too often couples spend little time simply focusing on and being proud of how well they have done.

A third goal is to go beyond identifying specific strengths and help the couple apply these strengths in upcoming situations so that the next 6 months are even better than the last 6. Because the therapy seeks to make the couple dependent on their own relationship strengths and abilities right from the beginning, the follow-up process seeks to promote ongoing growth in the marriage. It is hoped that the couple will not just maintain gains and avoid relapse, but that the relationship will be even stronger at the end of the follow-up process than it was at termination.

In summary, it is hoped that, for most couples, the time for therapentic helping is done—or substantially done—at the point of termination. But if the couple is stuck during follow-up, it is the therapist's job, minimally, to lead them back to the progress they had made. The therapist may then defer to them to define what they need to do to promote marital health over the next 6 months. Additionally, the therapist should help a relapsed couple be realistic about how far they have relapsed and recommend whatever additional therapy might be necessary. If major assistance is needed, it is possible that the termination was premature. A couple may have encountered a new circumstance that challenged them beyond their level of growth at termination or last checkup. Pregnancies, job loss, family death, and the like can certainly stretch any of us beyond our level of marital strength.

At follow-up, the therapist should assume first that the couple has created the resources to address any life crisis and do "more therapy" only if it is indicated. The balance to be struck here is to not foster more dependency on the therapist than necessary, while also not leaving the couple to their own devices when they really need the therapist's help.

The central question at follow-up and at each successive 6-month interval is: "Are the gains you made at termination still in place after 6 months?" The benefit of the 10 criteria list is that it helps the couple examine each aspect of the relationship for its current strengths or weaknesses, rather than making a more global assessment of the relationship as either all good or all bad.

Each of the posttermination sessions begins by outlining the structure and purpose of meeting. The four basic parts are an overview of the last 6 months, a request for any specific agenda for the session, a review of the 10 criteria for termination, and planning for the next 6 months. The therapist begins by requesting that the couple list any major changes they have made or that have happened to them since the last meeting.

This meeting also gives the couple an opportunity to provide the therapist with a global perspective on the relationship, be it positive or negative, although sometimes the details brought out by the 10 criteria list may belie the global assessment. If the report is primarily positive, the therapist may ask for specifics so that each person gets to brag about his or her contribution and also can compliment the partner on his or her good work.

Then the therapist asks if there has been some particular difficulty that the couple wishes to use the session to work on. Although this session's purpose is to provide an overview, working on a specific problem in the relationship may be part of the process. It is also an opportunity to assess whether the relationship has relapsed or if the couple could really be handling the problem on their own without assistance.

At times, couples want to work on a specific issue that has become gridlocked. When this is the case, the therapist should, after helping the couple reach some resolution on the specific issue, review what tools were most helpful, hopefully ones the couple learned in their original therapy. The therapist then helps them determine why the tools didn't work when they tried using them at home and what they need to do to make them work the next time.

REVIEWING THE TEN CRITERIA

In the follow-up session, the therapist asks both partners to define to what degree they think they were doing each item. Each person rates the relationship with a number from 1 to 10, with 10 being high, on how he or she thinks they performed as a couple on each of the 10 criteria during the last 6 months. The therapist then discusses at length the items where there are discrepancies between their ratings and the areas where the criteria are rated low by both. Mutually highly rated categories are emphasized to reinforce progress and to celebrate together.

Finally, the therapist and couple talk about the future. They reflect together on what criteria need strengthening and the process needed to do so. They also anticipate upcoming challenges such as the birth of a baby, death of a parent, or other significant events that are external to the marriage. The couple is then asked if they want to continue the follow-up process by having the therapist call them in 6 months.

During the follow-up process, it is especially incumbent upon the therapist to continue to help create full independence. The final follow-up appointment at 2 years posttermination must call on the couple to talk together about what their plan will be for sustaining gains and how they will create their own follow-up process without the therapist.

It is possible to start using the 10 criteria and doing follow-up with a couple even if the therapist did not begin therapy with this model. It is clear that the 10 criteria for termination are also goals that should be kept in mind from the outset. If the 10 criteria model was used at the beginning of treatment with the couple, it can be used throughout treatment to track their progress. During treatment, the therapist can consider, whether the couple's behavior reflects any of the 10 criteria and then identify which interventions can strengthen weak areas.

ROY AND MARIE

Therapy with Roy and Marie presented many challenges. First, I had not used the Gottman method from the outset. Changing a whole therapy model midstream is far from easy for the therapist or the couple, and it makes structuring termination and follow-up more difficult. Second, the work with this couple was unusual because it was so lengthy (48 hours over 4 years). Third, both spouses had had extensive previous therapy and were in individual therapy, which had reinforced each person's belief that the marital problems were located inside the partner and not between them. Fourth, Roy had done some property damage during a fight, so a careful domestic violence assessment was necessary.

By the time Roy and Maria started therapy, they had lived together for 9 years prior to the marriage and had been married for 8 years. They had a 20-month-old daughter and Marie was pregnant. This couple had been in either individual or couples therapy for almost all of their relationship. Both were committed to the relationship and were convinced that there "must be more if they could only work harder" on their individual issues. Each said they believed that ultimately therapy was necessary and thought that it probably had kept them together. They still had hopes that they could be happy with each other and wanted to continue to use therapy to achieve that.

When I first began seeing them, Roy complained, "I feel that she is not comfortable with me being angry at her," and Maria complained, "When I get angry with him, he hits things." He had, indeed, put a hole in the wall by hitting it. "That was the last straw," she said. "You are the one with the problem. Look, you can't even control your temper!" Although they were both convinced that he would never hit her, the incident was unsettling to them. They said, "We go along and do really well, and then we have very bad times."

The first year of therapy with Maria and Roy consisted of addressing numerous crises and repetitive mutual hurts. She wanted recreational time to herself without childcare responsibilities. He complained that he worked long hours and watched their daughter frequently and didn't have time to support more time away for her.

A constant theme was scarcity of time. Both protested that there was not enough time in the day for work, family, and the marriage, too. Both were consistently on edge and tense about the pressures of just living their lives. One or the other of them was chronically late for our sessions. Marie interpreted this as an unconscious lack of commitment to the marriage on Roy's part. He attributed it to having to squeeze sessions into an already-full schedule.

They also became very emotionally disconnected during and after fights. No matter how committed they acted toward each other before a fight, there was little or no carryover of that security after the fight. Both highly mistrusted the goodwill of the other after any conflict.

Because their orientation to the couple relationship was through the lens of individual therapy, they had a difficult time leaving an individual perspective behind. They tended to want to analyze their partners and themselves. They "knew" about unconscious motivations because they themselves knew *they* had them. This was a vehicle for blame between Roy and Marie.

Part of what complicated the shift to the SRH model was the fact that the first year of work with them was devoted to helping them look at their unconscious motivations. I did a lot of interpreting, translating, and reframing; exercises and assignments were based on my perception of what their process was. I asked them to practice more "I messages" and to ask directly for what they wanted.

It was hard for them to work on building positives instead of concentrating on eradicating negatives. At first they protested that it couldn't possibly be as easy as "If we work together and do things we both enjoy, our marriage will get better." After all, they said, the other partner had deep and significant emotional issues that needed to be resolved before the marriage could improve at all. It was important that this couple actually show more affection and express their positive feelings more openly. They also needed to develop a common vision or dream.

Marie gave birth to their second daughter 4 months after we began couples work. They took only a 5-week break from therapy to have the baby and then they simply brought the baby along.

Eight months after we started, I began working in the SRH model, and I gave them the diagnostic packet of questionnaires developed by the Gottman Institute. I hoped that GMCT would give us a clearer picture of the areas of the relationship that needed work and help us set clear goals in SRH terms. A diagnostic picture was needed.

Then several sessions elapsed not either thinking of or talking about Sound Marital House concepts. After almost a year we began talking about the existence of the four horsemen. We used the metaphor of the emotional bank account and they learned about turning toward. When Marie said, "I don't want to make deposits," I was at a loss as to what to do next. Roy returned the next week and complained that he didn't like the direction the sessions were going. Marie disagreed. Roy said, "I want my fear addressed that there might be another destructive conflict." Now I really didn't know what to do next!

THERAPY

What finally became the turning point of therapy was what John Gottman called "the fundamental attribution error." This translates into "I have only one problem—you!" In order to illustrate this concept for Marie and Roy, I placed an empty chair in the office in front of them and "put" the problem in it. I then asked them to work together on *it*. It was the first time they began to see that GMCT was about gaining collaboration between the partners in the couple against the problem. About that same time, I presented the 10 criteria for termination, which gave them a clearer vision of what we were trying to accomplish.

Although Marie reported that externalizing the problem in this way was "transformative" for her and took away her need to defend her actions so much, she still protested that the problem was so big that "just externalizing it" would be insufficient—it didn't solve the problem of Roy's "serious emotional issues."

The couple appeared to be married to the idea that the problem was enormous. They hadn't considered the power that increasing their respectfulness for each other could have. If their marriage was to improve, they couldn't just decrease conflict; they also needed to do things that promoted liking and caring about each other. I gave them small assignments designed to help them do that. They had to start believing that their partner wasn't "the enemy."

This idea of doing small things for each other as a way to heal the relationship struck a cord for Marie. After a long time of only focusing on how to work together without blame as a strategy, Marie said during one session, "I think this is going to make things better." For the first time they really began to believe that they were going to get past all this and have the marriage they wanted.

It was helpful to compile a folder of SRH interventions and handouts for them. We returned to the questionnaires I had set aside and discussed an assessment of the relationship in SRH terms. The 10 criteria spelled out the general goals for a healthy marriage. We also switched to a primarily dyadic approach where most of the conversation in the sessions was now between them instead of between them as individuals and me.

When each of them began telling the other about little courtesies they had noticed the other doing, their attitudes toward each other changed dramatically. Each was able to make more of the kind of relationship omissions and errors that people are likely to make without its meaning that the other person was out to hurt them. The fondness and admiration system turned on like a switch. After that, they were able to identify multiple ways that the other had turned toward them. It had been happening all along, but it had been invisible before. They were now very pleased that the other had noticed and appreciated so much of what they were doing.

TERMINATION AND FOLLOW-UP

It became clear to them that as we headed toward termination, their therapy needed to focus on learning how to regulate intimacy and not just conflict. Each had their limits in this area. When they got too intimate and vulnerable, conflict would erupt. In the SRH model, it is not always necessary to work on these issues until the couple can be "really intimate." There is more room for accepting people's limitations and abilities without trying to change them. Both Roy and Marie were learning to accept their personal limitations and not experience the other's actions as rejections of themselves. The couple benefited from focusing on strengths as long as they both felt secure that they could limit the amount of intimacy to something within their comfort zone.

After 2 more years, the 10 criteria were introduced as a progress check and as a way of consolidating the use of the SRH model to view the relationship. When the couple reviewed the 10 criteria for termination, they decided that they had made enough progress and that they could, in fact, terminate and begin the follow-up process. At termination, the relationship looked like this:

- The markers of divorce (defensiveness, criticism, stonewalling, and contempt) were definitely removed.
- The fondness and admiration system was strong.
- Love maps were current for each of the partners.
- Both partners agreed that accepting influence was a challenge but both knew how to do it and had some successes.
- Turning toward was consistent.
- Repair was still taking a long time. It was usually successful but both partners were still feeling very hurt during conflicts. We examined this carefully and both agreed that the deep hurt was a function of personal vulnerabilities and not the result of the partner's being abusive. However, both were still capable of escalating a conflict quickly.
- Respectful influence was still shaky during escalations, but calm discussions were more frequent. When conflict flared up quickly, they hurt the other first and asked questions later.
- Both were being more soothing to the other, but there was still room for improvement.
- Both agreed that they had the tools to return to a conversation that did not go well and do it better the second time.
- The marital poop detector was activated sooner and issues were brought up with a softened start-up more frequently.

The one thing that seemed very abnormal to the couple was to not be working on the relationship by engaging in emotional discussions about "heavy issues." They felt like they were neglecting the relationship when they just enjoyed time together, played with their two daughters, and supported each other's interests and goals. Both were getting angry at times; however, because escalations were less fregrent and less volatile, anything that got "out of control" seemed like a quirk to them, not a central problem in the relationship.

The first follow-up was scheduled for 3 months from the termination at the couple's request. However, they cancelled and reset the appointment several times, citing as a reason that the session would interfere with some couple or family social event. We finally met 5 months posttermination. They came to the session a few minutes late, but this time they were laughing about it.

When they checked in, they reported that there had been no major conflicts in the last 5 months, that there was an abundance of positive sentiment override, and that fondness and admiration was high. Marie tearfully talked to Roy about how much she valued his consistency in a world she considered scary and shaky. This consistency had previously been labeled as rigidity and one of his serious character flaws. Both expressed deep respect and valuing for the other.

They had no current issue to address. As a therapist, I did very little that session. We simply celebrated their progress together. The Gottman positive adjective checklist was used as a way of reinforcing and further building the positivity. It was in the context of this exercise that Marie expressed her gratitude to Roy for his consistency.

They also reviewed the 10 termination criteria. Both agreed that the areas that had improved were accepting influence and doing repair. In light of having had no major conflicts in 6 months, a record for this couple, it was clear that the poop detector and softened start-up mechanisms had improved also. The couple was still not spending a lot of time together, as they kept their lives very busy, but both had a sense of peace and balance about that.

At the second follow-up session 6 months later, the relationship was showing signs of relapse but also continuing strength. They came separately and both were 20 minutes late. Marie was angry about a returning pattern of Roy' lateness, but the argument did not escalate. Each stated their reasons for being late, and both reacted nondefensively. They elected to not make an issue of the lateness and to use their time to review the 10 criteria. That they could actually set this aside and work on other aspects of the relationship was a sign of strength.

Their 10-criteria review during that session was as follows: They had virtually eliminated negative sentiment override and consistently maintained a sense of positive sentiment override. Both agreed that fondness and admiration and love maps were still strong. However, accepting influence, especially about the allocation of tasks inside versus outside the house, had become a tug of war. Failure to sooth the partner during conflicts was still a problem. Although they were not throwing as much gas on the fire, both agreed that this was a temptation that was hard to resist. Sometimes they just didn't care and did it anyway, even though both stated that they knew how detrimental this pattern could be.

Based on the 10-criteria report, the tentative assessment at the outset of the appointment was that their relationship gains had been solid but the couple was, at times, neglecting to use the tools they had. However, I also had to stay open to the possibility that the gains might not be as solid as I thought, or that the couple might have opened up a new problem area that they had not encountered before, making more therapy necessary. My initial stance during the session was to mirror for Roy and Marie that they indeed had a solid foundation. It appeared that they had all the tools they needed to address any relapse and to figure out how to make it better. Then they talked together while I observed.

They did very well and made significant headway in the session. Marie was able to be much more reflective about what had been transpiring. Even as she reported problems, she consistently referenced the positives that counterbalanced them for her. Roy was very nondefensive even when Marie was recounting complaints she had. He repeatedly expressed appreciation about how she had diffused multiple potential escalations. He also saw her as particularly supportive and understanding of his struggles at work and his need for down time. They asked to meet the following week to see if they could consolidate more of their gains and get a clearer focus for the next 6 months.

This presented an interesting theoretical dilemma. It is essential in the follow-up process that the therapist strike a balance of progressively continuing to fade his or her involvement but be ready to resume therapy if the couple needs it. This couple was at the 1-year follow-up point and had been functioning exceptionally well for 18 months. The question was. "How much continued therapy is too much?" It might not be helpful to move back into doing therapy and have them become dependent in an ongoing way. However, new circumstances may have tested their limits, so I needed to be prepared to restart therapy if that was necessary.

The couple was 15 minutes late for the session the next week. When I asked if they had sustained their gains from the previous session, they reported a global feeling sense that it was marginal at best. Another review of the 10 criteria was done in detail because of their negative answer. As we looked at each criterion, the couple spontaneously reported multiple interactions for each category that were examples of significant growth. This discrepancy was puzzling in the light of the global negativity they reported.

The source of their doubts appeared to be that each of them had not been respecting his or her own limits as far as the capacity for intimacy was concerned. We once again addressed the need to tailor intimacy to each of their tolerance levels. This was not a reframe, but a respecting of their enduring vulnerabilities regarding risk and being close. There is no optimal level of intimacy that every couple should match.

Reluctantly, they also reported that they had had a conflict during the last week in which Roy had punched a hole in the wall. After 3 years of therapy and a year of follow-up, it was quite surprising to be hearing about property damage during a fight.

Marie, said, smiling, "Yeah, I immediately went and got a magic marker and put a heart around it." Roy smiled sheepishly and said he felt pretty foolish. They both were able to see that his reaction was a product of his difficulty dealing with stress. Although certainly a problem, there was little risk of his turning this frustration toward Marie or the children through violence aimed at them. The effectiveness of Marie's repair was also a clear indication that the fundamentals of the relationship had changed and that the fondness and admiration system had provided a container for Roy's actions. The rest of the session was spent reviewing the fundamentals of flooding, time-outs, and self-soothing.

The couple decided that two sessions were enough to keep them on a positive track and asked to return in 6 months. Restarting therapy again was not needed.

The third follow-up session was held in December. They were only a couple of minutes late and were very warm and affectionate with each other. They gave their "state of the relationship report" and it was quite positive. The couple reported significant, ongoing dialogue about issues with no major conflicts over the past 6 months. They said that the four horsemen were limited, and there was no contempt. When disagreement arose, repair happened swiftly. The marital friendship was strong, and both said they believed that their spouse was actively supporting their dreams both as individuals and for the marriage. When asked to explore what was most meaningful in life to them at this point in time, they both said the most meaningful thing to them right now was parenting and giving their daughters the love, support, and connection that they did not receive as children.

Because of many complications in their lives, the fourth follow-up session did not happen until the following August. Roy had been carefully listening to his body signals and had been very attentive to some unusual symptoms he experienced. He decided to seek medical attention, and was able to head off an impending stroke and take significant preventive steps using medication to remove an arterial blockage.

There were no problems to be addressed here, so I inquired about what meanings the couple derived from all these events. They then shared meanings that involved the gratitude they both felt for being married to each other. During the medical crisis, they had supported each other well and their appreciation of each other had deepened. They altered their work schedules and were spending much more time together. Even though it appeared that little was done in the session beyond celebrating their success, they requested to continue the 6-month follow-up sessions indefinitely as an accountability measure.

When they came for their fifth follow-up session, the couple was on time! Both reported the relationship as solid. They struggled now not with each other, but with their daughter, who had developed learning problems. They were frequently at odds about how to address this but both said those differences represented a tension, not a division. There were many avenues open to them to attempt to help their daughter, and the philosophy of each was different enough to offer an opportunity to try many of them. The couple was committed to using their differences as a strength.

I used Likert scale of 1 to 10, with 10 being the highest, to assess the couple's progress on the 10 criteria. They did this playfully, with neither of them scoring any area lower than 7, except Roy, who gave himself a 6 on his ability to soothe Marie. Interestingly, she disagreed with him and cited multiple examples of times he did or said something that helped her calm down in conflict. They were still not spending much time together, but they seemed to have worked out a rhythm that suited their personalities.

I then asked them what they attributed their ability to sustain gains over such a long period of time to. Marie said, "the Sound Relationship House model." She went on to say that its simplicity, clarity, and usability, as well as its emphasis on positive relationship building, meant that she didn't have to struggle through all of their unconscious material to work out an issue. She laughed.

They noted that at first they did not believe that the small turning toward actions would have much effect because their problems seemed so large. Roy especially noted that it had a profound effect on reducing the intensity of their escalated conflicts and that the results spoke for themselves.

They also said that they were now more mindful and aware of how they treated each other and of when a negative perspective was creeping in. They felt that they had the tools now to reverse that. It was fascinating and rewarding to hear them say that they used to think that the differences between them were the problem. This left them hopeless because the differences were real and were not about to change. Now they said that they realized that it was how they managed the differences between them that had been a problem, and they had been very successful in changing that.

FOLLOW-UP SURVEY

In order to assess couples' progress and the evolution of their relationships following termination, nine couples were surveyed by in October of 2001. The purpose of the survey was to track the progress, maintenance, or relapse of the couples following termination. The survey was not structured as a rigorous research project; rather it was an attempt to determine whether the couples perceived that their relationship was substantially better than when they started therapy, even after 2 years posttermination. Because other studies have shown that after anywhere from 6 months to 2 years posttermination, 70% of couples return to pretherapy distress levels, positive results on the questionnaires would suggest that the combination of the therapy and the follow-up was helpful in maintaining long-term change.

Each couple, with one exception, was given the Gottman "17 areas" questionnaire, the Weiss-Cerretto marital status inventory and the Knox problem inventory at the outset of therapy. Because the questionnaires are given prior to any assessment or therapy sessions, they represent each person's perception of the state of the relationship before meeting with the therapist. These questionnaires, and the Gottman relapse questionnaire, were then sent to the couples after termination. Some of the couples had had only one follow-up session and others had had four (which represented the 2-year mark). Couples were asked to answer each of the questions according to how they were now experiencing their marriage after therapy and the follow-up process. In addition, the couples were given a survey developed by the Gottman Institute asking them to evaluate the benefit of the follow-up process to them. Of the nine couples polled, six returned questionnaires. The answers to these questionnaires were then compared to the original questionnaires.

Of the six couples who responded, none was considering divorce at the time of the surveys. Earlier, at intake, three of the couples had been considering divorce, two of which were dealing with a recent affair, were separated, and had scored at 10 on the Weiss-Cerretto (the cutoff for predicting divorce is 4 items marked). The husband of one couple had been considering divorce but at a very low level. Because it is not unusual for a therapist to complete what looks like a successful therapy only to find out later, often by chance, that the couple has divorced, it was encouraging that none of these couples during their posttherapy time were currently considering divorce.

All six couples reported that the numbers of disagreements between them on a range of issues and the severity of problems were reduced at follow-up. It is interesting that for some couples, the severity rating of some areas actually increased after termination, but in those couples the numbers of problem areas had diminished. This seems to indicate that global dissatisfaction had decreased, but with the improving of the relationship, some areas had become more apparent hot spots.

The Gottman relapse questionnaire was used as a crosscheck. It is a list of possible problem areas that closely parallels the more detailed 17 areas questionnaire. The client simply selects between "doing fine" and "a problem now" on a list of possible problem areas. None of the couples checked more than two areas as "a problem now," and the couples who did check areas as "a problem now" added a comment that qualified the intensity of the problem. Typical comments were along the lines of "We are doing fine, we regularly spend time together talking, avoid bringing up problems when we are flooded, are better at hearing each other and moving on." These kinds of qualifiers seem to suggest that when problem areas are marked, the couple is indicating what the current issue is rather than indicating that their relationship has relapsed. This questionnaire is a good indication of global satisfaction or dissatisfaction. Each partner in each of the couples indicated broad global satisfaction with the relationship at whatever stage of follow-up they had reached.

CONCLUSION

There is reason to believe that simply doing therapy and then terminating may not be enough to assist couples in maintaining lasting change, which of course, should be the goal of any marital therapy. Having a clear benchmark against which to measure progress is an essential aspect of therapy for couples. The use of the SRH model, combined with the 10 criteria list, makes this possible.

During the follow-up process, the therapist and the couple can constructively address even small relapses in a very brief time. Couples are then able to make needed course corrections and maintain their gains independent of the therapist for another 6 months. It appears that couples who are able to maintain gains for 6 and 12 months are able to keep those gains for 2 years. If they are able to maintain gains for 2 years posttermination, it is more probable that they will be able to avoid the high rate of relapse shown in research studies and maintain their gains indefinitely.

Many of the couples in the follow-up survey also reported that the care of their therapist beyond the termination of the therapy was a positive factor in maintaining change. This makes it abundantly clear that this is not simply a mechanical behavioral process, but a very human endeavor. The person of the therapist and his or her caring for these couples is a powerful healing force.

Couples also frequently mentioned their ongoing accountability as an important aspect of the follow-up process. Knowing that they would have to give an account when they went back for a therapy session gave them pause when they were tempted to disregard what they had learned. Having someone to answer to may be a universal need, no matter what our ages or stage of marriage.

If accountability and checkups with someone who cares about the marriage are essential, it might be that couples need to find a way to create a community that will make this possible. Most of the nine couples in the survey had no other couples to talk to about their marriages. When outside conversations about the marriage occurred with others, they consisted of each partner complaining individually to a friend about the other partner.

A lesson taken from their experience is that when termination is nearing, the therapist might consider initiating discussion about support systems for the marriage other than therapy, so that when the follow-up process is completed, couples will have ongoing support from one another.

Sustaining gains after termination of therapy is a significant challenge for all couples and for those of us who work with couples. Seriously considering how much sustaining gains needs to be built into the therapy may help many couples in the future to live out their married years with fondness and affection and with conflict that does not destroy the marriage. In turn, their marriages can leave a legacy for their children and grandchildren that demonstrates that marriage can be a lasting and loving place to embrace.

REFERENCES

Boegner, I., & Zielenbach-Cronin, H. (1984). On maintaining change in behavoral marital therapy. In K. Halweg and N.S. Jacobson (Eds.), *Marital interaction: Analysis and modification.* (pp. 27–35). New York: Guilford Press.

Gottman J. M., Coan, J., Carrere, S., & Swanson, C. (1998). Predicting marital happiness and stability from newlywed interactions. *Journal of Marriage and the Family, 60,* 5–22.

Gottman, J. M., & Levinson, R. W. (1992). Marital processes predictive of later dissoluton: Behavior, physiology, and health. *Journal of Personality and Social psychology, 63,* 221–233.

Jacobson, N. S., & Addis, M. E. (1993). Research on couple therapy: What do we know? Where are we going? *Journal of Consulting and Clinical Psychology, 61*(1), 85–93.

Jacobson, S. M., Schmaling, K., & Holtzworth-Munroe, A. (1987). Component analysis of behavioral marital therapy:Two year follow-up and prediction of relapse. *Journal of Consulting and Clinical Psychology, 53*(2), 175–184.

Index

dream-within-conflict intervention (*countinued*)
  in case example of Pat and Paul
    (psychodynamic plus Gottman
    methods), 189
  in case example of Peter and Angie
    (emotionally distant), 117–120, 129
  in case example of Tom and Lindsey
    (marathon therapy), 178
  therapist's use of, conflict re two couple
    models, 184
dreams, 2
  conflict and (*see* dream-within-conflict
    intervention)
  embedded in gridlocked perpetual
    problems, 8
  loss of, 105, 108, 193, 195, 199
  unfulfilled, 174
Dykan, E., 2

emotion(al)
  bank account, 139, 140
  coaching, 97
  disengagement, overview of, 109–110
  meta-, 103, 136–37, 146, 147
  in psychodynamic vs. Gottman approaches,
    183
  see also affect regulation
enduring vulnerabilities. *see* vulnerabilities,
  enduring
equilibrium, in couples therapy, 11, 14,
  28
expectations
  attachment, 186
  relational, 185
  role, in stepfamilies, 132
  thwarted, 159
  unrealistic, in case example of Lisa and
    Dave (stepfamily), 138, 139, 145,
    147–48

family-of-origin issues
  in case example of Frank and Judy (affair),
    52–53, 60–62
  in case example of Jack and Barbara
    (parenting conflicts), 201, 210–11
  in case example of Jan and Jack (depression),
    75
  in case example of Janet and Steve (sexual
    dysfunction), 103
  in case example of Lisa and Dave (stepfamily),
    137, 151
  in case example of Marina and Derek
    (trauma-related violence), 31–32
  in case example of Mike and Alice
    (equilibrium), 20–21, 26, 27
  in case example of Myra and Thomas
    (borderline), 91
  in case example of Pat and Paul
    (psychodynamic and Gottman methods),
    194
  in case example of Peter and Angie
    (emotionally distant), 111–12

  in case example of Tom and Lindsey
    (marathon therapy), 171–72
  internal working model shaped by,
    186
  therapist dealing with own, 12
family therapy, structural, 13
feedback
  in case example of Jack and Barbara
    (parenting conflicts), 202–4
  in case example of Jan and Jack
    (depression), 76
  in case example of Mike and Alice
    (equilibrium), 21–22
  in case example of Peter and Angie
    (emotionally distant), 114–16
  questionnaire-related, 19–20, 171
flashbacks
  in case example of Marina and Derek
    (trauma-related violence), 32, 33, 40
  childhood abuse and, 29, 30
flooding
  in case example of Frank and Judy (affair),
    55, 58
  in case example of Jack and Barbara
    (parenting conflicts), 205
  in case example of Jan and Jack (depression),
    82, 85–86, 87
  in case example of Janet and Steve (sexual
    dysfunction), 104
  in case example of Lisa and Dave (stepfamily),
    150
  in case example of Mike and Alice
    (equilibrium), 20–21, 26, 27
  in case example of Marina and Derek
    (trauma-related violence), 33
  in case example of Peter and Angie
    (emotionally distant), 125–26
  in case example of Tom and Lindsey
    (marathon therapy), 179, 180
  childhood abuse and, 29
  laughter depotentiating, 26
  see also diffuse physiological arousal
follow-up sessions
  in case example of Roy and Marie (follow-up
    work), 220–25
  criteria used during, 214
  GMCT's process of, 215–17
  survey, 225–26
  termination intertwined with, 213
fondness and admiration
  affair, impact on, 48–49
  assessing, 19
  in case example of Jack and Barbara
    (parenting conflicts), 212
  in case example of Jan and Jack (depression),
    77, 79
  in case example of Janet and Steve (sexual
    dysfunction), 104
  in case example of Lisa and Dave (stepfamily),
    135–36, 139, 146
  in case example of Mike and Alice
    (equilibrium), 21–22

marathon therapy
  case example of, 170–180
  client contraindications for, 168–69
  overview of, 165–69, 180
"marital poop detector," 214, 221, 222
marital satisfaction
  affairs and, 48
  children and, 197
  conflict regulation and, 186
  criteria evaluating (*see* healthy marriage,
    criteria for)
  management strategies and, 166
  stepfamily, factors affecting, 132
"mass and fade approach," 215
meaning
  affair, impact on, 49
  in case example of Lisa and Dave (stepfamily),
    138, 144, 147, 153
  in case example of Myra and Thomas
    (borderline), 93–94, 99
  in case example of Pat and Paul
    (psychodynamic plus Gottman methods),
    189
  in case example of Peter and Angie
    (emotionally distant), 114
  in case example of Roy and Marie (follow-up
    work), 224
  of conflict (*see* dream-within-conflict
    intervention)
  in emotionally distant couple, 110
  internal working model formed by, 186
  of love, in case example of Janet and Steve
    (sexual dysfunction), 105
  overview of, 8
medication
  in case example of Marina and Derek
    (trauma-related violence), 44
  for depression, 70, 73–74, 83, 122, 126–27
metaphor(s)
  of the blind people and the elephant
    (subjective realities), 156–58
  of the car and the tennis court (accepting
    responsibility), 160–61
  eases client's anxiety about new concepts,
    155–56, 162, 163
  of the healing hip (self-soothing), 161–62
  of lemon yogurt (clear expression of needs),
    158–160
  for marathon therapy work, 169
  of real estate negotiation (compromise),
    162–63
Milan school, 12
Minuchin, S., 11

narrative therapy, 13
National Opinion Research Center, 48
needs, emotional
  competing, 175–76, 194
  expression of, 66–67, 125, 151
  metaphor conveying, 158–160
  shame of, 60

negative sentiment override
  affair, impact of, 49
  in case example of Jan and Jack (depression),
    77
  in case example of Mike and Alice
    (equilibrium), 16–17, 23
  in case example of Myra and Thomas
    (borderline), 97
  in case example of Peter and Angie
    (emotionally distant), 114
  definition of, 4–5
  in traumatized couples, 29–30
  see also "four horsemen of the apocalypse";
    turning away or against

oral history interview
  in case example of Frank and Judy (affair),
    50–55
  in case example of Jack and Barbara
    (parenting conflicts), 198–201
  in case example of Jan and Jack (depression),
    72
  in case example of Janet and Steve (sexual
    dysfunction), 102–3
  in case example of Lisa and Dave (stepfamily),
    133–37
  in case example of Tom and Lindsey
    (marathon therapy), 173–75

Papernow, P. L., 132
parallel lives, of emotionally distant couples live,
  110, 112
paranoia, in case example of Marina and Derek
  (trauma-related violence), 43
parenting styles
  conflict over, 203, 204
  differences in, 197, 208
  observing, in case example of Jack and
    Barbara (parenting conflicts), 210
positive sentiment override
  in case example of Roy and Marie (follow-up
    work), 221–22
  definition of, 4–5
posttraumatic stress disorder (PTSD)
  affairs and, 48, 54, 55, 67
  in case example of Marina and Derek
    (trauma-related violence), 33, 34
  DPA interacting with, 35
  education about, 34
  reinforced by couple's negative sentiment
    override, 30
  see also abuse
powerlessness, sense of, 70, 86–87, 94, 97, 98,
  144
prediction, course of discussion, 5
Primal Wound, The (Verrier), 200
problems, perpetual, 2
  in case example of Jack and Barbara
    (parenting conflicts), 208
  in case example of Jan and Jack (depression),
    84–85